AUBREY AND THE DYING LADY

By the same author

ARTISTS AND WRITERS IN PARIS

AUBREY AND THE DYING LADY

A Beardsley Riddle

MALCOLM EASTON

(COL).

When darker forms of doubt appal,
And new false lights have birth

SECKER & WARBURG
LONDON

First published in England 1972 by
Martin Secker & Warburg Limited
14 Carlisle Street, London W1V 6NN

First published 1972
© Malcolm Easton 1972

SBN: 436 14070 5

185892   03   9200   02

Photoset and printed in Great Britain by
BAS Printers Limited, Wallop, Hampshire

Illustration Acknowledgements

The author and publishers wish to thank the following sources for permission to include illustrations.

Illustrations 10 and 11 are reproduced by gracious permission of Her Majesty The Queen.

Miss Stella M. Alleyne (3, 4); Mrs I. J. Bealby-Wright (87, 88, 90, 96); Bournemouth Public Library (52, 53); Brighton Public Libraries (52); Anthony d'Offay, Esq. (29, 30); The Fogg Art Museum, Harvard University (80); W. G. Good, Esq. (1, 47, 71, 102); The Harari Collection (59); Mrs Viva King (frontispiece); The National Building Record (12, 37); The National Portrait Gallery, London (24); Lady Page (48); private collection (50, 51); Giles Robertson, Esq. (29); J.-P. B. Ross, Esq. (31, 85); *The Scotsman* (38); The City Art Gallery, Southampton (7); The Tate Gallery, London (25); Victoria and Albert Museum Library, London (59); Dr Paul Winckler (39).

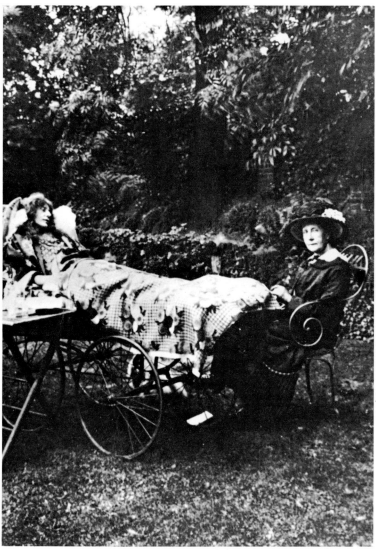

Mabel Beardsley (1871–1916), sister of the artist, with Mrs Beardsley, Hampstead, 1913. The photograph exactly recalls the opening of Yeats's poem 'Upon a Dying Lady', *her lovely piteous head amid dull red hair Propped upon pillows.*

To
Brian Reade

Contents

List of Illustrations

Prefatory Note and Acknowledgements

If one thing has supported me through the difficulties of writing this book, it has been my belief in the abiding excellence of the artist's work. I complete it with my conviction renewed that Aubrey Beardsley is the greatest of English pen-draftsmen, and it is appropriate in the centenary year of his birth to re-affirm one's faith. A misunderstanding very much to the artist's disadvantage exists here. He has been judged not by his original drawings, but by the zinc-block 'facsimiles' made of them. How unjust this estimate is, I discovered for myself when I examined every available original drawing at close range, off the wall and out of its frame. The climax of an unforgettable experience was reached one day at Messrs Wildenstein's, when I was privileged to go through the examples owned by the late Ralph Harari: the finest private collection of Beardsley originals in the world. I am quite sure that this artist will never receive his due until he is judged, as all his fellows are, by the work as it left his hand and not by the mechanical reproduction. The difference, particularly in the *Lysistrata* and later (and undervalued) pen-and-wash drawings, is nothing less than staggering.

I speak of difficulties. These were inherent in the task I had set myself: an attempt to explain the drawings through an account of Aubrey's sexual psychology and his relationships with friends and family. All existing Beardsley studies showed that this must be the next step; but once embarked upon the enterprise I became aware of the daunting lack of material. The letters are far from explicit. We know very little about the artist's friendships (I have devoted my Introduction to this topic); about his father and mother, almost nothing. Of his sister Mabel not even the beginning of a glimmer of knowledge existed when I sat down to write an account which was to estimate her importance so highly. It may be felt that she fails here to achieve a sharp enough outline, that I exaggerate the part she played in Aubrey's life. While I see a certain justice in such criticisms, I can say only that, at the end of my labours, I hold as strongly as when I started the view that—despite the lack of solid,

Aubrey and the Dying Lady

satisfactory proof—the mysterious, intangible figure who became Yeats's 'Dying Lady' must be linked with any final understanding of her brother's art and character.

It has been my intention to do something to enrich Beardsley studies by concentrating on the least-known aspects: the physical details of his illness, for instance; the transvestist and trans-sexual elements in his work; and the argument (an argument it must remain) about incest. From the start, I wanted to avoid duplication of the continuous narrative of Aubrey's life and the catalogue of his productions so admirably carried out already by Mr Brian Reade, and reinforced by Mr Stanley Weintraub's biography of a year or two ago. To supply some equivalent for the missing sequence of events as a whole (my division being by topic), a short chronology has been provided.

I have received throughout very generous encouragement and help. First from Secker & Warburg themselves, who most courage-ously entrusted me with yet another book on Beardsley; in particular, Mr T. G. Rosenthal and Mr John Blackwell gave me some much-needed advice on presentation and style.

In the special area of Beardsley studies, I should like to acknow-ledge outstanding debts to Mr Brian Reade, whose pioneering work is so universally respected; to Mr W. G. Good, my earliest and unfailing helper;* and to Mr Henry Maas, both as private critic and co-editor, with Dr J. L. Duncan and Mr Good, of the in-valuable recent publication, *The Letters of Aubrey Beardsley*. To these three scholars and the publishers, Cassell & Company Ltd, I owe a gratitude that all succeeding Beardsley students will share. For the first time we have beside us the artist's complete corres-pondence within the covers of one volume, and I am initiating a practice that will become invariable from now on, I am sure, when I give 'MDG' page-references to all quotations which would previously have been credited to Gray's *Last Letters*, Walker's *Letters to Smithers* and the several additional sources.

In the fields of psychiatry and medicine, Dr J. Amor Ardis, Dr Richard Pugh and Dr Robert Raines (whom I could consult in

*Both Mr Reade and Mr Good read drafts of my book and suggested alterations, almost all of which have been adopted, to the great improvement of the final text.

Prefatory Note and Acknowledgements

his capacity as art historian as well as physician) have given un-wearied attention to my inquiries: and it remains for me to stress that any misconceptions or too-fanciful conclusions must be laid at my door, not theirs. It was an unexpected piece of good fortune for me to make the acquaintance of Dr John Randell of Charing Cross Hospital, the leading authority on transvestism and trans-sexualism, just before my book was completed, and to be able to discuss some relevant Beardsley problems with him.

One of the pleasures relieving the hard grind of my work has been the friendship it led to with Miss Jane Bacon, the actress (Mrs I. J. Bealby-Wright), widow of George Bealby Wright, by his first marriage the husband of Mabel Beardsley. From Miss Bacon I gained my first knowledge of Mabel's theatrical career, difficult as it would have been to fit the details of it together otherwise. It was of enormous help to me to be entrusted with a substantial packet of original letters to Robert Ross from Aubrey, Mabel and Ellen Beardsley (the artist's mother). Sir Rupert Hart-Davis accepted responsibility for taking this very sympathetic action, and I am most grateful to him, as also, of course, to the owner of the letters, Mr J.-P. B. Ross, by whose kind permission I quote from them extensively. I wish to thank Mr John Smithies for drawing my attention to the Wagner churches in Brighton; and Miss Stella Alleyne and Sir Sacheverell Sitwell for helpful corres-pondence that goes back some years. Sir John Rothenstein, Mr Cecil Farthing, Mr Anthony Symondson, Mr Giles Robertson, Mr Anthony d'Offay, Mr W. G. Good, Fr Brocard Sewell, O. Carm., Lady Page and Mrs Viva King have all been most generous over illustrations.

For permission to reproduce in full the poems entitled 'Upon a Dying Lady' and to quote at length from Yeats's published letters, and shortly from *The Trembling of the Veil*, I have to thank Senator Michael Yeats, the W. B. Yeats Estate and A. P. Watt & Son, together with the publishers, Macmillan & Co. and Rupert Hart-Davis Ltd. My thanks go to Mr Michael Rhodes and University College, London, for help in consulting the Lane papers housed there. Reading University's Librarian showed me the same courtesy in connexion with its Beardsley holdings.

Grateful acknowledgement of short passages quoted is made to

Aubrey and the Dying Lady

the authors, editors, heirs or estates, and publishers, of the following: the magazine *Blackfriars*, in respect of two articles by Marc-André Raffalovich; C. B. Cochran, *Secrets of a Showman*; Desmond Flower and Henry Maas, *The Letters of Ernest Dowson*; John F. Gallagher, 1961 edition of Frank Harris's *My Life and Loves*; Sir Rupert Hart-Davis, *The Letters of Oscar Wilde* and *Max Beerbohm: Letters to Reggie Turner*; M. Montgomery Hyde, *The Trials of Oscar Wilde*; Cecil Lewis, *Self-Portrait taken from the Letters and Journals of Charles Ricketts, R.A.*; Faith Compton Mackenzie, *As Much as I Dare*; Margery Ross, *Robert Ross: Friend of Friends*; Sir William Rothenstein, *Men and Memories*, Vol. I; Netta Syrett, *Strange Marriage* and *The Sheltering Tree*; R. A. Walker, *A Beardsley Miscellany*.

Among a number of helpers on the staffs of libraries, I should like particularly to express my thanks to Miss Marianne Winder, of the Wellcome Historical Medical Library, Miss Eileen A. Hollingdale, of Brighton Public Libraries, and Mr Morley Case, of the Central Library, Bournemouth. I have also had the constant help of an old colleague in the duplicating process, Mrs Betty Brundrett, to whom I am once more very grateful.

Finally, I wish to record the noble way in which my wife has endured a total disruption of our life together during the composition of this book; in particular, for the whole of one Long Vacation when all waking moments had to be devoted to it. I cannot thank her too warmly for her sympathy and support, which mean everything to me.

Chronology

I Mabel and Aubrey Beardsley

1871   Birth of Mabel on 24 August to Vincent Paul Beardsley and Ellen Agnus Pitt, married in Brighton, 1870.

1872   Birth of Aubrey Vincent Beardsley on 21 August.

1885   Aubrey a boarder at Brighton Grammar School, in the town where he was born and spent his earlier childhood. Since 1883, it is thought, the Beardsleys' home had been in London.

1888   Aubrey leaves school for his first employment in a surveyor's office, and shortly afterwards with the Guardian Life and Fire Insurance Company in the City.

1891   Mabel and Aubrey meet Burne-Jones, who advises the boy to train for a professional career in art. As a result, Aubrey puts in a brief attendance at the Westminster School under Fred Brown.

1892   Aubrey is introduced to Robert Ross on 14 February and soon becomes a member of a group whose most celebrated personality is Oscar Wilde; produces his first Japanese-style drawings; and, in the autumn, secures a contract from Dent to illustrate *Le Morte Darthur*. By the end of this year he has taken Burne-Jones's advice and turned professional.

1893   Marks Aubrey's meteoric rise to fame, heralded by Joseph Pennell's article on his work published in the first number of *The Studio*. He is made much of in Paris as well as in London.

1894   Publication of Aubrey's most important early work, his illustrations to the English edition of Wilde's *Salomé*. In spite of this, Aubrey sees to it that Wilde plays no part in *The Yellow Book* for whose art-work he now becomes responsible. Volume I appears in April, taking him to the peak of his notoriety. In receipt now of a regular salary, he has been able to move with his family from lodgings at 59 Charlwood Street to a house of their own, 114

Aubrey and the Dying Lady

Cambridge Street, nearby. At the end of her summer term at the Polytechnic School for Girls, where she has been teaching, Mabel makes her début as a professional actress at The Assembly Rooms, Malvern, in a touring version of *A Woman of No Importance*.

1895   Wilde is arrested on 5 April. Shortly afterwards, a group of Bodley Head authors demands Aubrey's dismissal, because of the artist's association (in the public mind) with Wilde. His designs for Volume V of *The Yellow Book* do not appear, and he leaves Lane's employ for that of Leonard Smithers. With Smithers and Arthur Symons (and Mabel) in Dieppe he helps to plan *The Savoy*. Marc-André Raffalovich enters Aubrey's life, giving financial support.

1896   The first number of the magazine appears in January. It ushers in Aubrey's finest year's work, itself lasting exactly the twelve months. In the same year which witnesses the publication of a shortened version of *Under the Hill* (*The Story of Venus and Tannhäuser*), with its superb illustrations, and the technically astonishing *Rape of the Lock*, followed in the summer by the drawings for *Lysistrata*, Aubrey's health—he suffers from tuberculosis—breaks down. One crisis is survived in Brussels, but from now on the struggle continues against hopeless odds. Aubrey moves from Epsom to Boscombe. In November Mabel leaves for a tour of Canada and the States in *The Chili Widow*, later transferring to an American company under Richard Mansfield.

1897   *A Book of Fifty Drawings* published. Aubrey and his mother move from Boscombe to Bournemouth in late January. Encouraged by Raffalovich and John Gray, he becomes a Roman Catholic on 31 March. In April, with help from Raffalovich, mother and son depart for France. The search for health leads them from the Hôtel Voltaire, Paris, to St-Germain. Mabel, back from her American tour, is able to rejoin her family for a brief holiday in June, and later in August, by which time the scene is Dieppe. In December, Aubrey and his mother

Chronology

travel south to Menton. Death now stares the artist in the face, but this year has seen the production of some of the most remarkable of his drawings, including the illustrations for *Mademoiselle de Maupin*. Mabel pursues her theatrical career, in minor roles and short runs.

1898   When his rapidly-failing strength allows, Aubrey continues work on illustrations (begun late in 1897) for *Volpone*. He discusses with Mabel the possibility of bringing out a new Catholic quarterly magazine, but is unable to leave his room in the Hôtel Cosmopolitain after 26 January. A critical haemorrhage occurs about 5 March. On 7 March Aubrey writes his letter to Smithers, begging the publisher to destroy all copies of *Lysistrata* and '*all* obscene drawings', the envelope being addressed by Mrs Beardsley. Mabel is summoned from London, where she has been playing at the Garrick Theatre, and is in time to see her brother before he dies, aged 25, *either just before or just after midnight* on 15 March (the date always accepted up till now, based on Mabel's letter to Ross of the same day, is 16 March). Requiem Mass is celebrated in the Cathedral in Menton, and later, on 12 May, in the Jesuit Church in Farm Street, London.

II   Mabel Beardsley

1899   Is engaged to play the Duchess of Strood in a tour of Pinero's *The Gay Lord Quex*, but retires due to ill-health. Lodges with Mrs Erskine, in Gloucester Place, where she is observed by another guest, Faith Stone.

1900   Returns to the cast of *The Gay Lord Quex* in January. Writes for *The Idler* and reviews for *The Saturday Review*.

1901   Is described by Max Beerbohm as creating a 'great sensation' in Dieppe, where she takes a holiday in September.

1902   Plays in a revival of J. T. Grein's *The Degenerates* at the Imperial Theatre; at the St James's, in a matinée performance of *The Finding of Nancy* by her friend Netta Syrett; and in *The Lion Hunters* at Terry's Theatre, where she meets her future husband George Edward

Wright, who acts under the name of George Bealby and is always referred to as George Bealby Wright. Mabel is thirty-one, Bealby Wright twenty-five.

1903　On tour in South Africa in Mrs Lewis Waller's production of *The Marriage of Kitty*. On 30 September, with her father as a witness, she and Bealby Wright are married in the Roman Catholic Cathedral in London.

1906　Appears in a Drury Lane tableau (Ellen Terry's Benefit) designed by Bealby Wright's friend, James Pryde. From about 1905 Mabel, having given up the stage perhaps for health reasons, conducts a *salon* at 48 Charlwood Street attended by some of the most eminent men of the day, among them J. M. Barrie, H. B. Irving, Captain Robert Falcon Scott, as well as by friends of her brother, like Max Beerbohm.

1909　Death of Vincent Paul Beardsley from progressive muscular atrophy on 17 July. He was 69.

1910　Attends the Artists' Ball at the Grafton Galleries, but a photograph of her in fancy dress suggests a serious deterioration in health.

1911　Oswald Birley paints her portrait as 'An Elizabethan Age'.

1912　At some time before October, she enters a nursing-home in Holford Road, Hampstead. This is established by the Michael Fields' diary, which refers to the cause of her illness as cancer. At Christmas she receives the gift of a tree decked with toys and presents, an occasion immortalized by W. B. Yeats, a frequent visitor and correspondent from now on, though Edmund Davis, Charles Ricketts's patron, and Ricketts himself seem to have been its moving spirits.

1913　Yeats completes the seven short poems recording the incident, under the title of 'Upon a Dying Lady'. His letters written to Mabel, now in the collection of the University of Texas at Austin, cover the years 1913 and 1914.

1913–　Apart from one letter written by Mabel in July 1914 and
1916　another undated fragment, probably a little after the

outbreak of war, we have no more precise information on the last stages of her illness than is provided by Raffalovich's posthumous article in the magazine *Blackfriars*, of November 1928. At the last stage she leaves the nursing-home for her mother-in-law's house, 75 Lansdowne Road, Holland Park, where she dies on 8 May. The death certificate records the cause of death as cancer uteri, though this may be questioned. She was 44.

1917   'Upon a Dying Lady' appears in *The Little Review* and *The New Statesman*, before its publication in book form in 1919 in *The Wild Swans at Coole*.

1932   Ellen Agnus Beardsley dies on 15 January, aged 85.

Introduction:

How little we know

'Aubrey Beardsley now speaks for himself,' declared the Revd John Gray,[*] as long ago as 1904; and again, 'Of the work there remains probably nothing to be said.' Even in this centenary year of his birth, the chief objection raised against another book on Beardsley will be that everything has been written already. Yet Gray was wrong, and today we still know really very little about the artist. I shall devote my Introduction to a typical illustration of the problems ahead.

On the death of an old friend, in 1949, I found myself heir to his library. He had had a wonderful nose for rare editions and bibli-oddities of all kinds, and with other pickings I selected a badly singed green volume, a copy of the first (small-paper) edition of Ernest Dowson's *The Pierrot of the Minute* (Fig. 1), published in 1897, for which Aubrey Beardsley provided the frontispiece, an initial letter, a vignette and a cul-de-lampe.[†] The combined charms of poet and artist compensated for the book's miserable condition. Without examining it further, I slipped it into my bag with the others and travelled back to Devon. For fifteen years, the last eleven of them spent in Yorkshire, my whole time was absorbed by general problems of art history, and *The Pierrot of the Minute* remained forgotten on its shelf.

Then, one day, I happened by chance to open it, and found to my surprise that it contained an autograph letter from the artist on the fly-leaf and a note in the original owner's hand pasted to the inside front cover. The letter ran as follows:

Bournemouth, March 22nd.

My dear Julian

So glad to get a letter from you. I have been abominably ill all this year, and am now off to France for a change of everything. As this month's *Idler* will inform you I have 'not long to live'. Still I hope to make out twelve more months before I go away altogether.

[*]In his edition of *The Last Letters of Aubrey Beardsley*. John Gray (1866–1934), was a poet who became a Roman Catholic priest.
[†]Now in the collection of Mr W. G. Good.

Introduction

London will never see me again, for bacilli flourish rather too vigorously in its giddy atmosphere. Chastity has almost become a habit with me now, but my dear Julie, it will never become a taste—Sweetest messages to Mons Morgan.

Ever Yours

Aubrey Beardsley

1 Julian Sampson's copy of *The Pierrot of the Minute*, the discovery of which (badly damaged by fire) set in train the present writer's Beardsley investigations. Lettering and figure are stamped in gold on green cloth.

And the note in the recipient's hand read:
This *Pierrot of the Minute*—among the very few books rescued from the fire in Gray's Inn—was given to me by Aubrey Beardsley; and, in spite of its shocking condition, I keep it for the sake of his letter to me on the first page which is very characteristic of him. It has never been reproduced, and is unknown except to a few of my friends to whom I have shown it.

Julian Sampson 9.7.31.

Aubrey and the Dying Lady

No book on Aubrey Beardsley, or the Beardsley period, had ever mentioned any connexion between the artist and Julian Gilbert Sampson, to whom this letter is addressed in terms which suggest a considerable degree of intimacy. The letter was easy enough to place in its context. The year was 1897, and the book one of the complimentary copies for which Aubrey wrote to thank Leonard Smithers, its publisher, on 10 March; for *The Pierrot of the Minute* had appeared only a few days earlier.

The gloomy forecast printed in the March issue of *The Idler* reflected not just a whimsical delight in shocking the reader (since Aubrey virtually dictated this article) but a desperately sick man's courage in facing the truth. The year before, he had suffered a particularly terrible haemorrhage while walking in the Chine, and he had been much taxed, more recently, even by a trifling move from Boscombe to Bournemouth, where he was now staying in a boarding-house called Muriel in Exeter Road. On 7 March he had already told Smithers that his doctor would not hear of his returning to London, but was recommending Normandy or Brittany instead. On 31 March he was received into the Roman Catholic Church. In April he and his mother left for France. When death all too soon overtook him at Menton, in March of the following year, he had failed by five or six days to 'make out' the twelve months hoped for in his letter of 22 March 1897. And, lest it be supposed that I exaggerate our ignorance concerning the artist, I may add that I have just (November 1971) received official corroboration from the archives at Menton that Aubrey died, *effectivement*, as the French say, not on 16 March—the date given in every dictionary and autobiographical account and catalogue so far published—but on 15 March 1898.

This is not the place in which to give a full account of the obvious but nonetheless necessary lines of inquiry I had to pursue. It was not difficult to discover that Julian, the younger son of Colonel Thomas Sampson, landowner, of Moor Hall, Ninfield, in Sussex, and on his mother's side the grandson of a French nobleman, the Comte de Méric de St Martin, had been born in 1870 (two years earlier than Aubrey) and had died in 1942. Closer identification proved less easy. Sir Sacheverell Sitwell, with whom I was in correspondence, remembered being introduced to Sampson by Mrs Ada

Introduction

Leverson at an exhibition at the Leicester Galleries in the later 1920s. It seemed to Sir Sacheverell that Aubrey's friend had been tall and thin, and an impression of great elegance remained. Unfortunately, Mrs Guy Wyndham, the daughter of Mrs Leverson, had no recollection whatever of this dandy. And the elegance itself came to be momentarily challenged when I received word from the late Oliver Brown, whose omniscience was legendary, of a Café Royal-frequenting Sampson, forty years back, white-haired, white-bearded and stout.

The letter from Oliver Brown was followed by one from Vyvyan Holland, Wilde's younger son, then still living, but he had scarcely seen any of his father's and Aubrey's friends before about 1908, and he could form no mental picture of Julian Sampson. Meanwhile I was pursuing various elderly men-at-law who had once lived on Sampson's staircase at Gray's Inn, or had acted, or might be presumed to have acted, professionally for Julian and members of his family. This looked like being the most promising source of all: till the courteous Messrs X. and X. (of indecipherable signature) broke the news to me that the sole Sampson relict of Julian's generation had entered a Closed Order which proscribed correspondence. Mrs Allfree, widow of that unjustly neglected artist, Geoffrey Allfree, and once a neighbour of Aubrey's mother, strove bravely to recall some scrap of Pembroke Road conversation relating to Julian: without success.

In these circumstances, I placed an advertisement in *The Times*. It elicited but one response, with superscription printed in red on the pale blue paper, thus:

'Finis coronat opera'

The humour of 'Hogsnorton' its historian has had the high honour to depict before the Queen's Majesty and the Most Exalted Personages in this Realm of England.
ONE GAINSLEA COURT, DERBY ROAD, BOURNEMOUTH.
25187
There followed a typescript from Mr Gillie Potter (for the

writer was none other than the distinguished comedian, records of whose monologues on Hogsnorton we had collected in my boyhood), in which he showed the greatest interest in my advertisement. He had known more than one Sampson, but most particularly Evelyn, nephew of Julian. With Evelyn, a youthful Potter had been coached in Greek in a Cornish vicarage before the First World War. This member of the family had been the son of Julian's brother Gerald by his first wife, Miss Bonham; but he remembered, too, visiting 'Uncle Julian' in Arlington Street. Without question, Julian was Sir Sacheverell Sitwell's tall, thin pattern of elegance, not Mr Brown's squat, stout, white-bearded diner at the Café Royal.

Fascinated as I was by the Sampson family tree which 'Professor' Potter inventively sketched out, it will not be supposed that I ever allowed myself to lose sight of the real object of my investigations. Regrettably, the sudden restoring to life of a friend and patron of Aubrey (old lists confirm that Julian once owned the watercolour 'Hermaphroditus' and a sketch in chalks of Ada Lundberg (Fig. 2) had thrown no light on the circumstances or character of the relationship between the two young men—or three, if Morgan's proved a personality to be reckoned with. Correspondence concerning Sampson continued to flow in sluggishly from one non-*Times* source and another. Miss Katherine FitzGerald was able to supply me with expert information from the register of Sir John Lavery, who had painted a portrait of Sampson in 1905. Professor Denis Gwynn, Lavery's son-in-law, remembered meeting Julian with his mother, 'a formidable old lady of the Empress Eugénie period', at the Hôtel Meurice, Boulogne, during the 1920s. But it was all too late. Even Oliver Brown's memories had not stretched back to include Aubrey himself. Sir Gerald Kelly told me that Aubrey and he had once been invited to the same party, but the painter, then unknown, had been shy of attracting the attention of so celebrated a fellow-guest.

Just when the situation seemed quite hopeless, some outdated inquiry drew an answer at last—from Singapore, from Lieut-Colonel Richard Sampson: I was now in correspondence with the great-nephew of Aubrey Beardsley's friend Julian. Colonel Sampson made references to the family's descent from George IV on the

Introduction

2 Ada Lundberg, music-hall artiste: Aubrey's sketch of 1893. Drawn with coloured chalks on brown paper, it perished in the fire from which *The Pierrot of the Minute* was rescued.

male side, and to an old green trunk at Sutton-on-Hone, in which would be found a photograph of Lavery's portrait of his great-uncle. The original, as Lavery noted in his register before he died, had perished in the disastrous fire at Gray's Inn. This represented the most promising line of investigation yet. And Colonel Sampson was good enough to put me in touch with his step-aunt, Miss Stella Alleyne.

Her first letter inspired me with the highest hopes:

I think I knew him [Julian Sampson] as well as anyone of the family, whose memory would not go back so far. My mother married—a second marriage on both sides—Gerald Sampson,

Aubrey and the Dying Lady

Julian's elder brother. I was then about seven and often saw
Aubrey Beardsley (a sad, delicate-looking young man) and his
mother and sister, who had wonderful red-gold hair, at the
Vicarage of St Barnabas, Pimlico. The Vicar, Alfred Gurney,
was a very rich man and knew many artistic and literary people.
His niece, Helen, a child of my age and a daughter of Edmund
Gurney, the Psychical Research author, composed poems. She
read one of them to me (not a very attentive listener, for it was
of Homeric length), and I remember her saying: 'And Mr
Beardsley has drawn pictures for it.'

In April 1966 my wife and I drove to Cuckfield and spent
the afternoon with Miss Alleyne, who could summon up the
late 1880s as though it had been yesterday and was, I would
hazard, the only person left in the whole world who could remember Aubrey in the days of his early youth. Waiting for me, as
promised, was the photograph of Lavery's perished portrait of
Julian Sampson. It showed a handsome and effeminate man of
thirty-five, his features having that slight Hanoverian cast which
Gillie Potter, in discussing the facial characteristics of all the
Sampsons, had referred to as a 'touch of Prinny'. A dandy, if ever
there was one, Julian had been depicted holding in his right hand a
delicate statuette, presumably in bronze. As this might be the
handiwork of Ricketts (if not of Rodin), the connoisseur, too, was
thus suggested.

There were more photographs, of a perceptibly homosexual
character. In one, the same elegant young man, exactly Aubrey's
'dear Julie', dreamed, Narcissus-like, in eighteenth-century costume (had I not my own theories, newly-formed, about the
influence of that period, Gallic in source, upon the Nineties?).
In another, he sat as it were enthroned, very much the dominant
partner with what appears to be a current love in woman's finery
leaning seductively over his shoulder (Fig. 3). In another photograph still—and memories of Jerome K. Jerome made all three
of us smile as we examined it—were gathered together three

*I discussed with Mr Brian Reade the fascinating possibility that this could have been
'Bertram Lawrence', pseudonym of J. F. Bloxham, author of the notorious *The Priest and
the Acolyte* under his own name, but contributor of poetry to *The Artist* as 'Lawrence'.
Mr Reade showed conclusively that it could not be.

Introduction

3 Julian Sampson, Aubrey's mysterious friend,
photographed with a conjectural male partner
dressed as a girl.

flannelled friends: Julian; a youth Miss Alleyne spoke of as
'Bertie Laurie'*; and George Thomas Morgan himself, wearing a
straw-hat and golden, well-brushed, wide-winged moustaches.

After a short reign only, Morgan left St James's Square for
chambers in the Haymarket. Miss Alleyne remembered him well,
before a lovers' tiff interrupted the gay muffin-teas at No. 24, so
innocently enjoyed by the little girl and her mother, Julian's
sister-in-law. To Morgan succeeded Victor Miller, a stalwart
fellow whose likeness was also now available, posed with Julian
and an intruder from the opposite sex (Mrs Neville) in the grounds
of Lady Eldon's bungalow at Bourne End (Fig. 4); and, no
doubt, many more. But I was neither historically nor clinically
concerned with the general pattern of Sampson's existence; nor
with his wit (described by someone in the Lavery circle as 'Sitwell-

and-water') and connoisseurship (he and his cronies interested themselves in such topics as the 'fate of the door' in early nineteenth-century interior design). I had hoped to be exploring

4   Julian Sampson (left), Victor Miller, a homosexual partner, and Mrs Neville in the garden of Lady Eldon's bungalow at Bourne End.

the nature of the bond between this young sprig of fashion and Aubrey Beardsley. How and where had they met? At the St Barnabas parsonage? This had seemed to me likeliest. The Beardsleys were often entertained at Gurney's table, which, again, would have supplied Julian with as fine a dinner as he could wish for, to say nothing of the probable company, too, of his brother Gerald and his cultured sister-in-law.*

But Miss Alleyne was not so certain. Truth to tell, she found it difficult to believe that her cheerful step-uncle and the melancholic, drooping Aubrey had ever been close friends. If Julian came to the Vicarage, she surmised, it would not have been for the pleasure of meeting the young artist (then an unknown, poverty-stricken amateur), or his sanctimonious brother Gerald, but to call on Willie Gurney, reputed 'wild', even Wildean. I also began to have second thoughts. I had been to some trouble to study Aubrey's varied, and strangely conflicting, epistolary styles since my discovery of the Sampson letter. It seemed to me now too 'brilliant' in tone to have sprung from the deepest attachment. For the closer friends of the artist, few aphorisms, or departures into the heroical, lightened the long, harrowing accounts of blistering and blood-spitting. So I was back more or less where I had started, the richer for three or four photographs. Miss Alleyne could tell me no more about Aubrey himself in those far-off days: and in 1966 one had little hope of meeting another observer of Aubrey from the life.

It was on the whole, therefore, in a spirit of disappointment that my wife and I drove south from Cuckfield through the lengthening shadows, the names and features of the terrain, associated with the long exile of school, adding for me their own nostalgic sadness. Ditchling, Lewes, Firle: now we were bumping along the track which leads to remote Charleston, where, at the very foot of the Downs, Duncan Grant has his studio. The eighty-one-year-old painter, from whom my university was to buy a characteristic work, had been ten when the Wilde affair exploded and Aubrey lost his post as art editor of *The Yellow Book*. Unfortunately (for the purpose of these researches) Grant had been brought up in India, not Pimlico, and had never attended a late-Victorian Sunday service at St Barnabas.

I had now spent two or three years trying to find out something as elementary as the plain facts of a friendship between Aubrey Beardsley and this wealthy young man with whom he must have

*The Revd Gerald Sampson was one of Father Gurney's curates.

been on at least affectionate terms. A couple of postcards, so Mr Henry Maas was to tell me later, show that the pair had been known to each other from 1893, and the letter in *The Pierrot of the Minute* was written four years afterwards. Four years (if not five) in the artist's mere six effective years of adult life must testify to more than a fleeting acquaintance. Add to this, that Sampson acquired for himself not only the 'Hermaphroditus' and sketch of Ada Lundberg, but one of the *Lysistrata* drawings as well. How many more friends of Aubrey's were there of whom we know nothing? How many other aspects of his life and character are still withheld from us?

Gray, in fact, was much mistaken when he suggested, even in 1904, that the artist's life had always been an open book. As to there being nothing more to say about his work, our new permissiveness has barely loaded its starting-pistol. Nor, as the next few pages may I hope suggest, will the problem of Aubrey's style (or styles) be found to have yielded up every mystery.

A Young Marcellus

One

Almost as unfortunate as Chatterton, Aubrey Beardsley equally deserves the title 'marvellous'. Indeed, in both genius and courage, he can be reckoned Chatterton's superior.

Born on 21 August 1872, he died on 15/16 March 1898,* having outlived the poet by eight years, yet still barely reaching maturity. 'Brutally clipped, a victim of victims,' so Henry James, bewailing the talent less, bewailed the artist.[1] And long afterwards André Raffalovich† wrote: 'When I remember him, I remember his youth.'[2] Young as he was (twenty-five years and close on seven months, at his death), he craved to be younger still; and compilers of reference-books were for a long while ignorant of the year or two habitually subtracted from his age in any *curriculum vitae*.

Yet he had never been a prodigy to match the infant Thomas Lawrence or the golden-haired, pre-adolescent Millais. The Royal Academy Schools would not have been much impressed by his performance at eleven. Piety, if piety governed the counsels of John Lane,‡ has preserved Aubrey's juvenilia: sketches already in pen and ink that go back to his twelfth and thirteenth years. For a draftsman of that age they are neither particularly bad nor particularly brilliant.

'On my first day at dinner,' recalls the impresario Charles B. Cochran, who had arrived in the same term (January 1885)§ at the Brighton Proprietary Grammar and Commercial School, 'I sat next to a delicate-looking boy, thin, red-haired, and with a slight stoop. He was a particularly quick talker, used his hands to gesticulate, and altogether had an un-English air about him.'[3] Though Cochran thought more highly of his study-mate as an actor than as an artist, other boys seem to have been impressed by

*See Chronology.
†Marc-André Raffalovich (1864–1934), Aubrey's 'Catholic conscience' and benefactor from 1895. See 'Passionate Friends'.
‡1854–1925: the most important of Aubrey's early publishers.
§Autumn 1884, if Cochran refers to Aubrey's arrival as a day-boy.

1

the sheer range of the newcomer's accomplishments (Fig. 5).

The following ex-prefect's account, bleak as the world of ink-wells and gnarled desks from which it springs, usefully supplements Cochran's and has not, to my knowledge, been published before:

He was in a sailor suit and knickerbockers, which made him look younger than the others. He had reddish hair. I said to

5   Aubrey Beardsley at the beginning of his schooldays.

him: 'What's your name?' He said: 'Beardsley.' 'What else?'
'Aubrey.' [When, many years later, the artist was staying in a
house called 'Muriel', he told a friend: 'I feel as shy of my
address as a boy at school is of his Christian name when it is
Ebenezer or Aubrey.'] I said: 'What can you do? Are you any
good at cooking?' He said he was not much good at cooking. I
said: 'What *can* you do?' And he replied: 'What do you want
me to do?' 'Well, apart from what I want you to do in the study,
have you got any accomplishments?' He said: 'Well, one or
two.' 'What are they?' 'I can sketch a bit.' I said: 'All right,
sketch me then,' and he sat down and did a very good profile of
me. I said: 'That's pretty good. What else can you do?' He said:
'Would you like some music?' I replied: 'Yes, let's have some
music.' 'Would you like something original?' I said: 'Yes.'
There was no piano in the room, but he went to a little har-
monium, sat down and said: 'I'll give you something original.'
There were several boys looking on and we thought his composition was very good. I said: 'Well, that's good. What else can
you do?' He said: 'Do you like poetry? Would you like a
recitation—something original?' I said: 'Yes.' So he immediately
went to the other end of the room, stood up and recited a piece
called 'The Pirate' which appeared [apparently as 'The Valiant']
in the School Magazine afterwards.[4]

If the reader supposes that such brilliance (which did not include
cutting any sort of a dash on the playing-field in the Old Shoreham
Road) brought Aubrey popularity, he cannot know much of
British schools, day or boarding. And though there are reports to
the effect that the artist held his own among the young philistines,
the system had not won his approval. 'The education of children
in England,' he observed later, 'is indeed a thing to make one
aghast.'[5] A. W. King,* a master, was kind and encouraging, however, and drawing began to take precedence over Aubrey's other
interests.

Some sketches guying Virgil and his Headmaster have a dentist's
waiting-room humour about them. Two illustrated letters written
to a Miss Felton during his schooldays offer a hint of the economy

*1855–1922. Later of the Blackburn Technical Institute.

of line which was to become so memorable—but a hint only. In *The Uncollected Work* Lane gave an elaborate showing to the programme-designs made by Aubrey for family entertainments between 1884 and 1888. They mark the stages of his growing-up, but none along the path to *Salome* and *The Yellow Book*.

Two

Among the Lane papers is a note from another Brighton master, Fred Carr. He must have seen something of Aubrey after the boy had left school at the end of 1888, and asked him how he was getting on. Aubrey is said to have replied that he 'spent his evenings [in London] walking the streets . . . it was there he saw the subjects which he drew and elaborated on his return home'.[6] This sounds like a recollection in senility on the part of Carr, who must have been getting on in years by 1920. I cannot see Aubrey at any time taking Gavarni's advice about putting out his lamp, pulling on his breeches and slipping off for twelve hours—or even one hour—into the hundred-and-one activities that 'churn the streets into mud'. The drawings which belong to the immediate post-school period have more to do with books and plays. Aubrey was a Mannerist: he created his images from within.

All the same, London (whither his family had moved about the year 1883)* remained his first and last love; and, whatever damage it did his lungs, no other environment better suited satire and invention. The close chambers and tenuous galleries of the city's labyrinth wonderfully concentrated his fancy. In the midst of the maze was his first place of employment, a surveyor's office, sometimes referred to as an architect's office, since E. Carritt, his immediate superior, acted as architect as well as surveyor to the District of Clerkenwell and a part of Islington, at 3 Wilmington Square, W.C. Aubrey spent but a short while there, before he moved on to the City, to the Guardian Life and Fire Insurance Company's head office in Lombard Street.

His clerkship does not seem to have been especially humiliating or demanding. Mr Anthony Symondson has examined the unpublished papers of Sir Ninian Comper,† from which it appears

---

*I have never been able to find proof of this, but it is respectably vouched for.
†1864–1960. Church architect and designer.

that there were men in the Fire Office aware of Aubrey's promise as an artist.[7] And the dullness of his existence was enlivened by the shop of Jones and Evans in nearby Queen Street, where his drawings were taken in exchange for books.

About this time, Aubrey attended an occasional reunion of the Old Boys of his school. One of them, H. S. M. Grover, recaptured something from his memory of such events, held annually in London. A glimpse is thereby given us of another, and for my purpose not irrelevant, side of the young artist-clerk: 'We were discussing the sex question and he [Aubrey] wound up the conversation by remarking forcibly that if a woman were possessed by a man, she wanted to be, and that was all about it.'[8] One can imagine the fluttering hands and high staccato tone adding to the shock of this announcement, flung with such conviction at less sophisticated Old Grammarians. For Aubrey, quite apart from his preoccupation with the 'sex question', the need to *épater les bourgeois* seems to have been paramount from the beginning.*

Three

A pencil-drawing, typically and grandiloquently entitled 'Hamlet patris manem sequitur' (Fig. 6), of about 1891, seems to bring the juvenile productions to a close. Lacking the emotion of an early 'Tannhäuser' and the malice of another youthful work, the 'Litany of St Mary Magdalene', this 'Hamlet' is oppressively derivative.

Indeed, Aubrey's early dependence on fellow artists reminds one of Raphael who, in Roger Fry's witty phrase, burrowed through his elders like an earthworm. The two were similar in their apprenticeship attachments, Raphael to Perugino, Aubrey to Edward Burne-Jones,† for there was the same cloying sweetness to emulate (Fig. 7). In July 1891 occurred a personal encounter between the nineteen-year-old employee of the Guardian Life and Fire Insurance Office and the venerated painter at The Grange, North End Lane. Praise was bestowed. Letters of advice and

---

*This was the opinion of Wilde, a good judge in such matters, expressed in a letter to Robert Ross, January 1899.
†Sir Edward Burne-Jones, Bart (1833–1898), was at the height of his fame from the early 1880s.

6   Hamlet patris manem sequitur: published in *The Bee*, 1891.

encouragement followed. Burne-Jones recommended a course of study: 'You must learn the grammar of your art, and its exercises are all the better for being rigidly prosaic,' he said.[9] It was at his suggestion that Aubrey presented himself to Fred Brown at the

7   Sir Edward Burne-Jones, 'The Arming of Perseus', *c.* 1875. The painting provides a good example of a woman (albeit Minerva) who might well be a man suffering from gynaecomastia, with breastplate adjusted to meet this contingency, and a man himself in an advanced stage of atrophy of the testes. Aubrey is often thought to have caricatured these sexual ambiguities in *Le Morte Darthur*: in fact, it is more likely that he genuinely shared Burne-Jones' taste for the epicene.

Westminster School of Art,* instead of applying to South
Kensington. Brown (that unacknowledged star of late nineteenth-
century English painting) was man enough to swallow the
'grotesque' element in the specimens presented and paid handsome
tribute to Aubrey's promise. All these early pieces of professional
good fortune—soon to include election to the New English Art
Club and a warm welcome at the Salon of the Champ de Mars in
Paris—can be traced back to the kind offices of Burne-Jones. The
circumstances favouring this dominating influence were therefore
exceptional. Nor need we be too apologetic about it: Morris's
right-hand man had an impeccable sense of design.

Four

It could have been admiration for Burne-Jones, too, that attracted
Aubrey to Prince's Gate in the first instance, for a number of the
painter's best known works there were on public exhibition. Of
this visit, still in July 1891, he wrote to G. F. Scotson-Clark,† a
school-friend trying his luck with Cochran in the States: 'Yesterday
I went to Mr Leyland's house. His collection is GLORIOUS.'10
He went on to list what was so glorious: the Rossettis, the Ford
Madox Browns, Millais's 'Eve of St Agnes' (certainly one of the
basic documents of the Aesthetic Movement) and, of course, the
bevy of Burne-Joneses. Leyland's purchases from the Casa Pacci
received mention, Botticelli and Filippo Lippi being raised to the
same exalted status as the Pre-Raphaelites.

   But Frederick Leyland had been most notably the champion of
Whistler. What brought the public to Prince's Gate was not so
much its Old Masters, genuine or attributed, Rossetti's somnolent
ladies or Burne-Jones's bloodless ones, as the excitement of behold-
ing that supreme memorial to the wayward artistic temperament,
Leyland's dining-room, the Peacock Room.‡ Aubrey, too, gazed
with admiration at Whistler's painting, 'La Princesse du Pays de
la Porcelaine': this we know from a charming little water-colour
note of it sent to Scotson-Clark. In the same letter there is evidence

---

* Frederick Brown (1851–1941) left the Westminster School for the Slade in 1892.
† 1872–1927. He left for America with C. B. Cochran in 1892.
‡ J. A. McN. Whistler (1834–1903) decorated the Peacock Room for F. R. Leyland,
founder of a Liverpool steamship line, in 1876–7.

of the visitor's delight in the blue-and-gold decoration opposite, the peacocks themselves, shining out undimmed by fourteen years of London fog sieved through the grimy sashes (Figs. 8, 9). Wings spread, eye-feathered trains swirling round them, they must have

8   The dining-room, or 'Peacock Room', decorated by Whistler, at the house of Frederick Leyland in Prince's Gate.

made the deeper impression; for not only would a similarly arrogant subjection of nature to decorative ends, and marshalling of empty space to sharpen the silhouette, become important factors in Aubrey's art, the actual Whistlerian shorthand is taken over by the younger artist in design after design.

There was something else in the Leyland dining-room: before Whistler painted his peacocks, an architect called Thomas Jeckell* had set up shelves to carry splendid examples from the shipowner's collection of porcelain. The principle of this delicate scaffolding (which inspired The Butterfly to 'ruin' Leyland's Spanish leather at the outset), a subtle play of vertical against

_____
1827–1881. He made his name with a splendid piece of ironwork known as the 'Norwich Gates'.

horizontal, is a cross between the Gothic and the Japanese. In a sense, too, it takes us back to Rossetti (a blossom-strung trellis, gold on the black buckram of his sister's *Poems*) and forward to Charles Ricketts (and the felicitous binding for *The Sphinx*).*

Going thro' the rooms

9   Aubrey's impression of Mabel and himself on the occasion of their visit to Prince's Gate in the summer of 1891 to see Whistler's 'Peacock Room'.

Aubrey's own dallying with this panel-motif, glimpsed first perhaps in its perfection at Prince's Gate, was especially momentous. Mediaeval and 'Japonesque' unite in those drawings in which he initiates the style that marks him out as a great original artist.

Five

In another letter of 1891, Aubrey spoke with enthusiasm of Hampton Court. Above all, he relished the Mantegnas (Figs. 10 and 11). Not long ago, with Aubrey in mind, I re-visited the Palace to

---

*The books carrying these designs appeared in 1861 and 1894, respectively. D. G. Rossetti (1828–82) exercised a powerful influence for many years. Charles Ricketts (1866–1931), founder of the Vale Press, designed other books for Oscar Wilde besides *The Sphinx*.

10 Andrea Mantegna's 'Triumphal Car' from the series known as *The Triumph of Caesar* at Hampton Court Palace (Royal Collection), begun about 1477 and acquired by Charles I in 1629. Mantegna remained Aubrey's favourite model from early youth till his death. He might well have taken his 'V' for 'U' in the signing of his name from the fine piece of painted lettering above.

look again at those nine noble, sculpturesque canvases completed by Andrea Mantegna during the last years of the fifteenth century and acquired by Charles I for the Royal Collection in 1629. By good luck I was able to see them while still under the hands of the restorer in the Queen's Guard and Presence Chambers. In Aubrey's day, the compositions forming what is called 'The Triumph of Caesar', apart from their dirt and overpainting, hung behind glass, facing windows. Splendid as they now appeared to me (Verrio's re-touching scraped off), it must have been almost by a process of divination that Aubrey could style them 'tremendous' and an 'art training in themselves'.[11]

Fine they are, of course, and everything Aubrey claimed for them. They formed, besides, an antidote to the willow-willow-waly-O of Ned Jones, for if ever a great master stuck to facts, Mantegna did. Which does not prevent the facts of the 'Triumph'— the soldiers' kilts and buskins, swords, lances and Eagles, the faithfully rendered Corinthian columns, the chariot-wheels encrusted with ornament—being, all of them, turned to decorative purpose. Of the human figures rendered by Mantegna, a scholar has written 'We may call it logic or responsibility: they stand where they are placed, by necessity. Nothing in them is accidental, and their presence elucidates the laws governing art.' The very

11   'The Elephants', from the same series at Hampton Court. One is inevitably reminded of Aubrey's early visits to the Palace by his initial 'V' for the *Volpone*, carried out in Menton.

impersonality of Mantegna, his coldness accentuated by the sandy grounds painted over in stone colour, made him the more valuable model for Aubrey. Wit and mockery could be added, but the pen-drawn figures would still share with Mantegna's that character of severe deliberation.

12 Wren's Fountain Court, Hampton Court Palace.

There was much else in this artist's work to hold Aubrey's attention, not just at the impressionable stage but throughout his life. The treatment of garlanded fruit and foliage, massed treasure, urns on pedestals seen *sotto in sù*, even the 'Triumph of Caesar' elephants which supply inspiration for a *Volpone* Initial just before his death: all may be traced to Mantegna, whose prints covered the walls of the hotel bedroom in Menton where Aubrey spent his last hours. Strangely enough, Mantegna's dominant trait as an engraver, the lavish oblique shading, he ignored, except in one instance of relevant *pastiche* (Fig. 101). Of all artistic borrowers, Aubrey was the subtlest and most selective.

Hampton Court itself, whither Mrs Arabella Fermor, Belinda of *The Rape of the Lock*, was rowed in her painted vessel,

The sun-beams trembling on the floating tides,
remained a favourite rendezvous for Aubrey; and when it could no
longer be that, a nostalgic dream: 'How I envy anyone who is able
to spend the summer on the Thames,' he wrote to Raffalovich
from Boscombe, in 1896, 'and be within punting distance of the
ever gracious Hampton Court.'[12] The *charm, preciseness and grace*
which Agostino Taja found in Mantegna, together with that
astringent formality I have alluded to, are not restricted to the
'Triumph', though Aubrey considered it the Palace's chief glory.
These terms apply equally well to the buildings which house
Mantegna's pictures and to its pretty gardens. Throughout Aubrey's
work, one is reminded of Wren's Fountain Court (Fig. 12) and
garden façades. The stone swags on the mellowed brick, the
cloister lamps, the rich labels under their heavy cornices, a
pair of Terms flanking a fireplace, the elegant fenestration of the
Lower Orangery; and, above all, the garden vistas, clipped and
statued: these pass into Aubrey's natural vocabulary.

Six

We know from Robert Ross* that the young artist explored other
departments than the Print Room in the British Museum with
'extraordinary thoroughness'.[13] When tempted to ascribe the
quality of his line, the disposition of his simplified darks and
lights, exclusively to Harunoto or Utamaro or to over-emphasize
the influence of that *Book of Love* passed on to him by William
Rothenstein,† we do well to remember this. Japan, as Aubrey
would himself have been the first to point out, was not the whole
world.

The Greek vase-painters must instantly have attracted him.
Kylix, lethykos and rhyton, black-figure and red-figure, had
messages to convey to the young draftsman very different from
those of the 'statue standing still' which conversed with Housman
in his 'Grecian gallery'—a gallery tucked, too, one assumes, behind

*Robert Baldwin Ross (1869–1918), close friend of the artist and his mother and sister.
See 'Passionate Friends'. Mr Reade tells me that Aubrey's name is not among those
actually recorded as having used the Print Room.
†Sir William Rothenstein (1872–1945), a brilliant young draftsman specializing in por-
traiture and a prolific forger of links between art and literature.

Smirke's massive portico in Great Russell Street. These satyrs and revellers were far from advising a stoic: 'Courage, lad, 'tis not for long.' He knew, we can hardly doubt, of Pater's celebrated essay on Winckelmann,* yet did not feel obliged to turn to the author of the *Geschichte der Kunst des Altertums* to sanction his likes and dislikes, or restrict the qualities he looked for in art to 'noble simplicity' and 'quiet grandeur'. Studying the more mischievous products of the Ceramicus, he well understood that the hand elaborating the glans penis or brushing in the pubic curls had been shaken by the same gusts of sacrilegious laughter as his own. He found no élite here to look up to. Like the Shropshire Lad, he could have kicked his heels in contemplation of heroic marbles. He chose otherwise. Aubrey, indeed, lacked entirely the faculty of respect: though imposing its limitations, that was his great strength.

Seven

Almost every past style of painting drew him like a bee on the wing. In between, and passionately, he collected examples by the old steel- and copper-plate craftsmen: 'I have just found a shop,' he once told Rothenstein, 'where very jolly *contemporary* engravings from Watteau can be got cheaply, Cochin, etc.'[14]

As we know from the letters, he retained his love of Watteau. Much prized by him were the engravings after the paintings and drawings published by Watteau's patron, Julienne. These had been among the first to aim at facsimile quality rather than systematized reproduction, and they led naturally to the technical innovations of the eighteenth century in that field—in particular, to stipple, aquatinting and the use of the roulette—which, in turn, would be ingeniously simulated by Aubrey's clever pen. With Watteau, like himself a consumptive and graceful performer on two planes of meaning, the nineteenth-century artist must have felt a special kinship.

From J.-M. Moreau and Gabriel de Saint Aubin he was able to extract a less spiritual enjoyment; and to borrow, for the sheer fun

---

*Published in *The Westminster Review* in 1867 and subsequently in *Studies in the History of the Renaissance*, 1873, the book which established the reputation of Walter Pater (1839–94).

of it, details of furnishing and interior decoration—so that Pope's
Rape of the Lock, of 1712, is unconcernedly presented in a Louis
Seize setting.

Eight

But, given this noticeable switch in his work from the oriental to
the age of Hogarth, from sharply differentiated black and white to
grey (obtained by imitation of the close-laid lines of the Western
engravers), we have still not accounted for the mood in Aubrey
which it gratified.

His interest in the eighteenth century could have been stimu-
lated or heightened by a taste for Théophile Gautier.* The
archaizing foibles of the group of Romantics gathered together in
the Impasse du Doyenné during the early 1830s have been recorded
by Gérard de Nerval in his *Petits Châteaux de Bohème*. We learn,
specifically, of a revival of enthusiasm for late seventeenth and
early eighteenth-century art. The grey panelling of Rogier's vast,
dilapidated apartment in the Impasse was painted over with just the
kind of after-the-event *fêtes galantes* that Aubrey delighted in supplying to Smithers for *The Savoy* in the brief and dazzling St
Martin's summer of his genius. However, when all his debts to the
eighteenth century have been set down, Aubrey will be seen to have
thrown deeper roots into the seventeenth.

One of the first surprises experienced by young Cochran was
to find his twelve-year-old contemporary deep in the *Love in a Tub*
school of playwrights. 'Even in those days,' he recalled, 'Beardsley
preferred Congreve and Wycherley to the ordinary books of
boyhood.'[15] And it was back from Versailles bathroom-Rococo to
the robust Baroque, a *barocco* described in a late eighteenth-
century dictionary of the Fine Arts as the 'superlative of the
bizarre', that Aubrey's truest instincts directed him. He would
always, of course, climb up and down the chronological ladder at
will. Never, for instance, did he lose his taste for the Restoration
dramatists; and the comically elaborate Dedication from *Venus
and Tannhäuser* surely smacks of Otway at that writer's most
ingratiating. The painting and writing of the Baroque, early and

*Théophile Gautier died in 1872, the year Aubrey was born, but his most influential work
was done twenty to forty years earlier.

late, dually inspired him. One can well sense the swirling rhythm of Rubens's 'Last Judgement' reduced to an abstraction on the front-cover of *Volpone* (Fig. 13). And with the drawing for the

13 *Ben Jonson his Volpone: or The Foxe*, front cover, the design for which, though dated 'Paris 1898', was sent by the artist to Smithers from Menton early in December 1897.

frontispiece of the same work, Aubrey's agate-hardness of temper seems to have encountered its final and perfect foil in a Jacobean author, the robust Ben Jonson.

Nine

Besides the use he made of the art of the past, there has to be reckoned what was owing to *Zeitgeist* and *Zeitgenossen*. Once having acknowledged the role of Burne-Jones and the influence of Whistler, we find that Aubrey's debts to contemporaries are not extensive. He would, I think, have been distressed—and with reason—to see the entries in some popular dictionaries of art which present him as a 'chief exponent' of the style associated with Mackmurdo, Rennie Mackintosh and the Macdonald sisters.* His visions were of a classic clarity, quite different (once he had left extreme youth behind) from those of the Glasgow School still wreathed in the mists of Ossian. It is as absurd to call his work *art nouveau* as it would be to call Michelangelo a Mannerist: even in the realms of creative imagination the horse still comes before the cart.

Another suggestion, that Aubrey drew largely on the Frenchmen of his day can be traced to Arthur Symons,† in the essay published by him just after the artist's death in 1898.[16] Beyond his openly expressed pleasure in the work of Puvis de Chavannes‡ (a Gallic Burne-Jones, appealing to Aubrey at the same stage) and what we may assume he discovered in that of Degas and Toulouse-Lautrec, there seems little substance in this. Symons spent more than two of his twenty-four pages§ deploring the superficial cleverness of the French comic papers and posters, as though the English artist had been infected by their slick, eye-catching qualities. Aubrey loved Paris and produced posters himself: *ergo*, he must have studied the hoardings in the Boulevard de Clichy

---

*A. H. Mackmurdo (1851–1942) started *The Hobby Horse* with Herbert Horne: Charles Rennie Mackintosh (1868–1928), like Mackmurdo, was a designer and architect, and was married to an artist, Margaret Macdonald, sister of Frances. Aubrey did, of course, contribute to the *art nouveau* canon.
†1865–1945, critic and poet, who worked in close collaboration with Aubrey on *The Savoy* magazine in 1896.
‡1824–1898.
§*Aubrey Beardsley*, 1898, reprinted 1948.

with the rapt attention accorded by a young Florentine to the
Brancacci Chapel frescoes.

No doubt, he knew and appreciated the good points of Chéret,*
just as he would have enjoyed the drawings of Léandre and Caran
d'Ache—especially the last, with his finely-groomed line; but
leafing through *Gil Blas Illustré* and *La Vie Parisienne* for the
jokes (and, perhaps, in the month of August, for the fanciful
bathing-costumes), is a very different thing from becoming the
disciple of a particular style, and Aubrey could certainly have
learned nothing from Chéret himself, father of the contemporary
affiche. Chéret was preoccupied by the very things Aubrey avoided.
The Frenchman's posters are mere vignettes writ large. Crisp
outline is entirely absent. Form hardly exists. All is subordin-
ated to an illusion of gay, abandoned movement. Painstakingly
pretty and without any undertow of satrical comment, careless
(the kindest word) of the titling that accounts for a quarter to a
third of a *grand aigle* sheet, Chéret and his professional brethren—
with the possible exception of Grasset†—have little in common with the Aubrey of 'A Comedy of Sighs', the Todhunter
poster for The Avenue Theatre, of 1894 (Fig. 14). This and the
two T. Fisher Unwin posters, 'The Pseudonym and Autonym
Libraries' and 'Children's Books', and other posters and posterettes
advertising *The Yellow Book* and *The Savoy*, are all entirely
personal in form and colour and display the artist's characteristic
respect for the picture-area's boundaries which exercise their usual
influence on the deliberately severe and static design.

Ten

By the autumn of 1892, Aubrey was able to leave the Fire Insurance
Office and, as Burne-Jones had advised, take up art as a career.

'The best and biggest thing I am working on at present is
Malory's *Morte Darthur* (a splendid *édition de luxe*) for which I
am getting £200,' he wrote at this auspicious moment to his old
Headmaster in Brighton.[17]

The commission given him by J. M. Dent‡ to illustrate *Le*

*Jules Chéret (1836–1932).
†Eugène Grasset (1841–1917).
‡1849–1926. Founded his publishing house in 1888.

14   Poster for *A Comedy of Sighs*, 1894.

Morte Darthur started off, indeed, as God's gift to the young unknown, but was to become—so quickly did Aubrey establish his reputation—a bore and a misery before the drawings were completed. 'Variable' might aptly describe Aubrey's contribution to the *Morte*, which appeared in parts during 1893 and 1894, with a first bound edition in three volumes. There is some superb interlacing-pattern (this he seems to have been able to manufacture almost with his eyes shut), and a number of the chapter-headings will remain classics in that *genre*. The broad treatment of black and white also augurs well. But the figure-work is still a disconcerting echo of Burne-Jones; while, though the pen-line is grand throughout, the illustrative content and even the decorative invention (as Aubrey himself would have admitted) are often ludicrously skimped.

One must distinguish, however, between haste and deliberate simplification, between ignorance and caprice. If the spirit means more than the letter, there is no need to wince at the floral and faunal freedoms which shocked Aymer Vallance* (Fig. 15). All the same, we can amuse ourselves by speculating on the plant which so splendidly enlivens the spine and front-cover of the bound volumes (Fig. 16). Is it a Gloriosa Lily furnished with the leaves of the *Sagittaria*? Or is Mr Brian Reade correct in opting for a triple hybrid, combining the Passion Flower, *Clementis viticella* and the Tulip? One is left with the suspicion that, sinister or suffocating in their botanical eccentricity, all Aubrey's flowers are *Fleurs du Mal*; but I am grateful to Mr Derek Stanford for drawing my attention to Havelock Ellis's belief that the pear ought to be a female symbol,[18] since one of the full-page borders is loaded with pears and Aubrey, like some of the actresses he admired, specialized in the *double-entendre*. We shall have reason to return to Havelock Ellis, a contributor to *The Savoy*, when we come to consider in rather more detail, later on, the possible origin of Aubrey's images.

Of ironic significance in the *Morte* is the definition it offers of an illustrator's duty to his author and his author's readers. With some

*Aymer Vallance (1862–1943) was a connoisseur of the applied arts and authority on ecclesiastical architecture. Aubrey called him in as interior decorator, when he moved to 114 Cambridge Street in 1894. They had met through one of the High Church clergy at the Church of The Annunciation in Brighton.

Chap.
riv.

15 Chapter-headings, hermaphroditic in character, from *Le Morte
Darthur*, published 1893–4.

justice, the supplying of pictures to books may be regarded as auxiliary, a service. When Aubrey received his Malory commission, illustration certainly had that character. But it is doubtful if, even

16   Design for cover and spine of the bound *Le Morte Darthur* (Volume 2), published 1893–4.

in the first moment of thinking how lucky he was, he ever saw himself *serving* the time-honoured text, or Dent, or the great British public.

Aubrey, the *Morte* already made clear, was one of those distinguished masters, like his admired Mantegna, who—as Federigo Gonzaga had described it to the Duchess of Milan—*hanno del fantastico* (indulge their whim) and from whom one must accept what is offered. And as Aubrey began, so he went on: a law unto himself. From a practical point of view you could say that the embellishments he produced were almost totally off the point. But this disregard for the text ensured the preservation of his artistic integrity and helped nurture a genius that startled, and still startles, the world.

Eleven

Even before Evans, the bookseller, introduced him to Dent, the publisher, and the Malory was agreed upon, Aubrey had summed up his dull days at the Guardian Life and Fire Insurance Office in a gloriously unexpected drawing, 'Le Débris d'un poète' (Fig. 17), of 1892. Though the *Morte Darthur* would oblige him to linger in Joyous Gard for some while yet, in spirit he had already joined Kogo-no-tsubone on her moonlit verandah.

For the 'Débris' belongs to a series of Japanese-style drawings in the *tanzaku* format, recorded in a letter (to be precise, in two letters) of 1892, full of hope and excitement. Nearly two years had passed since the first haemorrhages laid him low, and for most of that time drawing was quite out of the question. Then: 'In certain points of technique,' recalled the artist in the autumn which gave him his freedom, 'I achieved something like perfection at once. . . .'[19] It is given to few of us to be able to substantiate a claim of this order. Aubrey felt he could; and the 'Débris' exists to prove him right. The 'perfection' arises from an extraordinary flair for energizing space, from the fine ease and flow of the line and from the hair's balance of pathos with mockery which Aubrey so often established in his best work. Note that this drawing is a foreshadowing only of the strict black and white of most of the designs for reproduction. Here the darks have been rubbed or blotted. And, to hold their own in a book or magazine, the thin hide-and-seek arabesques would have to be exchanged for bolder contours, themselves thickening further, alas, in the photo-mechanical line-blocks manufactured for the purpose.

It was the moment when Aubrey was getting to know Robert Ross. He had been recommended to Ross by Aymer Vallance, and the meeting took place in Vallance's rooms on 14 February 1892. Ross thus describes his first impression of the budding celebrity:

Though prepared for an extraordinary personality, I never

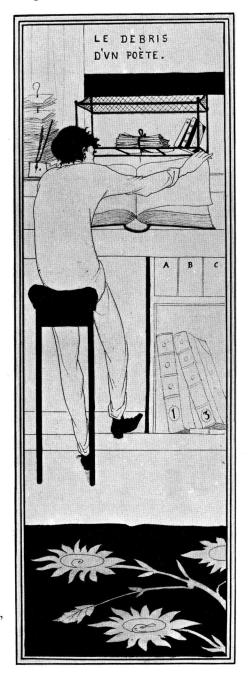

17 Le Débris d'un poète,
c. 1892.

expected the youthful apparition which glided into the room. He was shy, nervous and self-conscious, without any of the intellectual assurance and ease so characteristic of him eighteen months later when his success was unquestioned. He brought a portfolio of his marvellous drawings, in themselves an earnest of genius; but I hardly paid any attention to them at first, so overshadowed were they by the strange and fascinating original-ity of their author. In two hours it was not hard to discover that Beardsley's appearance did not belie him, He was an intellectual Marcellus suddenly matured.[20]

As befits a genius, his hair—brushed smooth and flat over his head and part of an 'immensely high and narrow brow'—has ceased to be referred to as red and become a respectful auburn. But the gauntness of the boy, what D. S. MacColl,* also present, called the 'consumptive's look of eager fire and hurry',[21] shocked and touched Vallance's friends.

Aubrey, however, did not look for sympathy, least of all for pity. Ten months later, by December 1892, he could report on Puvis's acceptance of him as a 'jeune anglais qui fait des choses éton-nantes'[22]; the *Morte Darthur* leapt ahead; several publishers besides Dent (Lawrence & Bullen, for instance, suggesting *Lucian's True History*) were buzzing round him; and in April 1893 *The Studio's* first number would appear, with wrapper design by its young *protégé* and a prestigeful puff from Pennell.†

---

*Dugald Sutherland MacColl (1859–1948), a minor artist and major art critic who wrote perceptively, but not sympathetically, about Aubrey's work.
†Joseph Pennell (1860–1926), American graphic artist, active at this time in England. Max Beerbohm thought the part he played in assisting Aubrey was later somewhat exaggerated by Robert Ross.

Passionate Friends

One

Mystic and Romantic, the French term *cénacle*—a literary club or coterie—well suits the later group of writers and artists on our side of the Channel whose pivotal genius was Robert Ross. Intellectually they looked to France. Balzac, Sainte-Beuve and Théophile Gautier were among their favourite authors and Aubrey, on 14 February 1892, could not have brought with him better credentials (in addition to a well-filled portfolio) than his astonishing familiarity with every detail of the *Comédie humaine*. A propitious St Valentine's Day—yet an ominous one: for an introduction to Ross meant an introduction to Wilde;[1] and through his association with Wilde Aubrey would experience the greatest disaster of his professional career.

Though Wilde humorously referred to him as 'our Scotch friend', Robert Baldwin Ross was born of a family long domiciled in Canada where his father had been Attorney General and his grandfather first Prime Minister of the old Upper Province. After the Attorney General's death in 1871, and following his expressed wish, the three Ross children were brought to England to be educated. Mrs Ross and her young family settled here, and in due course Robert went up to King's College, Cambridge, in 1888. Already in 1886 he had met Wilde, his senior by thirteen years. A journalist with an unusually witty and original touch, Ross approached the visual arts in a similar spirit (well demonstrated by the acute, ironic essay on Simeon Solomon in *Masques and Phases*), and when he could bring himself to turn from Aubrey, the hothouse intellectual and expatiator on Molière and *Manon Lescaut* and (even more impressively, since none of his audience was musical) on Wagner, to the owner of the portfolio, he perceived at once the unique draftsman with whom he had to do.

Few of us, probably, would have been as percipient. The 'Phèdre', the 'Beatrice Cenci', the two designs for *Madame Bovary* and the set for the Abbe Prévost's novel, which were then

27

or later acquired by Ross, are almost as feeble as the 'Francesca da Rimini' bought by Ross's close friend, More Adey.* We are not without means of guessing the kind of price Aubrey was paid for them: there is a cheque dated 13 May 1892 and made out to 'A. V. Beardsley' over the signature of Ross. It is for thirty shillings, and almost certainly relates to the purchase of a replica of Aubrey's 'Joan of Arc'. Bobbie (or Robbie), as his intimates— who soon included Aubrey—liked to call him, was giving a reasonable price for what were still juvenile and then as yet virtually unsaleable productions.

Ross would remain throughout the artist's life not only an admiring, but a warmly sympathetic and generous, supporter.

Two

This *Cénacle* had more than a general masculine mystique: its key figures were homosexual, the others at least latently homosexual. In the manner and argot of inverts, they were gay and often witty— but certainly never paragons of virtue.

Nobody, indeed, would expect to find the inflexible high-mindedness of Balzac's little band of the Rue des Quatre-Vents reproduced in real life in late-Victorian London. It is significant that it was Lucien de Rubempré, betrayer of the lofty principles of Lambert and d'Arthez, of whom the Wilde circle made a cult; though a rather touching mock-modesty required that they should express themselves on such topics with a smile. Thus it was long ago in Dublin, *when he was a boy*, Wilde told O'Sullivan,† that— with Julien Sorel—Lucien de Rubempré had become one of his two favourite characters,[2] and Max Beerbohm informed Ross that the death of Lucien de Rubempré would have been, *were it not for a certain misplaced comma in his first published work*, the one great tragedy of his life.[3] Among the more memorable sequences of the *balzacien* saga is that which lifts the beautiful young Lucien from the depths of ruin and despair in *Illusions perdues* to power and affluence in *Splendeurs et misères des courtisanes* before, at the

*William More Adey (1858–1942). With Ross, he was a co-director of the Carfax Gallery.
  Vincent O'Sullivan (?1868–1940), poet and novelist, American by birth.

conclusion of the second novel, ruin faces him again and he hangs himself in his cell. That the false abbé turns out to be a criminal, not a clerical, rescuer adds to the piquancy of the relationship between the two men. The theme has irresistible charm for an active or passive homosexual reader, who may identify himself either with the forceful Vautrin or the weak but fascinating Lucien.

But however francophil were Ross and his friends, they had grown up, the conventionally educated among them, under the influence of a *cénacle* of far greater charm and intellectual authority than that of d'Arthez, or of Sainte-Beuve, or of Gautier. 'Why were we at Oxford taught to read Plato and to regard the *Symposium* as a magnificent work?' plaintively inquired Lord Alfred Douglas,* many years afterwards.[4] He could go back further, and wonder why boys were brought up to read the *Eclogues* of Virgil at school, not excepting, in Byron's words:

> *that horrid 'un*
> *Beginning with* formosum pastor Corydon.

Mr Brian Reade has covered in great detail the whole field of educational and literary (as well as religious) influences working upon the public-school and university Englishman during the later nineteenth century. I must not repeat what is lucidly set out already in that useful book, *Sexual Heretics*, but shall merely suggest that to justify his homosexual predilections Wilde, the classical scholar and enthusiastic disciple of Pater, lived in part at least in a dream world, imagining himself back among the elegant and lively-minded young men who paced the courts of the palaestra. One cannot doubt that the *Symposium*, most delightful of Plato's conversation-pieces, was often in his mind, with its finely-woven argument in favour of a spiritual love between men. And he really seems to have persuaded himself into believing that a supper-party with a couple of male prostitutes sent round on approval from Little College Street constituted an agreeable 'Hellenic' evening out.

---

*Lord Alfred Bruce Douglas (1870–1945), son of the 8th Marquess of Queensberry, whose association with Wilde provoked his father's wrath and the disastrous consequences following upon Wilde's taking out a writ for libel against the Marquess.

18   Salome with the head
of St John the Baptist,
published in the first issue
of *The Studio*, April 1893.

Three

If (and unlikelier things have happened) it was Ross who introduced Wilde to homosexual practices, by the time Aubrey became acquainted with the *Cénacle* the latter was embarking on his tragic love-affair with Douglas, and Ross had taken as partner William More Adey, recent translator of Ibsen's *Brand*. No jealousies, however, disturbed the continuance of the original Oscar–Robbie *bon accord*.

Throughout the later months of 1892 and the early part of 1893 Aubrey's own relations with his new friend prospered. Ross introduced him to useful people, and Aubrey would report on his rising fortunes: nothing very out of the way—a new commission for the *St Paul's* magazine, a good notice in *Livre et l'Image*. They met frequently, drank tea and lunched together. It was certainly through Ross that Aubrey first saw a copy of Wilde's *Salomé*, printed in French and published simultaneously in London and Paris in February 1893.

His immediate reaction was enthusiastic, and he produced unbidden the drawing, 'J'ai baisé ta bouche, Iokanaan' (Fig. 18), in time for it to appear with Pennell's article in the April *Studio*. Without doubt, Aubrey was glad enough to cultivate Wilde at this stage, for in April, though nothing came of it, he spoke of a joint trip to Paris.[5] On the strength of the 'Iokanaan' design Lane decided to make an illustrated edition of the *Salomé*, translated into English. By June Aubrey's drawings were beginning to arrive in Vigo Street, where Ross was invited to drop in and admire them: that is to say, the artist thought them worthy of admiration, but there were strong protests in other quarters, and Lane himself scanned them anxiously, one by one, for indecencies deftly obscured. With Wilde ensued something like a quarrel.[6] Aubrey, however, was quite capable of standing up to both author and publisher.

It is true that three drawings had to be replaced. But even if he did not have things all his own way, *Salome* gave Aubrey his first real chance to excel. Wilde never liked the illustrations provided for his tragedy: how could he? (Figs. 19–23). On the other hand, there is plenty of evidence of good relations between the two men

19   Frontispiece from Oscar Wilde's *Salome*, published 1894: The Women in the Moon.

20 The Toilet of Salome: from Oscar Wilde's *Salome*, published 1894.

throughout 1893, from the inscription in a copy of the original edition, dated March: 'For Aubrey: for the only artist who, besides myself, knows what the dance of the seven veils is, and can see that invisible dance. Oscar,'[7] to the letter of December (all, otherwise, that survives in his hand to Aubrey), inviting the artist to a dinner at Kettner's at which Ross would also be present.[8]

When did Aubrey begin to harden his heart against Wilde? One cannot read much into a remark the former made to Ross, shortly before the Kettner dinner: 'Both of them [Wilde and Douglas] are really very dreadful people.'[9] 'Very dreadful,' in that homosexual argot that Aubrey was so quick to pick up, represents scarcely more than a titter and a toss of the head. But by January 1894 the situation must somehow have altered. For as art-editor-to-be of *The Yellow Book*, then under discussion, Aubrey made the firmest stipulation that Wilde should never contribute. Only recently I have come across Lane's statement upon this point. When have Aubrey's admirers had the honesty to admit that the artist treated Wilde as unceremoniously in this respect as William Watson* was to treat him, when, in the year following, *The Yellow Book* came under attack?[10]

Four

Aubrey may have had less of the spirit of forgiveness in him at this time when he was striving to play the part of a young man of fashion against the insistent warnings of ill-health.

He had blossomed out as a dandy. This was in the Brummell, not the d'Orsay, tradition: very sober, very spick-and-span. All muted greys, that year at the Salon of the Champ de Mars, his appearance had produced a mild sensation. His tailor we know, since Aubrey later found difficulty in settling the account, and the name of Doré, to be found traced across shop-fronts in Conduit and St James's Streets (and also, rather mysteriously, in the King's Road), suggests the height of elegance. Miss Netta Syrett† appears to have been bowled over by these dove-coloured ensembles when

*Sir William Watson (1858–1935), poet. He was one of The Bodley Head's authors.
†Miss Syrett's *Nobody's Fault* was published in 1896 in Lane's *Keynotes* series, so beautifully embellished by Aubrey. She continued to pour out works of the order of *The Mystery of Jenifer* and *The Shuttles of Eternity* throughout a long life which ended in 1943.

21 Enter Herodias: *Salome* design published in the 1907 *Portfolio*.

22 The Toilet of Salome (first version): expurgated *Salome* design published in *The Early Work of Aubrey Beardsley*, 1899.

23 Salome on settle (Maîtresse d'orchestre): *Salome* design published
in the 1907 *Portfolio*.

she visited 114 Cambridge Street.[11] Sir William Rothenstein,
hailing from the home of good cloth, was less easily pleased.
Looking back, he shook his head over Aubrey's 'butterfly ties' and

24   J.-E. Blanche's portrait of Aubrey Beardsley, painted at Dieppe
during the summer of 1895.

his 'too smart clothes with their hard padded shoulders'.[12]

At this distance in time, it is difficult for us to form a correct
opinion on the matter. The reader may consult J.-E. Blanche's
never-to-be-forgotten half-length of Aubrey in the National
Portrait Gallery, a harmony in brown and silver (Fig. 24). He can

25   Sickert's oil sketch of Aubrey, when attending
the unveiling of a memorial to Keats in the Parish
Church, Hampstead, July 1894.

turn to Sickert's fleeting register of the whole figure in the Tate
(Fig. 25).* And then there are some splendid photographs, the
best, perhaps, by Frederick Evans (Figs. 26, 27, 28). Alas, there was

*Both J.-E. Blanche (1862–1942), and W. R. Sickert (1860–1942) were personal friends of
the Beardsley family.

too little flesh to fill out Doré's suits, and the angular effects that disturbed Rothenstein may have been quite involuntary.

The dandyism, of course, must be seen as more than mere

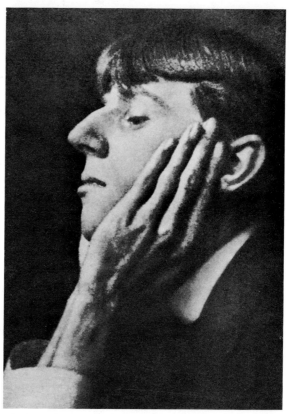

26 Photograph of Aubrey by his friend the book-seller, Frederick H. Evans. A man of unusual skill and enterprise, Evans produced magnificent platino-types of Aubrey's drawings which, without the photo-grapher's distinguishing mark, would be difficult to tell from the originals.

self-indulgence. It can certainly be taken as read that this sort of display carries with it the need of the artist to detach himself from the crowd ('On ne se pare que pour se séparer,' wrote Baudelaire), and, to preserve his self-respect, the pretence that he creates his works only to amuse himself.[13]

27 An extremely
rare photograph of
the artist, provenance
unknown.

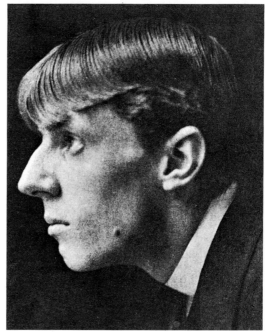

28 Aubrey: the
'gargoyle' photograph
by Frederick H. Evans.

Five

Wilde may really have announced that Aubrey was his 'invention'. Coarsened by success as we know him to have been, particularly as a result of taking too much wine, he could have been responsible for some injudicious act which deeply hurt the artist: whence *The Yellow Book* veto. Being marked by the stigma of homosexualism can hardly have been Aubrey's fear, for Ross, better

29   Robert Ross (1869–1918), Aubrey's early patron and staunch friend of the Beardsley family, with, (right) Reggie Turner (?1870–1938), Max Beerbohm's chief confidant.

known to the police than anyone for his Piccadilly importunings, was among the first to be told of the new magazine and invited to contribute (Figs. 29, 30, 31).

There was an occasion towards the end of 1893 when the combined activity of Douglas and Ross resembled a French farce rather than what Wilde, himself preoccupied with a series of unemployed grooms and valets who traded anal intercourse for

30   A very rare portrait of Oscar Wilde (1854–1900) during his American tour and dated 1882. It well expresses the Bunthorne manner and the ideal homosexual love of which he spoke so eloquently at his trial.

cash, liked to refer to as the 'noblest form of affection'. In a letter to Reggie Turner* (who had also loved Douglas not wisely but too well), Max Beerbohm reported:

Bobbie Ross has returned to this country for a few days and of

*?1869–1938, man of means, author and brilliant conversationalist. With Ross, he was present at Wilde's death in 1900.

114 Cambridge St
SW.

Dear Bobbie

If superfluous fresh air tobogganing & snow capped mountains, have not completely killed your love of the fine arts, I am sure you will be vastly interested to hear that Harland & myself are about to start a new literary & artistic Quarterly. The title has already been registered at Stationers Hall & on the scroll of fame. It is "THE YELLOW BOOK". In general get up it will look like the ordinary French Novel. Each number will contain about 10 contributions in the way of short stories & discursive essays from the pens say of Henry Harland Henry James, Crackenthorpe George Egerton & Max Beerbohm

31   Aubrey's letter to Ross, of early January 1894, announcing the foundation of *The Yellow Book*. Ross, currently involved in a scandal, was absent in Switzerland. He did not, in fact, contribute to the magazine. The scored-through address is the Hogarth, Beardsley's club, 46 Dover Street.

The drawings will be independant & supplied by Aubrey Beardsley, Walter Sickert, Wilson Steer, Will Rothenstein & other past masters. The publication will be undertaken by John Lane, & the price will be 5/-.

(No 1 appears on April 15th)

We all want to have something charming from you for the first number. Say an essay or a short story in which the heroine is not a beautiful boy.

Now do send us something soon in your most brilliant style & make up your mind to be a regular contributor

Our idea is that many brilliant story painters & picture writers cannot get their best stuff accepted in the conventional magazine, either because they are not topical or perhaps a little risqué. Let me have a line by return as we want to get No 1 ready as soon as possible. Ever yours Aubrey Beardsley

best wishes for N. Year from all

him there have been very great and intimate scandals and almost, if not quite, warrants: slowly he is recovering but has to remain at Davos during his convalescence for fear of social relapse. I must not disclose anything (nor must you) but I may tell you that a schoolboy with wonderful eyes, Bosie [Douglas], Bobbie, a furious father, George Lewis [the eminent solicitor], a head-master (who is now blackmailing Bobbie), St John Wontner [a less eminent solicitor], Dover, Calais, intercepted letters, private detectives, Calais, Dover and returned cigarette-cases were some of the ingredients of the dreadful episode.[14]

This is a convenient place for Max Beerbohm* to make his bow. He had been introduced to the *Cénacle* by Will Rothenstein at the end of the Oxford Trinity term of 1893, though he had met Ross himself a year to eighteen months earlier. Only aware of Max's existence since his visit to Oxford that May, Will reckoned he had discovered a genius and insisted upon everyone knowing it. First the University itself was informed; then, when Eights Week was over, he took Max to see his London friends: and among those whom he had not already had the pleasure of meeting was Aubrey (Figs. 32, 34).[15]

There were seventy-two hours between their birthdays, the Oxford prodigy being by that margin Aubrey's junior. They liked each other at once. The hardness which daunted Rothenstein was welcomed by Max as a refreshing element of common-sense, sadly lacking in Symons, Le Gallienne and Lionel Johnson,† those other 'Decadents'. The caricaturist in him could appreciate, too, the extraordinary combination of beak-like nose, lean jaw and formidable skull enclosed in its smooth brown shell of hair. (Fig. 33)

As far as two beings of precocious talent and in love with every kind of elegance could differ, they did: Max all plump, round curves, Aubrey (in Wilde's phrase) a 'silver hatchet'; Max's wit rarely paraded, Aubrey's jerkily, extravagantly hurled at all comers; Max composed in manner and movement, Aubrey restless as a

*Sir Henry Maximilian Beerbohm (1872–1956), equally celebrated for his wit as artist and writer.
†Richard Le Gallienne (1866–1947) and Lionel Johnson (1867–1902) typify the Romantic and Catholic (convert) elements in Nineties verse.

cat. They spent much time together at the Café Royal, at Angelo's, at the theatre. Max was put up for Aubrey's club, the Hogarth, and shared with him a couple of tickets for the double (Todhunter–Yeats) bill at The Avenue, being rewarded with a first glimpse of W.B.Y.

32   A portrait of Aubrey by William Rothenstein.

By September 1893 collaboration was in the air. Aubrey hoped to produce a series of drawings, and Max the verses, for a publication to be called *Masques*, or *The Masques*.[16] The project did not materialize. Another opportunity occurred at the turn of the year, however, which was not let slip. Max, with his 'Defence of Cosmetics', became a contributor to the first issue of *The Yellow Book* (Fig. 35). It was an ambiguous young man who went down from Oxford in 1894, 'too much interested in the moderns to have yet had time for the ancients'. One might describe him at this stage as still, if hesitantly, homosexual, accepting nothing more than jewellery from Reggie Turner. Highly critical of the *Cénacle*, he was, however, 'intrigued'—his word—to take his share

33 Max's caricature of Aubrey in *Caricatures of Twenty-Five Gentlemen*, 1896. 'Of course,' wrote the subject of it to Max, 'I like my own portrait best.'

of the *réclame* it offered. *The Yellow Book* brought him closer to Aubrey than he would ever be again.

The drawing 'L'Education sentimentale' particularly delighted him:

Aubrey has done a marvellous picture for the *Yellow B*: '*l'Education sentimentale*' he calls it. A fat elderly whore in a dressing-gown and huge hat of many feathers is reading from a book to the sweetest imaginable little girl, who looks before her, with hands clasped behind her back, roguishly winking. Such a

34   A print of the Frederick Holyer photograph of Aubrey inscribed on the back in what is thought to be Gray's hand: *Tous les vices avec leurs griffes/ Ont, dans les plis de cette peau,/ Tracé d'affreux hiéroglyphes.* With, added afterwards: *par les dieux jumeaux this is a very foolish quotation !*

strange curved attitude, and she wears a long pinafore of black silk, quite-tight, with the frills of a petticoat showing at the ankles and shoulders: awfully like Ada Reeve, that clever malapert, is her face—you must see it. It haunts me.[17]

The artist's influence can be traced in Max's article, 'A Defence of Cosmetics', which fits so closely into place with Aubrey's coquette looking into her street-lamped mirror, to appear as the cover-design of Volume III of the magazine. Though it might seem that Max was the specialist in matters of couture and

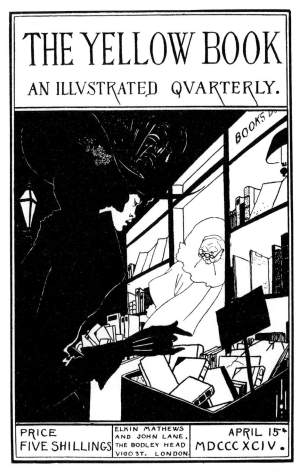

THE YELLOW BOOK

AN ILLVSTRATED QVARTERLY.

BOOKS

PRICE
FIVE SHILLINGS

ELKIN MATHEWS
AND JOHN LANE,
THE BODLEY HEAD
VIGO ST. LONDON.

APRIL 15ᵗʰ
MDCCC XCIV.

35   Prospectus-cover for Volume I of *The Yellow Book*, published April 1894.

self-embellishment, Aubrey, we shall see, out-rivals him in these—as well as the more complicated—mysteries of the dressing-table.

Six

In spite of Max's 'Defence' essay and the contributions of Arthur Symons, of which the poem 'Stella Maris' is the most celebrated, the special character of *The Yellow Book* was conferred upon it by

Aubrey, and Aubrey alone.[18] The creation of a so-called Beardsley Woman had already earned him the epithets 'libidinous and asexual'. In the main expressed in starkest black-and-white, his originally decorative preoccupations gave place to satire. Precisely what he was satirizing is a matter of speculation, and I shall do my share of this, as opportunity provides; but the drawings caused much offence and, as a result (Aubrey told Henry James), the greater part of the 'thunderbolts'—the most violent, perhaps, from 'The Thunderer' itself—fell on the art-editor's head.[19] To this attack he stood up with remarkable self-assurance. He knew his value. A blow here and there might make him wince, but of the kind of harsh notoriety that had scared Max, Aubrey could not have enough.

Meanwhile, as the quarterly issues followed one another in July and October 1894 and January 1895, filled pictorially with Aubrey's grimacing wit, the Wilde–Queensberry drama was developing. Wilde, his criminal libel charge against the Marquess, Douglas's father, having petered out and led to his own total discredit, left the Cadogan Hotel under police guard for Holloway Prison on 5 April 1895. Under his arm he was supposed to have been carrying a primrose-paper copy of Pierre Louÿs's *Aphrodite*,* which was noted by a reporter as a 'yellow book' and in the newspapers naturally became transformed into *The Yellow Book*.

On 6 April Wilde and Alfred Taylor, a rather pathetic trader in young men, were charged with offences under the Criminal Law Amendment Act of 1885, the police 'horn-book', one might call it, which covered 'gross indecency' between males. On the 8th, spurred on, it is said, by Mrs Humphrey Ward, William Watson cabled Lane, then in New York: 'Withdraw all Beardsley's designs or I withdraw all my books.' Ironically, Watson was not (as he is often made out to be) a champion of bourgeois convention, but as fearlessly independent in outlook as Aubrey himself. However that may be, Lane visualized a mass exodus of the Bodley Head's leading authors, and sanctioned Aubrey's dismissal from *The Yellow Book* just as Volume V was about to roll off the presses.

*But Wilde's friend Pierre Louÿs (1870–1925) did not publish this licentious and celebrated work till 1896.

The *Cénacle* scattered. Ross made for Calais again, not this time on account of the 'schoolboy Helen of Troy'. Douglas, at the urgent request of Wilde's lawyers, had crossed the Channel, too. Max's confidant, Turner, judged it discreet to make himself scarce in the same way. Looking back, we must still wonder at Wilde's decision to remain to face the music—when he had only to get into a brougham, and a fast pair of horses would have taken him to Erith, whence, by yacht, he could have reached Boulogne or Dieppe in the hours between dinner and breakfast.

One speech in particular, during his trial, evoked for the man in the dock a volley of applause and hisses. It occurred on the third day of his second grilling, when he had been questioned on the meaning of a poem by Douglas:

'The Love that dare not speak its name' in this century is such a great affection of an elder for a younger man as there was between David and Jonathan, such as Plato made the very basis of his philosophy, and such as you find in the sonnets of Michelangelo and Shakespeare. It is that deep, spiritual affection that is as pure as it is perfect. It dictates and pervades great works of art like those of Shakespeare and Michelangelo, and those two letters of mine [to Douglas], such as they are. It is in this century misunderstood, so much misunderstood that it may be described as the 'Love that dare not speak its name', and on account of it I am placed where I am now. It is beautiful, it is fine, it is the noblest form of affection. There is nothing unnatural about it. It is intellectual, and it repeatedly exists between an elder and a younger man, where the elder has intellect, and the younger man has all the joy, hope and glamour of life before him. That it should be so the world does not understand. The world mocks at it and sometimes puts one in the pillory for it.[20]

The *Cénacle*, therefore, as envisaged by Wilde in a moment of eloquent self-pity, consisted of an heroic group of sexual deviants despised and persecuted by a rabble of top-hatted John Bulls, themselves the philistine *profanum vulgus*.

Seven

It is in the context of this trance-like apologia that one begins to understand the relationship between the two most brilliant members of the coterie, the 'smiling giant' with his gift for words and the crabbed, bent youth whose pen was put to the other use. Harris* (Fig. 36) saw Aubrey as Wilde's evil genius. 'It is im-

36 Frank Harris (1856–1931), as seen by Max Beerbohm: from the latter's *Caricatures of Twenty-Five Gentlemen*, 1896.

portant,' he says, 'to remember that it was Beardsley who influenced Oscar, and not Oscar who influenced Beardsley.'[21] While it is perhaps even more important to remember that Harris himself, with his 'Yes, Frank', 'No, Frank', 'Of course, Frank' interpretation of past events, is rarely to be trusted, he was right

*Frank Harris (1856–1931), variously editor, short-story writer and biographer, all in the same erratic but colourful manner. A passage from his *My Life and Loves* is referred to later.

to show that, in some curious way, Aubrey got the upper hand where Wilde was concerned.

The passionate declaration of the virtues of homosexual love made at the Old Bailey will throw light on the problem. This speech exhibits one of Wilde's most fatal flaws. He was a mass of self-deception. His more indulgent friends might admire the speech—and it is a marvellous piece of off-the-cuff oratory—but they could hardly take it seriously. There was nothing very 'beautiful' or 'fine' about Douglas, Wilde's blue-blooded, temperamental consort, or about Ross (the worries of whose life were, not surprisingly, prematurely depriving him of his hair), or the unhappy young clerk Shelley and the doggedly debauched Parkers, or the degrading evidence of chambermaids at the Savoy Hotel. It may be that we have come to accept much that Victorian society winced at. We do not demand of every aspect of love between men, or of love between men and women, that it shall be 'fine' or 'beautiful': on the contrary, we know it cannot be. And so, with his superior intelligence, did Wilde. But he would pretend.

Aubrey, I believe, dropped on this pretence like a hawk. Opportunities were not wanting for a continuous, malicious appraisement of the chasm between practice and precept. There was another pretence, too: Wilde's posing as a connoisseur of the visual arts. To Aubrey these Olympian pronouncements about Michelangelo and Praxiteles must have been infuriating. The connoisseur himself had elected to live in what would then have been described as a 'bijou town residence' (No. 16 Tite Street, with Godwin's white woodwork wriggling round it), at the same time, demonstrating his taste in pictures by hanging up for contemplation Simeon Solomon's 'Triumph of Eros', a Monticelli and a favourite self-portrait from the brush of a mediocrity called Pennington. And this was he who created the exquisite Lord Henry Wotton, the lovely house and the treasures there accumulated by Dorian Gray!*

Nobody, as Mrs Beardsley once implied, ever got the better of Aubrey.[22] And the *Salome* illustrations are an instance of it. Wilde

---

*I accept that Godwin, Solomon and Monticelli all have their merits, but the bathos is still laughable.

must have been entirely bewildered, but he knew that Aubrey had discovered an essential weakness in him and dared not argue on pictorial aesthetics with so sharp-tongued a collaborator. No precedent exists, surely, for such cavalier treatment of a text. Artists will continue to applaud the arbitrary content of the drawings, authors still gasp at Aubrey's impertinence. Consider the treatment of the moon in this Maeterlinckian prose-drama of Wilde's translated back into English by Douglas and re-honed and polished by the Master: for Salome herself, it is a virgin; for the Young Syrian, a dead woman; for Herod, a mad or drunken woman. For the author, clearly, the femininity of the moon was never in question. Yet it is the moon which Aubrey turns into a caricature of Wilde himself (Fig. 19).

'Enter Herodias' (Fig. 21) is an interesting drawing for us, though it must have shocked and angered Wilde; for it combines harsh satires on both forms of male appetite, with little to choose between the naturalness of the 'unnatural' and the unnaturalness of the 'natural'. Sexual references proliferate. No wonder the beauty of Wilde's play, and in spite of its extravagances it is beautiful, has been completely overlooked by the questing eye that cannot take in text as well as illustrations.

Could Lane have been right in assuring the 'ingenuous Yankee' that Aubrey was a prophet lashing out against the 'O.W. tendencies of the age'? Or was Vallance justified in being highly amused by this: '*Figurez-vous* the young man of the period, hovering between the choice of two courses and finally deciding in favour of orthodox vice through gazing upon the charms of the Beardsley woman'?[23]

Eight

On 25 May it was all over. Wilde and Taylor were each condemned to two years' hard labour. The rescue of Aubrey from his own predicament—loss of face, job, income—was almost as spectacular as that of Lucien de Rubempré.

Before his Vautrin arrives, however, and still respecting the chronology of events, we have an opportunity to consider a rather curious point connected with Aubrey's attitude to Wilde and homosexualism. After his dismissal from *The Yellow Book*, the Beardsleys' changed circumstances obliged them to leave 114

Cambridge Street and they split up, Aubrey's mother and sister returning to a nearby lodging in Charlwood Street and Aubrey himself seeking other temporary accommodation on his own. By October 1895 he had settled (it was to be for longer than usual) at Geneux's private hotel, 10–11 St James's Place, running off St James's Street just north of the Palace (Fig. 37).

37   10–11 St James's Place, formerly Geneux's Private Hotel. Wilde wrote the greater part of *An Ideal Husband* here. Why did Aubrey elect to move into the same set of rooms in 1895, shortly after the débâcle of *The Yellow Book*?

It has been suggested that the more central position was chosen as convenient for his association with a new publisher, Leonard Smithers,* then in Arundel Street, Strand. At the same time, the choice of furnished rooms available in the West End of London in those days was very considerable, and one wonders at Aubrey's decision to move into just this ground-floor set in St James's Place. One wonders, because Wilde himself had rented these very rooms from October 1893 till the end of March 1894, and had in fact written most of *An Ideal Husband* there. This might have lent them some distinction, you would think. On the contrary, the hotel during Wilde's stay had been highlighted as a place of assignation. Sidney Mavor and Charles Parker, both male prostitutes, had been invited there. 'I visited Wilde at his rooms in St James's Place,' Parker related at the Old Bailey. 'Taylor gave me the address. Wilde had a bedroom and a sitting-room opening into each other. I have been there in the morning and to tea in the afternoon'; and he went on to describe in open court an act of gross indecency which had occurred there between them on one of these occasions.[24]

So Aubrey, in his drawings a castigator of homosexuality and (in the *Salome* illustrations) of the deviant sexual practices, if not sodomy, of Wilde himself, chose to recommence life—after the *Yellow Book* crisis—in a pair of rooms permeated with associations of performance and performer. This leads us to reconsider the extreme position suggested by Mrs Beardsley, for instance, that there was bitter enmity between her son and Wilde, and urges us, somewhat bewildered, in the opposite direction. Or are we to suppose (and we can suppose anything) that it gave Aubrey, in his hostility to the man who, indirectly, had lost him the best job he ever had, a special thrill to recline on Wilde's sofa and lie on Wilde's bed, while the late occupant languished in a cell at Wandsworth and Reading Gaols (he was moved to Reading on 13 November 1895)? The problem, I think, is not resolved by the fact that Ross may have chosen these rooms, as he had a previous set at 17 Campden Grove. Of course Aubrey was glad to make use

---

*Leonard Charles Smithers (1861–1907). He became successively solicitor, bookseller and publisher. His relationship with Aubrey is dealt with in detail later on.

of Bobbie's good offices when it came to the wearisome business of apartment-hunting. But the final decision would have been his.

Nine

We now return to the artist's rescue, which can be dealt with in two parts. The first concerns Marc-André Raffalovich,* if not a

38   André Raffalovich (1864–1934). The photograph stood on top of the bookcase in Aubrey's room at the Hôtel Cosmopolitain, Menton, during the last months of his life. (See Fig. 102.)

Russian prince, a Russian wealthy enough to pass muster as such (Fig. 38). He had been educated in France and England and about

*He arrived in London from Paris in the early 1880s, before his twentieth year.

him, and perhaps unjustly, there clings a legend of literary amateurishness and social inadequacy. This unfortunate reputation appears to be based largely on the comments of Wilde, the wittiest of his detractors. If 'André', in a letter written by Wilde in 1886, refers to André Raffalovich, then it was he who at some party ludicrously 'introduced' a Forbes-Robertson to his own sister![25] 'Little André' had earlier aroused Wilde's indignation by speaking of the 'lumpy' character of the tuberose and giving that liliaceous plant its correct three syllables, when Wilde himself had decided there were only two. The latter had been reviewing Raffalovich's four books of verse for *The Pall Mall Gazette*, a task which wearied him. The ensuing exchange of letters amused everyone except the poet. There were other causes of resentment: Wilde said Raffalovich had come to London to found a salon and had succeeded only in founding a saloon. But the advantage gradually turned in favour of the Russian, whose wealth enabled him to detach from his tormentor the clever and handsome John Gray (Fig. 39) long before the Queensberry scandal blew up.[26]

According to his own testimony, Raffalovich first saw Aubrey at a friend's house in 1895 and, disagreeably impressed by what seemed to him 'some hardness, much affectation', he had felt no desire to embark upon a closer relationship.[27]

Then, not many weeks later, in the spring of the year and just after the *Yellow Book* crisis, Aubrey appeared one morning on the Russian's doorstep in South Audley Street. 'Mr Beardsley said he would wait,' the butler told Raffalovich, himself arriving back from an early call. Aubrey was discovered studying Gustave Moreau's 'Sappho'.* Turning to Raffalovich, he said he had come at his sister's suggestion. He was in a 'fix'. Soon they were conversing amicably, and the first impression, so little favourable to the artist, was quite reversed. We can take it that the friendship began, as it would continue, with a loan or gift of money. Aubrey then immediately returned to Paris.[28]

Back in London in the early summer of 1895, the acquaintance ripened. Thus Raffalovich:

---

*In reporting this, Raffalovich could well have been making a sly allusion to Mabel, on whose lesbian relationships he is elsewhere more explicit.

At the time I was thirty and he twenty-three. We called each
other Mentor and Télémaque, more out of affectionate playful-
ness than because he could then brook interference or guidance.

39   John Gray (1866–1934). The author of *Silverpoints* is seen here with Raffalovich and Mabel's
'godmother', Miss Gribbell, about 1893. They are in
the garden of Heathside, Weybridge, a country house
rented by André for several summers during the
1890s.

Of course, I admired him; he arrested me like wrought iron and
like honeysuckle; hardness, elegance, charm, variety. I delighted,
of course, in his fame, in his notoriety. Wherever we went he
was gazed at. They sang about him at the Gaiety; Max carica-

tured him; strangers credited him with unfathomed perversity; acquaintances all recognized his simple boyishness.[29]

Aubrey's letters to Raffalovich begin in 1895 and make up the largest surviving group addressed to a single correspondent. By May, less than a month perhaps after their meeting, they had already become Mentor and Télémaque to each other. The names, as Miss Brigid Brophy recently pointed out, are taken from Fénelon, not from the *Odyssey*.[30] One may add that, in Fénelon's *Télémaque*, Mentor, though in appearance a wise old man, was in reality the goddess Minerva disguised!

Ten

In practical terms, this friendship proved of incalculable service to Aubrey. On 23 May 1895 Vallance wrote to Ross: 'By the way, Raffalovitch (I don't know how to spell it) is financing Beardsley to any amount.'[31] Exactly when a regular allowance began to be made to the artist we do not know, but from a remark of Aubrey's about 'material things', thanks to André, no longer being 'a trouble to me', it seems likely to have been established by at least late 1896.[32]

Strictly, Ernest Dowson and Charles Conder* were members of the *Cénacle*, as Raffalovich was not; one might therefore expect the poet and the painter, with whom Aubrey had spent many festive evenings, to rank as closer friends. But, no: the artist instinctively recoiled from Dowson, whose self-neglect disgusted the dandy in him; and it was equally painful to see Conder, despite continuous heavy drinking, enjoy the good health he himself had been denied. On the other hand, Raffalovich had many more faults than they as an artist (either in prose or in verse). His style is turgid and his meaning ambiguous. He was appallingly careless. What would Yeats have thought of his *Wild Swans* being transferred from *Coole* to *Goole*?[33]

No doubt Aubrey soon became aware of his Mentor's failings, but the devotion paid him by this strange man was as necessary as it was flattering. Without André's books, flowers and expensive

*Ernest Dowson (1867–1900), is forever associated with the celebrated refrain: 'I have been faithful to thee, Cynara! in my fashion.' Some critics think that Aubrey was in some debt to Charles Conder (1868–1909), artist of charm and distinction.

boxes of chocolates, the invalid's life would have been intolerable; without the gifts of money, taking ultimately the form of £100 a quarter,[34] he could not have travelled south to the Mediterranean in a last bid to recover his health.

For such advantages, a raised eyebrow or two in the *Cénacle* could be ignored. Indeed, as his illness made it more and more difficult for Aubrey to take part in social life and his exile from London itself lengthened, he saw scarcely any of his old friends except the faithful Ross. The brief intimacy with Max faded out. MacColl had never really approved of his drawings, Symons did not care for him personally. When Wilde came out of prison on 19 May 1897, Raffalovich's dislike, whatever may have been Aubrey's feelings in the matter, would have been an effective inducement for the artist to avoid his old associate.

It has also to be remembered that Aubrey was received into the Catholic Church a few weeks before Wilde's release largely through the encouragement of Raffalovich, himself a recent convert, and Raffalovich's friend John Gray, who in 1898 would relinquish his librarianship at the Foreign Office to study for the priesthood, finally taking Holy Orders in 1901. The nature of Aubrey's faith is something we shall discuss later on: here it will suffice to point out that, in the growing despair he must have experienced with the advance of his disease, the enthusiastic spiritual support of Raffalovich was something to cling to. When he could not draw, when he was too miserable to read, prayers served him better than Dowsonian sighs, and he thanked Raffalovich, now no longer Mentor but Brother (in Christ), for sundry kind 'Pater[noster]s', though confessing that he was a 'sorry beadsman' himself.[35]

Eleven

It will be perceived that a financially rewarding relationship with a man of homosexual tastes like Raffalovich, author of *L'Uranisme, Inversion Sexuelle Congénitale* (published in France in 1896),* must inevitably bring us to the question which in any case had to be asked: was the close friend of Robert Ross, the one-time crony

---

*The first publication to cite the Wilde affair, and one which supports the theory then current that homosexuality is congenital.

of Max, the fleeting associate of Wilde and Douglas, himself a homosexual?

Whether or not an answer can be given to this question, it seems clear that men thus orientated found Aubrey attractive. Wilde once likened him to an orchid—a high compliment from one eccentric botanist to another. For Aubrey's part, he could address the undoubtedly homosexual Julian Sampson as 'my dear Julie' and send 'sweetest messages' to George Morgan, Sampson's lover.[36] The letters to Raffalovich, however, exhibit nothing of this flirtatious mood. The artist is on his best behaviour. Was it, then, Good Samaritanism and nothing more?

Raffalovich himself, typically enough, provides a clue which leads us to suppose that the relationship had its strongly emotional (along with its missionary) aspect. If a mystery could be solved by the substitution of another mystery, that, too, would have been very much to the taste of the pseudonymous Alexander Michaelson.* We are directed by him to look for a portrait of Aubrey in George Moore's little-known story, 'Hugh Monfert'. It appeared in the volume entitled *In Single Strictness*, the 1922 edition, but in a re-issue was dropped to make way for another tale.

There can be little doubt that the character, Percy Knight, is a fictional painting of Aubrey, 'a youth of seventeen or eighteen, hollow-chested and pale, with large, eloquent eyes, whose talent as an illustrator Hugh set above any man of his own time'. And, most surprisingly, this Hugh Monfert's features, as described by Moore, closely resemble Raffalovich's (to judge by the photographs and Sydney Starr's portrait in oils);† like Raffalovich, Percy's (i.e., Aubrey's) admirer is a convert to Catholicism, a man of great wealth who, having rejected the idea of entry into the priesthood, busies himself with plans to build a Roman Catholic church: Raffalovich himself was financially responsible for the building of St Peter's Church, Edinburgh, for his friend John Gray.[37] George Moore, of course, knew Aubrey, and was early hostile to his work, being the leader of what the artist described as the 'fronde' highly critical of the *Salome* illustrations. Then, later, so Lane tells us,

*The name adopted for Raffalovich's *Blackfriars* articles.
†The last reproduced in *The Letters of Aubrey Beardsley*, 1971.

Moore performed an aesthetic somersault, as he had over Japanese art, and became Aubrey's fervent admirer.[38] Aubrey's sister Mabel was also known to the author of 'Hugh Monfert', appearing in the story without question as Percy's sister Beatrice.

Does what Moore wrote reflect what actually happened between the three parties in real life? Were it not for the deviously twisting, guilt-ridden, masochistic spirit of Raffalovich, and his delight in hints and signs and half-revealed mysteries, and, above all, his habitual indiscretion, I should find this difficult to believe. Would a minor writer allow a major writer to take some of the most private incidents of his emotional past and serve them up to the public in ill-concealed fictional form during the former's lifetime? Yes, if that minor writer were Raffalovich, I think he might!

This is George Moore at his dullest, and we need not concern ourselves with a detailed account of 'Hugh Monfert'. As a brief summary, what follows will be sufficient for the purpose. Hugh is devoted to Percy, the artist. Mrs Monfert is anxious for her son to marry, so that there may be an heir to his great estates; and when he shows interest in Percy's sister Beatrice, she does every-thing possible to bring the two together. It comes, in fact, to marriage. Not till the first night of the honeymoon does Hugh discover that he had only supposed himself in love with Beatrice: it was her brother he loved. He applies to Dr Knight, his father-in-law, for help and advice. The marriage should obviously be annulled, but ought Hugh to escape from the world and join an Order? How can he continue to live in a heterosexual society? Dr Knight argues the case with greater philosophical calm than would most fathers of daughters placed in the same predicament, and ultimately persuades Hugh that he will be of more use to the Church in his lay capacity as a wealthy and important landowner. At this point we move into the future, in which Beatrice re-marries and Percy (who has given every warning of doing so) dies of pulmonary tuberculosis. 'I may boil my pot and carry my can,' concludes the bereft Hugh, 'but the spring of life is gone for ever out of me, as it has gone out of Percy.'[39]

The reader may remember that it had been Aubrey's sister who suggested his going to South Audley Street for help that early spring of 1895. I shall be turning to the subject of Mabel Beardsley

later: however, one must point out that not only did Raffalovich
make a close friend of Mabel, the lady in charge of his household,
Miss Florence Truscott Gribbell,[40] constituted herself Mabel's
'godmother', and may well have nursed the hope that André,
whom she loved as a son, and Mabel, of whose brother André had
become so fond, would make a match of it. The coincidences here,
while not to be pursued further than the evidence will allow, are,
I think the reader may agree, extraordinary enough to suggest
that Aubrey, Mabel and Raffalovich may have been emotionally
entangled in some way. What seems to emerge is that the relationship between Aubrey and his Mentor or Brother was latently
homosexual, on the part of the Russian at least.

Twelve

And is not this explained by the little anecdote which Yeats
relates in *The Trembling of the Veil*?
    Aubrey has called upon the poet in Bloomsbury, about the time
his association with Raffalovich was beginning, or about to begin:

> He is a little drunk [says Yeats] and his mind has been running
> upon his dismissal from *The Yellow Book*, for he puts his hand
> upon the wall and stares into a mirror. He mutters, 'Yes, yes. I
> look like a Sodomite', which he certainly did not. 'But no, I am
> not that', and then begins railing against his ancestors, accusing
> them of that and this, back to and including the great Pitt, from
> whom he declares himself descended.[41]

The usual interpretation of this passage, when it has been
noticed at all, is that Aubrey could not therefore have been involved in homosexual relationships. Quite apart from doubts we
may legitimately harbour as to the accuracy of Yeats's recollection,
I submit that the man reflected in the mirror, while displaying no
crudely obvious homosexual character, had still that about him
(admitted by Aubrey, if denied by the poet) which attracted the
cultured homosexual in quest of a partner. Though Max stated
that Yeats and Aubrey did not meet till January 1896, I believe
the anecdote to be essentially authentic; especially because of the
little ancestor-diatribe. The romantic in Yeats would have care-

fully filed away this interesting connexion (by no means proven) with the Earls of Chatham.

Thirteen

I have referred to a rescue in two parts, for Aubrey's financial and artistic rehabilitation after his dismissal from *The Yellow Book* in April 1895 became the shared responsibility of Raffalovich—and Leonard Smithers (Figs. 40 and 41).

40 Leonard Smithers (1861–1907), Aubrey's publisher, with his wife and son Jack. In later days Jack did his best to defend his father's name, but his suggestion that Wilde nursed a hopeless passion for Annie Smithers detracts somewhat from the credibility of these memoirs.

41   A conversation-piece featuring Leonard Smithers (left), Ranger Gull (better known as 'Guy Thorne'), and Hannaford Bennett, minor writers of the period. The camera played a considerable rôle in Smithers's back-of-the-shop equipment. His close associates, according to Jack Smithers, did not hesitate to use it for blackmailing, as well as pornographic, purposes.

With less title than the Russian to membership of the *Cénacle*, Smithers played such a useful part as publisher of otherwise unacceptable material, and entertained so generously and advanced money with such good grace, that he came to be tolerated and even liked by Wilde, by Dowson, by Symons and by Aubrey himself. Although Smithers arrived in London from his native Sheffield as early as 1890–91, and he had entered into correspondence with Wilde before that in 1888, his first independent venture as a publisher may not have been till 1894.* In 1895 he published Arthur Symons's *London Nights*, and through Symons became acquainted with Aubrey. He was thirty-four, a genuine bibliophil, able and ambitious, but quite without scruples. And while his chosen authors and artist were remarkable for their weak motivation towards coitus, Smithers, by contrast, was a Don Juan of enormous (or boastedly enormous) appetite, reputed to keep a mistress in every postal district of the capital. Altogether, one can

*The taking-over of Wratislaw's *Caprices* from Gay and Bird, Mr Reade suggests.

regard him as better cast for the part of Vautrin than was
Raffalovich, though Aubrey's own virtue would never be at risk.

The partnership with Aubrey (the artist to receive a fixed income
in return for all the work he could produce) represented just the
kind of gamble that appealed to this adventurous publisher.
Aubrey's earliest surviving letter to 'Mr Smithers', dated 30 July
1895, was written from an address in Bennett Street, St James's,
which turns out to have been the consulting-room of a Dr L.
Vernon Jones, and it contains the writer's warning that he will
have to spend the next two days in bed.[42] Smithers, therefore, was
under no illusions about the health of the young man in whom he
had decided to invest a good deal of money. It was at this stage
that Symons, calling on Aubrey at Smithers's behest and unaware
as yet of his extraordinary powers of recuperation, assumed from
the blanched cheeks and graveyard cough that he had *come too
late*.[43]

It would have been strange if Aubrey, a cool enough observer of
human failings, mistook Smithers even at first glimpse for an
honest man. But whether or not Smithers was honest mattered
less at this juncture than his courage and receptivity to new ideas.
He was also amusing, and for that the invalid, so prone to depres-
sions, could be grateful. In one sense (that they are the least
inhibited) Aubrey's letters to 'mon cher Léonard' are among his
most natural: on the one hand, the homosexual endearments go
by the board; on the other, the religiosity (as when addressing
André), the 'brave face' (kept up for Ross), the spongeing-
avuncular manner (adopted towards the undergraduate Pollitt).*
Instead, and in spite of a pleasant outspokenness about money and
the practical affairs of printing and publishing, another element no
more natural than the effeminate is blatantly displayed: a kind of
feverish heterosexual bravado, which seeks to vie, absurdly
perhaps, with the singular prowess of his correspondent.

In the summer of 1895, both in London and Dieppe, a rival to
The Yellow Book was discussed. Smithers would publish it, with
Aubrey responsible for the artwork and Symons as literary editor.

*H. J. C. Pollitt (1871–1942). He commissioned Aubrey to design the cover of a Cambridge
magazine.

When plans for this new magazine, *The Savoy*, began to take
definite shape, Symons and Aubrey worked intensively together
for a month, their meeting-place Sickert's favourite Café des
Tribunaux on the Dieppe waterfront. During this time Symons
observed the artist's peculiar ways, and drew on the recollection
for the essay published in 1898:

> Beardsley . . . imagined himself to be unable to draw anywhere
> but in London. He made one or two faint attempts, and even
> prepared a canvas for a picture which was never painted, in the
> hospitable studio in which Jacques Blanche painted the ad-
> mirable portrait which now remains with us. But he found
> many subjects, some of which he afterwards worked out [e.g.,
> 'The Bathers' and 'Moska', both illustrations to the article en-
> titled 'Dieppe: 1895' by Symons, published in No. 1 of *The
> Savoy*], in the expressive opportunities of the Casino and the
> beach. He never walked; I never saw him look at the sea; but at
> night he was almost always to be seen watching the gamblers at
> *petits chevaux*, studying them with a sort of hypnotized attention
> for that picture of *The Little Horses*, which was never done. He
> liked the large deserted rooms, at hours when no one was there;
> the sense of frivolous things caught at a moment of suspended
> life, *en déshabille*.[44]

Fourteen

I thought I would reserve discussion of *The Savoy*, that most
enchanting of vehicles for Aubrey's printed work, till Smithers's
appearance on the scene, since it is as a tribute to his initiative that
we must first consider Number 1. The design by Aubrey for the
cover of this January 1896 issue had passed through the hands of
the admirable zincographer Paul Naumann and a perfect impression was secured by the printer—H. S. Nichols, originally
Smithers's business partner*—upon pink paper boards. I have no
doubt that Aubrey himself chose the pink, his favourite tint with
black pen-work. And when, in the third number, the pink was
exchanged for a greenish-blue paper, the titling in a coarse red,

---

*Nichols remains an obscure figure. He later went to the United States, where he was
responsible for an exhibition of the crudest Beardsley forgeries masquerading as originals.

the magazine loses (for me, at least) much of its visual charm.[45]

The first two *Savoys* are, indeed, Aubreiana to prize. As in the Sistine Chapel, small changes in the interests of decency have not ruined the original grandeur of conception. The cherub on the cover of No. 1 no longer stands poised—or, indeed, equipped—to urinate on a copy of *The Yellow Book* (Fig. 42), a dig at Lane

42   Original design for the front cover of *The Savoy*, No. 1, January 1896. In the published version the cherub's genitals were expunged.

the latter thoroughly deserved; yet what a splendid composition it is! Aubrey has well and truly 'burrowed through' Burne-Jones by now. He has since hobnobbed with many schools of engravers and comes up triumphant with this noble female with her riding-crop in the grounds of some Vanbrugh-like palace. The necessary touch of viciousness (Aubrey must stick to his last) is present only in the deliberately tortured lettering. Within, the magazine's pages are generous in margin and the typography exceptional for the period. In addition, this number contains a superb reproduction of one of his masterpieces, 'The Abbé' (Fig. 69).

And much of the credit for all this must go to Smithers. He was responsible for the appearance of the magazine in eight parts, which were later issued in three volumes bound in purple-blue cloth, a few copies being specially put up in vellum. These hard-back copies of *The Savoy*, even in the cloth edition, constitute one of the finest brass-blocked bindings of the time.

In direct contrast to such work produced at the height of his prosperity is the *Venus and Tannhäuser*, with text and illustrations by Aubrey, produced in 1907, the year of Smithers's death. Its cheapness and drabness pathetically reflect the ruin to which he had sunk. One thinks of the luxurious dress that must have been intended at an earlier stage for Aubrey's story which, as 'Under the Hill', had first appeared in the pages of *The Savoy*, and, whatever his misdemeanours, one's heart goes out to the bankrupt publisher. Nor can we forget the infinite pains Smithers went to, in 1897–8, over the title-page for Wilde's *Ballad of Reading Gaol*, which no one else would publish. As Wilde himself admitted, the typographical design, on which Smithers spent an entire day and for part of which (though the rest was type) he insisted on a special block being cut, turned out a notable success in its own *genre*.*[46]

Fifteen

'I thought Smithers had an evil influence on Beardsley,' Sir William Rothenstein reflected afterwards.[47] But an early result of their collaboration was the totally innocuous *Rape of the Lock*, innocuous, that is, in comparison with any other of Aubrey's ambitious series (Fig. 43). The savage irony of which he had shown himself a consummate master is excluded from these drawings, most of them entering into the category of 'prettiness', the last we might have anticipated from his caustic pen. A copy of

---

*Mr Reade has pointed out to me that, to his knowledge, this is the first example of titling aligned to the right, rather than the left.

The Rape of the Lock was, in fact, exhibited among the wedding-
presents at Marlborough House on the occasion of the marriage
between Princess Maud of Wales and Prince Charles of Denmark

43   The Toilet, from *The Rape of the Lock*, published 1896.

in July 1896. It was a gift to the royal couple from Lady Alston,*
who had employed Mrs Beardsley as a governess and become a
family friend.[48] How could the Prince and the Princess have
imagined that the same artist was currently crowing with laughter
and triumph in an Epsom hotel over the erotic extravagances of his
Lysistrata? The two works (the *Lysistrata* for private circulation)
have, technically, something in common: the play of solid line
against stipple, for instance. But whereas *The Rape* would have
been a gift as suitable for Victorian children as Victorian Royalty,
seventy years had to elapse before the *Lysistrata* drawings became
generally available in the bookshops.

Also under Smithers's aegis came the verse playlet by Dowson,
The Pierrot of the Minute (Fig. 70), with a few decorations by
Aubrey still in the innocent manner of *The Rape of the Lock*. It
appeared in March 1897. Those who have been faithful to Dowson
in their fashion tend to stress Aubrey's alleged unkindness
towards this tender dreamer. But the Aubrey who sneered and
snarled and never forgot a slight, and habitually lifted up his eyes
at his friends' shortcomings, seems to have been very largely the
invention of Vincent O'Sullivan.† Irritation and goodwill are about
evenly mixed in the artist's recorded references to the man with
whom it was at one time proposed that he should collaborate in an
English edition of *Les Liaisons dangereuses*.

Rothenstein, however, was right to blame Smithers for encouraging Aubrey to take part in expeditions beyond his strength
and sit up drinking in cafés when he ought to have been in bed.
We shall return later on to the disastrous result of their meeting in
Paris and going to Brussels together. Then there was the artist's
utter dependence on Smithers as publisher of his work: from the
autumn of 1897, Aubrey's fears on this score began to grow. Was
he not producing ideas and drawings for a man whose business
showed signs of running downhill so rapidly that even small sums
of money might soon be hard to come by?[49]

Adding to Smithers's problems, Wilde dogged him from various

*Sir Francis Beilby Alston (1820–1905), Chief Clerk at the Foreign Office, married Emily
Taylor in 1862.
†It is his *Aspects of Wilde*, 1936, which gives Aubrey this unpleasant character.

addresses in France and Italy during this first year of his release. Prison had not made Oscar an easier man to deal with. A penniless social outcast, he suspected the motives of his most faithful friends. In any case, it may well not be true that Aubrey, out in Dieppe with Conder and Blanche one day, steered them into a side-street to avoid a meeting, and that Wilde was bitterly upset as a result.[50] On the contrary, the references to Aubrey in Wilde's letters of July and August 1897 express the greatest goodwill. That Aubrey felt some embarrassment on this score, however, seems certain. A letter of his to Raffalovich from the Hôtel Sandwich, Dieppe, where he and his mother were staying, hints at it in the form of 'undesirable complications'.[51] In September a scheme was afoot to get Aubrey to do a frontispiece and decorations for *The Ballad of Reading Gaol*. The following passage from Smithers's estimate of what would come of it is worth bearing in mind, when the publisher himself has had to face so many charges of unreliability:

> I yesterday sent you back your poem [he wrote to Wilde]. I showed it to Aubrey and he seemed to be much struck by it. He promised at once to do a frontispiece for it—in a manner which immediately convinced me that he will never do it. He has got tired already of *Mlle de Maupin* and talks of Casanova instead. It seems hopeless to try and get any connected work out of him of any kind.[52]

By 1897, Smithers and Raffalovich between them were supporting a dying man whose capricious flitting from one project to another (Casanova would be forsaken for *Volpone*) is less astonishing than his will to work at all, as the end approached. From November of that year and over the first months of 1898, which were Aubrey's last, Smithers's weekly payments of about £12 a week began to arrive with mercifully greater regularity again. And, once more, the publisher's steadfast loyalty to his artist demands acknowledgement. He himself was to pay dearly enough for this generosity, and one is glad at least that Aubrey did not linger on, helpless, for another two years. For in 1900 Smithers went bankrupt. His residence in Bedford Square and shop in the Royal Arcade were given up, and, in the seven years following, the

Smithers family (husband, wife and small boy) descended, stage by stage, from the grandeur of a Bloomsbury mansion to the squalor of three dingy rooms in Cubitt Street, Islington. Later, Jack Smithers, the publisher's son, related the mysterious circumstances of his father's death in 1907. The corpse was stretched out on a bed—the only article of furniture—in an empty house in Parsons Green. Not a stitch of clothing remained. Even boots and monocle had been spirited away.[53]

Hogarth could have made something of the 'progress' of Leonard Smithers. How much was due to profligacy, how much to muscular rheumatism? And what role in his partner's downfall was played by H. S. Nichols? Who made greater use (in a back room, felt-fitted) of the double-crown Wharfedale printing-press multiplying pornography? If the wrath of heaven really does descend on wrong-doers (doing wrong, that is according to the *corpus juris* of their day), then Smithers had certainly provoked it in his own manner. It was he who, two years before meeting Aubrey, had published a limited edition of *Teleny, or the Reverse of the Medal*, a sodomitical tale of the utmost freedom;[54] and his last fling, as has been noted, was the unexpurgated edition of Aubrey's *Venus and Tannhäuser* which is frankly and, as many would have felt, unforgivably out to shock.

We come, therefore to the question of that last letter from Aubrey to his publisher, which runs thus (Fig. 44):

Menton

Jesus is our Lord and Judge

Dear Friend

I implore you to destroy *all* copies of *Lysistrata* and bad drawings. Show this to Pollitt and conjure him to do same. By all that is holy *all* obscene drawings

Aubrey Beardsley

In my death agony

Aubrey would have intended by this the illustrations to Juvenal's Sixth Satire as well as those to the Aristophanes. Pollitt was the Cambridge undergraduate to whom he looked for gifts of money as well as payment. Postmarked 7 March 1898, the envelope had

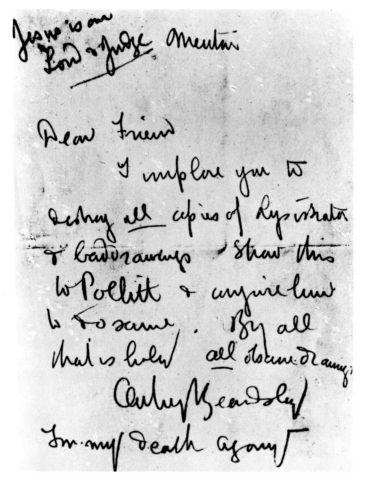

44 Aubrey's last letter to Smithers (the envelope, postmarked 7 March 1898, was addressed by his mother).

been addressed by Mrs Beardsley. Did she have a hand in the composition of the letter itself? If so, she never admitted to this at any time during the thirty-four years she survived her son. Smithers, characteristically, saw no reason why he should obey the injunction, however solemn. He had been Aubrey's paymaster:

the drawings, whether obscene or not, were his investments. He continued, therefore, to make what use of them he saw fit; and it may have been on this account that Ellen Beardsley so hardened her heart against him.

What surprises me about the letter is the lack of any reference to the manuscript of *Venus and Tannhäuser*, also in Smithers's possession. Can it be that this document, going certainly as far in words as any of its author's drawings, was known to Mrs Beardsley only in the expurgated version of *Under the Hill*? Blind, perhaps wilfully blind, to the implications of Aubrey's graphic art as we shall find her, she could hardly have been expected to share with him the amusement he derived from the full scope of Venusberg activity.

Sixteen

I am grateful to Mr Brian Reade for an opportunity to bring out three further points that may help towards establishing Aubrey's attitude towards fellow-members of the *Cénacle*, and may even bear on the problem of his sexual orientation.

Two of these points arise from remarks made to Mr Reade by the late Vyvyan Holland, Wilde's second son, who, shortly before Aubrey's death was taken as a boy of eleven or twelve to visit him in Menton. Holland remembered the particular kindness with which the artist spoke of his father: a natural thing, in the circumstances, yet it somewhat tempers O'Sullivan's spiteful tales. Aubrey was then confined to his room and never again to leave it, and Holland (who himself died recently) must have been the only person outside the family and those directly attending on the dying man who ever saw him with a beard. Wilde, separated from his children and in Paris, expressed to Smithers, a day or two after Aubrey's death, how greatly shocked he had been to read of the event, and, in another letter of March 1898, he commiserates with Smithers in the latter's genuine distress. The second point concerns the story that Mrs Leverson (Ada Leverson, 'The Sphinx')* seduced, or set out to seduce, Aubrey. Holland, who met most of his father's friends—themselves often friends of Aubrey's—about

*1862–1933. Wilde's faithful friend: a novelist and journalist.

the time he went up to Cambridge, at least vouched for the story having been in common circulation. What we are to make of it is another matter.

Finally, there is the paper-knife, with a silver handle inscribed 'TIM dd Aubrey'.[55] It was discovered (along with a scrapbook and the painting 'A Caprice' and other oddments) by a Mrs Pugh, who took over 114 Cambridge Street after the Beardsleys left the house in the summer of 1895. Mr Reade identified the handle's half-obliterated hallmark as Birmingham, probably early in the 1890s. Who was Tim? Mr Reade has wondered whether there could be covert reference here by the knife's donor to Howard Overing Sturgis, a pupil of the homosexual poet Cory at Eton, who published in 1891 a first novel entitled *Tim*. The theme of *Tim*, the reader will not be surprised to learn, is that of Douglas's poem, of Wilde's burst of oratory at the Old Bailey, of much of the literature and almost all the close human contact enjoyed by Aubrey: 'the love that dare not speak its name'.

The paper-knife exists, but the question of its provenance still awaits an answer.

It is a conclusion we are inevitably driven to, that neither an examination, however careful, of Aubrey's drawings by themselves, nor any study we can hope to undertake, at this distance in time, of the group of men with whom he spent his short active life, offers any real help when it comes to the deeper mysteries. There is no other English artist, become a household name, whose character is so difficult to determine. What does one drawing tell us of him that the next does not contradict? With all his apparent gregarious-ness (the term is Ross's), his flittings to and fro—in days of health— within the *Cénacle*, he had, thought Symons, 'scarcely a friend in the fullest sense of the word'.

'I doubt,' continued Symons, 'if there were more than one or two people for whom he had any real affection.'[56]

If love is the spring of action and artists resemble other men in their need and avowal of it, it will clearly assist us greatly to know who may be covered by that phrase 'one or two people'. The obvious place to look for them now is in the family circle, a domain where the infant mechanisms of adjustment to love or deprivation first come into play. We shall begin by exploring the relationship between mother and son, a relationship (since Aubrey's mother was also his nurse) that will inevitably involve us in a fresh appraisal of his fatal illness. It is, I think, high time such an appraisal was made. For nine-tenths of his working life Aubrey was an invalid, for a third of it dying: we can therefore hardly separate the genius from the sick man.

Ellen and the Invalid

One

Ellen Agnus Pitt, born in India in 1846, was the daughter of an Army surgeon (Fig. 45). The Surgeon-Major (as he became) retired to Brighton, and it was there that Ellen met her future husband, Vincent Paul Beardsley (Fig. 46), who—to paraphrase the condition of Joyce's Mr Daedalus—was something in a brewery. The meeting took place on the pier: while Ellen was sketching, it has been suggested, to minimize her indiscretion. But most of what passes as fact about this not unimportant encounter and the marriage, which followed in 1870, is a matter of conjecture. I think R. A. Walker,* doyen of Beardsley scholars, may have painted too black a portrait of the artist's father, whose origins (they have a whiff of Nottingham mud and labourer's corduroy) were less respectable than the mother's.[1] Walker was primed direct by old Mrs Beardsley and, after her death, by a family retainer, equally prejudiced against the husband, then long dead. The result is a picture of a total idler, waster, boor and, in youth, philanderer, which I have found hard to reconcile with his glowing testimonials for reliability from the New Westminster Brewery and Crowley's Alton Ale Stores.[2] Let us leave it that the marriage involved some clash of caste, that the partners, though they never formally separated, were not happy together (Fig. 47).

The Beardsleys' first child, a daughter, was born on 24 August 1871. The birth was normal and Mabel a healthy baby. Aubrey's arrival followed in just under the twelve months, on 21 August 1872. But this time Ellen fell seriously ill with puerperal fever, and her second child, delicate enough to inspire alarm, had to be removed till she passed the crisis. Undoubtedly we have to take account of Aubrey's tenuous hold on life from the beginning. And this first separation from his mother was by no means, even in early childhood, the last. Because of some unexplained inadequacy

*Author of the invaluable *A Beardsley Miscellany*, 1949.

79

of her husband's, Ellen herself had to work as a teacher of French and music—to children more fortunate than her own.

She seems to have been a successful governess, and in her spare time a good, stern, sermonizing mother. But we must certainly

45   Ellen Agnus Beardsley (1846–1932): an early photograph of the artist's mother.

46   Vincent Paul Beardsley (1840–1909), the artist's father.

abandon any notions of a love-starved Ellen overwhelming her 'little man' with maternal solicitude, over-wooing and over-coaxing him through endlessly prolonged rituals of meals and bath and bed like some mothers of delicate children. In their lodgings at 2 Ashley Villas (never identified, but probably a house in Vauxhall Bridge Road, near the brewery),[3] at 32 Cambridge Street and at 59 Charlwood Street, all Pimlico addresses and, no doubt, selected for their proximity to Mr Beardsley's place of employment, life was and would remain Spartan. However poor an example the father might set, the mother was determined to bring up her son a gentleman. It seems there was that in Aubrey which resisted the code laid down for him. Often (as Ellen confessed to Ross, years later) tantrums occurred: this little wisp of a creature possessed extraordinary powers of will. When, putting his faith in the privileges of the invalid, he risked a point-blank refusal to mend his manners, his mother whipped him.[4]

Two

But kindness alternated with sternness: Aubrey was so fragile. And at seven, when he suddenly went off his food with a cough and a little fever, the doctor reported ominously on a fine, moist crackle audible through the stethoscope. These must have been blissful nights, his cot set up in his mother's room; best of all, those occasions when he slept beside her in the place vacated (perhaps too willingly) by Mr Beardsley. What candlelight images imprinted themselves upon the sick child's memory? The watcher herself may well have been watched.[5]

¶ By contrast with any nascent sensuality that went unobserved, Aubrey's intellectual gifts were immediately recognizable. Long before he could walk, he thumped out the correct rhythm when his mother played Beethoven: 'I often used to change the time,'

47 Vincent and Ellen Beardsley in later married life. Mr Beardsley's rôle seems to have been negligible. He is not mentioned in his son's letters after 1892, and friends who visited 114 Cambridge Street assumed that Mrs Beardsley was a widow. This double photograph, hitherto unpublished, comes therefore as something of a surprise.

she related, 'in order to try and put him off—from four to six, and so on, but could never confuse him.' And then, as easily as he learned to read—the cabbalism of the printed page resolved itself miraculously—he took to the piano of his own accord, becoming something of a prodigy.[6]

Ellen herself played to the family every evening, choosing her programme carefully so that it should be a lesson in musical taste: just as the children were encouraged to read voraciously, but never rubbish. Mabel, whose forte was reciting, had raced through most of Dickens and Scott (Carlyle she frowned on) by the time she was six. But Ellen had no difficulty in deciding which of the two was destined for immortality. The boy's genius would carry all before it, whereas Mabel was to be the practical one. Genius or not, however, Aubrey was left in no doubt that he must behave like a surgeon-major's grandson.

Having this advantage over the rest of us, that he was personally acquainted with Ellen Beardsley in her old age, Walker confined himself to gallant references to her beauty (in youth), her charm and wit, and her courage in two terrible ordeals. It was from Ellen, he said, that Aubrey had inherited his high intelligence. And, of course, Walker was right. But privately he recorded his astonishment that so cultured a woman could have been so simple-minded.[7] If sexual innuendo, blatant as ever pen created, became the most striking feature (after its beauty) of the artist's work, does it not argue obtuseness on her part that she never observed it?

But she observed something. In an undated letter to Lane written long after her son's death, she recalled:

> Aubrey showed me a drawing one day I quite forget what it was—some awful female I daresay—and I said 'Oh Aubrey this is dreadful!' and he replied 'Vice is dreadful and should be [so] made or depicted' and then he added 'there is hardly a week that some comic paper does not contain a picture more corrupting than anything I have ever drawn.' On another occasion when there was something in some paper furiously abusing one of his drawings and I showed it to him he said 'Of course they are furious, they hate to see their darling sins.'[8]

Messianic or Mephistophelian, depending on which you like to make it, Aubrey's work must nevertheless have posed her consider-able problems, just as his health was another endless anxiety. However proud of his rapidly developing gift for drawing she may have been, she had not much more confidence in his taking up art as a career, when—in the autumn of 1892—it came to the point, than Aubrey's habitually dour and discouraging 'pater'.[9] Nor can it have pleased either of them that the decision was taken without so much as a by-your-leave. Quite apart from the financial risk, how could Aubrey's health stand up to working at all hours of the day, and against the clock, when publishers wanted designs completed in a hurry?

There was good enough reason for her fears on the latter score. By 1892 Aubrey must have been well acquainted with the con-sulting-room of Dr Edmund Symes-Thompson* in Cavendish Square, and have stared long and gloomily upon the fountain and old black mulberries in the private garden behind the house. Dr Symes-Thompson (Fig. 48), a distinguished physician, had given special attention to pulmonary diseases.[10] His earliest-known report is alluded to by the artist in a letter to A. W. King, dated 4 January 1890.[11] From this it appears that Aubrey's first serious breakdown occurred in late November or December 1889, when he was in his seventeenth year. During the interval following the initial infection in childhood, the lesion would have healed, only to recur, predictably, at the vulnerable approach of adult life. On the face of it, therefore, it is surprising to learn from Aubrey that the doctor's anxiety at this stage was on account of the heart rather than the lungs ('luckily not diseased'), particularly since a heart condition receives no further mention in his medical history.

Dr Symes-Thompson may have pronounced as he did (allowing always that Aubrey heard, or wanted to hear, correctly) to raise his patient's spirits; for, in fact, there had been a prolonged haemor-rhage which kept him away from the Fire Insurance Office for some while, even putting his job there in jeopardy. Drawing was out of the question. Instead, between crises of 'blood-spitting', he devoted himself to reading, particularly books in French, which

---

*1837–1906. There is a delightful note on the doctor's household in Cavendish Square by his daughter, Lady Page, in Gordon Winter's *Past Positive*, 1971.

48 Dr Edmund Symes-Thompson (1837–1906),
Aubrey's physician. He was the author, with his
father (Theophilus), of a standard work on pulmonary
consumption.

he had now mastered. His dazzling familiarity with the highways
and byways of that literature can be reckoned, indeed, a strange
benefit thrown up by the remorseless acceleration, from now on,
of the infective process in the lung tissue.

Three

The next serious breakdown took place in the spring of 1893, and
in September he was still complaining of the strained, weak condition in which it had left him.[12] He had now been dependent on
his own exertions as a professional artist for twelve months.

Frustration, it will be remembered, tormented him, as the onerous cut-price commission for Dent continued its demands.

There is a note in Ellen's hand about this state of affairs. She writes:

> Aubrey hated working to order. He grew very tired of the designs for the *Morte Darthur*, and it was very difficult to get him to do them. When Mr Dent became insistent and none were forthcoming, I went to Aubrey's room one morning and told him he must really get up and do them. He sat up in bed, rubbed his eyes and said:
>
> > 'A youth for a very small salary
> > Did a cartload of drawings for Malory;
> >   When they asked him for more
> >   He only said: "Sure,
> > They've already enough for a gallery." '[13]

To whom could she turn to make this difficult son of hers see sense? They were now living for the first time in a house all to themselves, for Aubrey's rising fortunes together, as is thought, with the aid of a bequest from his Great-Aunt Lambe had enabled him to take a lease of 114 Cambridge Street. In a real home of their own more ambitious entertaining was possible, and Ellen began to meet Aubrey's friends, among them the charming and sympathetic Robert Ross (Douglas's description of him as a 'rather pathetic-looking creature, in appearance something like a kitten' would not have been how Ellen saw one of her son's most influential admirers). But we have met Ross already in these pages, and I have only to explain that Ellen seems to have singled him out very soon as one in whom she could safely confide.

A group of her letters to him has survived, the earliest of which, written on 29 September 1893, seeks his help in the *Morte* problem:

> I am very uneasy [she says] at the way Aubrey is treating Mr Dent over the *Morte Darthur*, and horrified at hearing him propose throwing it over altogether. Please don't betray me by letting him know I have written to you, but you have great influence with him and I should be so grateful to you if you

would remonstrate with him on his behaviour. To me it seems monstrous that he should even contemplate behaving in such an unprincipled manner. His *Morte* work may be a little unequal—that is his own fault and because he is wilful enough not to exert himself over what he pretends he doesn't like—but take it on the whole, it is beautiful work and does him credit. But that isn't the point, he undertook to do it, and Mr Dent has spent money over it and subscribers too, and if Aubrey gives it up it will be disgraceful. It appears he is likely to be in for a good deal of undeserved rebuke and abuse, but if he treats Mr Dent as he proposes to do, I, for one, will say he deserves all he will get for such ungentlemanly conduct. . . . Please forgive me for troubling you, but you have always been [i.e., for nineteen months!] such a true friend to Aubrey that I feel sure you won't mind a distressed mother writing to ask for your help.[14]

One cannot fault Ellen's instinct for appreciating that here was her best ally. Not without reason did Siegfried Sassoon apostrophize Wilde's indefatigable aide in adversity:

O heart of hearts! O friend of friends!

For after, as well as before, Aubrey's death, Ross became in small matters and great the counsellor to whom Ellen (and her daughter) never had to turn in vain.

In this instance, Ross must have persuaded Aubrey against what would without doubt have been an injudicious, to say nothing of an ungentlemanly, course. A note was sent, in which the artist begged his friend to come to lunch 'as early as you can, as I have much to say to you, and will expect of you counsel, advice and resolution': and posted in the same month, at least, as Ellen's letter.[15] The agreement with Dent was duly honoured.

The tone of Ellen's next letter to Ross in this group makes it clear that her confidence had not been betrayed. It has another interest for us, since it was written from a nursing-home at 90 Harley Street (Miss Tidy's Establishment for Invalid Ladies, as the Directory tells us), where, on Christmas Day 1893, she received, with Ross's 'beautiful flowers', visits from Walter Sickert, the Revd Alfred Gurney (of whom more anon) and a 'detachment' of Alstons. What of Ellen's own health? There is a curious reference to it as 'very bad' in a letter of Aubrey's as early as

1892.[16] Her trouble is described as chronic sciatica, 'and it seems there is nothing to be done for her', adds her son. Well, Ellen survived till 1932, long outliving both her children and remaining active almost up to the end. On this occasion it seems that she stayed in the Invalid Establishment for over a month, as a period of convalescence after an operation. I am bound to say that, while several visitors are recorded in Ellen's own letters, and in others,[17] no call upon his mother by Aubrey is mentioned. It does not seem that he came to Harley Street with his sister, even on Christmas Day. One remembers that, following on his reference to Ellen's chronic sciatica in the 1892 letter, his only comment had been that 'very soon my sister [Mabel was already teaching] and myself will have the "family" [their unsuccessful father and a mother unable to continue as governess] on our hands, so the money view of my art has to be kept keenly in view'.[18]

As against what appears to be heartlessness on Aubrey's part, where his mother was concerned, there is evidence that fog drove him to ground early in December 1893. At the same time, it is surprising to find no comment on his mother's illness in his own letters, ranging from late November of that year to early January 1894, addressed to Ross. Gallantly attentive to Ellen himself, Ross had to depend on Mabel for twice- or thrice-weekly bulletins.

Four

We begin to wonder how the situation stood between mother and son. If Aubrey had been 'wilful' before his rise to fame, how much more difficult the turn things had taken since would persuade him to be! To find oneself a vogue figure, yet admonishable in one's own home, would have been testing enough for a more patient young genius.

The tone of Ellen's letters to Ross, however, suggests that she looked to him to risk arguments with her son from which she shrank. She seems to have adapted herself well enough to Aubrey's circle of friends, Wilde only excepted. As the house was not hers, she was not in a position to object to Aymer Vallance's ideas on interior decoration. Netta Syrett's description of 114 Cambridge Street, transformed to his design, is perhaps the most accurate. Here is the drawing-room:

The light was so obscured by heavy lace curtains drawn across the windows that it was only when her eyes had grown accustomed to the gloom that she could take in its rather strange appearance. The walls, as she then saw, were painted a deep orange, and against them rose slender black pillars that spread out at the top into conventional interlacing twigs and branches covering an orange-coloured ceiling. The room was so full that very little of the furniture could be seen, but glimpses now of a gold and black lacquer cabinet, now of a Chinese screen, or of the carved and gilded arm of a chair gave an effect of rather oppressive richness, heightened by a faint all-pervading scent which made the air sweet and heavy.[19]

What excited the heroine of *Strange Marriage* was probably not much to the taste of the older generation to which Ellen herself belonged. And where was Mr Beardsley? One has to ask oneself whether perhaps his professional duties kept him much on the brewery premises; for the parents do not seem to have parted company, yet Miss Syrett never heard Vincent Beardsley's name mentioned, and never met him during her frequent visits to Cambridge Street in 1894–5. She came to the conclusion that Mrs Beardsley was a widow. Grass-widow Ellen certainly seems to have been for much of the time: which may have led her to identify herself more closely with her son and his circle, whatever the difficulty of keeping Aubrey's nose to the grindstone, and however depressing Vallance's orange-and-black décor and the smell of balsam (in Japanese incense-burners, no doubt). She had little choice, if she wished to play any part at all in the artist's life.

And, of course, caveats and criticism not excluded, Ellen was tremendously proud of Aubrey and delighted by the excitement his success added to her otherwise dull and culture-starved life. I have mentioned what Walker called her simple-mindedness. The following letter to Ross, dated 7 March 1894, seems to support his conclusion:

I cannot resist writing to tell you the latest joke. I have been credited with having done the *Salome* illustrations. An elderly Frenchman whom I met at the Harlands* the other day, having

*Henry Harland (1861–1905) and his wife Aline lived in the Cromwell Road, South Kensington. He followed up his editorship of *The Yellow Book* by publishing, in 1900, *The Cardinal's Snuff-Box*.

looked through the book with evident appreciation, took my breath away by suddenly saying to me 'C'est vous Madame qui a fait çela?' Although I fail to see any impropriety in them they don't strike me as being exactly what one would expect from the British Matron! But I was too overwhelmed to explain matters to him and fortunately Mrs Harland gallantly came to the rescue.[20]

How could any Frenchman, elderly or otherwise, have entertained so bizarre a fancy? English gentlewomen, flat-chested and with features tending to the equine (a fair description of Ellen), had long been the favourite butt of French comic artists, in particular for their *minauderie*. Perhaps this, too, was a joke, misinterpreted by the victim. The Harlands were not people who expected their guests to stand on ceremony with each other. One suspects that the Frenchman was amused by the complacent manner in which Ellen displayed her son's drawings for *Salome*, and that a shaft of wit was the result. It is a matter for greater astonishment that she could say to Ross, of these same drawings: 'I fail to see any impropriety in them.' Was there no 'impropriety' in the design entitled 'Enter Herodias' (Fig. 21)? Did an artist draw sexually-excited monsters every day of the week? She was right, at all events, to conclude that it was not 'exactly what one would expect from the British Matron'. While Ellen may be credited with assuming (or accepting her son's assumption) that his target was not the Victorian code of morals, but the transgressor against that code, this is as good as to credit her with the belief that the moon shining over Pimlico was made of green cheese. Ellen was no fool. If she deluded herself, it must have been for a very good reason. She loved and she was afraid of, and she feared for, her son. The deaf ear and the blind eye had to be: they went with the love and the ceaseless apprehension.

Five

Let us pass on to another letter to Ross, almost six months later (5 September 1894), and we shall appreciate the difficulties with which Ellen had to contend:

My holiday has been such a disturbed and unhappy one that I

never had the chance of making any nice little plan for our meeting. Haslemere was a failure, Aubrey took a dislike to the place directly he got there and wanted to rush back to town at once. I didn't quite see the sense of this so I persuaded him to stay on from day to day, but his depression was so great and the life he led me so dreadful that at the end of a fortnight I gave it up and let him come home. I couldn't stay there by myself so I went to St Peter's Home, Woking, for a week to stay with the Sisters, and gave myself up to good works and a cap! I am afraid I was wicked enough to feel it a little dull, I had sinful hankerings after a good time, and a community of women with a distant view of the Chaplain now and then didn't satisfy my cravings. . . . I am sorry to say Aubrey has a slight return of haemorrhage, but I hope he will get over being liable to these attacks, there can be no peace of mind for me while his health is so uncertain.[21]

As 1893 passed into 1894, the volume of work engaging Aubrey grew. To the frustration of completing the *Morte Darthur* were added the excitement of creating a fashion (when *The Yellow Book* appeared on the stalls) and the anxiety not only of meeting his own deadlines but, as art editor, of ensuring that others met theirs. He received a warning about his health in June 1894; and in August, Dr Symes-Thompson, a strong believer in the beneficent effect of climate upon disease, had packed him off with his mother to Haslemere.

Valewood Farm, where their fortnight was spent, still exists and can be found about a mile south of the town, near the Petworth Road. Besides his multifarious services to *The Yellow Book*, Aubrey had much else on hand: decorations, title-pages, posters and the like. He had not always time now to see the friend to whom his mother confided her fears. But work was not simply a matter of satisfying a long list of customers, it was a spiritual necessity as well.

The agony of that enforced holiday for the son as well as the mother can well be imagined. And though the drawing was not carried out till the following year, something of the intensity of the conflict between what was medically desirable and humanly en-

durable is expressed in Aubrey's design for *An Evil Motherhood*
(Fig. 49). The claustral stillness of the sick-room seems to hang
about this work. The larger forms are draped and muffled. The
books are obstinately shut. Anticipating Sickert's by nearly twenty

49 Second frontispiece for Ruding's *An Evil Motherhood*, published 1896.

years, it is Aubrey's 'Ennui'. This composition was produced under
duress in November 1895. He was even obliged to offer, in the
young man sunk in the chair, a portrait of the author of *An Evil
Motherhood*, Walt Ruding.[22] We cannot, therefore, read into it a

consciously autobiographical reference: but the artist, caught in a cleft stick by Elkin Mathews and in a fury of ill-temper, has certainly revealed in it something of his 'depression' and the 'dreadful' life he led his mother. Her solicitude—how often had he sulked, refusing to turn his head, though aware of his mother's presence in the room?—must have been as exasperating on these occasions as his own sense of helplessness. Haslemere had its beauties and inspired him with 'backgrounds for *Tannhäuser*', but for an idle Aubrey they soon became intolerable. Better overwork in the poisoned air of the great city than the almost lethal boredom of the country.

After he had gone back to Cambridge Street on 22 August, Ellen, as she told Ross, went to stay at an establishment connected with the St Peter's Sisterhood of Kilburn, evidently justifying her presence by helping with its sick poor, to accommodate whom the Woking Memorial Home had just been enlarged. This was not a Catholic institution: in 1894, none of the family had yet been received into the Roman Church. Though clearly devout, Ellen evidently preserved a great deal of her youthful spirit. Before withering to angularity, as we see her in the late photographs, she had been slim, noted for her good looks and full of fun. There is a letter of hers to Captain Robin Holway,[23] in which she mentions a fancy-dress ball at the Brighton Pavilion, when a still attentive Mr Beardsley had whirled her through that 'adorable suite of rooms' and

> *. . . the casement jessamine stirr'd*
> *To the dancers dancing in tune ;*

though it was a far cry from Tennyson to the resident laureate of *The Brighton Gazette*, who acquitted himself thus:

> *And then Mrs Beardsley,*
> *May her honours increase,*
> *Looked most picturesque*
> *As a native of Greece.*

To this early provincial idyll had succeeded the grinding poverty of their life in London. Then, out of an existence shabby-genteel at its most lugubrious, Aubrey's brilliant gift had suddenly raised them. Once more, as in the old days in Brighton, she was surrounded by gay and personable young men, still (as we know from their letters) ready to compliment her on her youthfulness and charm. Naturally, Aubrey had his share of professional vexations and disappointments, but these were days when all the clouds had a silver lining. The too impetuous spirit, nevertheless, ignored the body at its peril.

For, of course, amusements and feverish industry exacted their toll. By November 1894, Dr Symes-Thompson was prescribing a water-cure. On 14 November Ellen thus confided in Ross:

I saw Aubrey off today for Malvern, Dr Symes-Thompson wished him to go to a medical friend of his Dr Grindrod who has a Hydropathic Establishment there. The doctor himself was at Paddington and it went to my heart to deliver the poor little boy over to his tender mercies for 'treatment' whatever that may be. I feel sure he is at this moment (8.30 p.m.) being regaled on gruel, and perhaps warm Apollinaris water—or being packed in wet towels or something damp! I have never been to a Hydropathic Establishment but it sounds dreadful, and as if one was never quite sure if it was a poultice or one's dinner that was being placed before one. And I think of that poor little boy reduced to this. He was very depressed at parting with me, my last view of him was in a 3rd-class railway carriage sitting opposite Dr Grindrod and looking like a little white mouse caught in a trap! And what I looked like I'm sure I can't think, but I felt such a wretch for letting him go. But what else could I do but persuade him to obey the doctor? I've had the greatest difficulty in persuading him to go away at all, and he isn't fit to be alone anywhere. The doctors thought him much better the last few days and speak most hopefully about him, our own doctor says positively there is no disease and that if he rests he will get quite well. I'm only afraid he will rush home in about a week and say he couldn't stand it. I am terribly anxious about him.[24]

Had Ellen known more about hydropathic treatment, she might have watched the train steam out of Paddington with an even heavier heart.[25] Charles Grindrod's father, Ralph, a disciple of

Priessnitz (the 'Columbus of Health') and of Hahnemann of Graefenberg, had been one of the first to introduce into this country the compressed-air bath, an iron chamber in which were installed a dozen fully-dressed patients, while Dr Ralph Grindrod at the controls slowly advanced the pressure half an atmosphere and noted their reactions through a glass panel. I have seen it stated that, in his day at least, those in the last stages of pulmonary tuberculosis were carried into the iron chamber. However old-fashioned these remedies—supported by prescriptions for pulsa-tilla of the twelfth potency and a duodecillionth of a grain of ipecacuanha—may have appeared to some medical practitioners in the 1890s, Dr Symes-Thompson was not one of them. He had, in fact, published a paper, jointly with Dr Charles Grindrod, on the place of hydropathy in medical science, expressing the view that the profession had given too little encouragement to English health resorts for water and air treatment.[26] And nowhere could one find drier, more bracing hill-air or purer, softer hill-water than at Wyche Side, Malvern Wells, the Grindrod clinic.

Nevertheless, the mystery of what such treatment might be supposed to do for Aubrey remains impenetrable. The stock Wyche Side patient was a chronic dyspeptic, an extravagantly dining and wining Londoner, who came down to Malvern for a periodic blow on the hills, regular diet and system of baths designed to relieve the organs of digestion. The importance of this episode is that it emphasizes the general helplessness of the medical profession, even of its highly-regarded specialists, when confronted with such cases as Aubrey's, though more than ten years had passed since Koch's identification of the tuberculosis bacillus.

Six

At Malvern, as at Haslemere, he was forbidden to draw. However, Ellen's 'little white mouse' was cerebrating in another way: as at Haslemere, so at Malvern, weaving words for his Penelopean tapestry, *The Story of Venus and Tannhäuser*. Presumably he had not brought the manuscript itself to Grindrod's, for he describes himself as sitting all day 'moping and worrying about my beloved Venusberg'.[27]

How fully was Ellen allowed to enter into her son's literary preoccupations at this moment? Rothenstein describes the shock he felt when he saw the erotic prints he had given the artist framed upon the wall at 114 Cambridge Street.[28] Aubrey certainly teased the modesty of his womenfolk. And the extravaganza slowly accumulating for Smithers (which we shall shortly be examining for ourselves) enters the class of overt pornography. But if Ellen knew what was going on, and deeply disapproved (observing that here *was* some impropriety), how could she have had the heart to call her ailing son to order? It was on her, however little it pleased him, that he would increasingly depend. To care for Aubrey must be her role in life, and the risk of crossing him had now, even through Ross, to be avoided. We shall not hear any more from Ellen on the subjects of 'principle' and 'gentlemanly conduct'. The problem would be to keep Aubrey alive.

It seems all too likely that he cut short his 'cure' in Malvern, as she had feared. It had been, he confessed to Frederick Evans, a very severe haemorrhage, leaving him 'horribly weak'.[29] But, almost as serious, he had temporarily lost his nerve. Once it was regained, he abandoned hydropathy and took the train back to London, where he was soon immersed once more in those dangerously stimulating tasks for *The Yellow Book* and the hundred-and-one extravagances that a *succès de scandale* entailed.

Yet probably, and Ellen was of this opinion, the shock and chagrin resulting from the cancellation of his art-editorship in April 1895 did him more injury than overwork. From overwork, of course, it by no means released him. Now he had suddenly to face the loss of his regular salary, the hurried disposal of 114 Cambridge Street and all the anxieties and humiliations attendant on finding new employment of a kind to recoup his losses. The timely appearance of Raffalovich and Smithers has been described already. Their help was invaluable. Yet the effects of the cruel blow he had suffered were not so easily repaired. A further haemorrhage occurred in July 1895 and, as we have noted, one of Aubrey's earliest communications to Smithers was dashed off in a doctor's consulting-room.

Living and working independently of his family meant that he did not receive the same care and attention. There were frequent visits to Dieppe, more pleasurable than wise, in that summer of 1895, and Aubrey, concerned with the planning of *The Savoy*, would often 'relax' far into the night in Smithers's raffish company. This magazine, though coming into existence so opportunely to keep his name before the public, was to tax his strength to the utmost, particularly when transformed from quarterly into monthly. Early in 1896 he took the injudicious step of leaving London, where his family and Dr Symes-Thompson could at least watch over him from near at hand, to go and live in Paris. There he flung himself into the *Savoy* commitments and his exacting designs for *The Rape of the Lock*. In the midst of this toil he was visited by Smithers, with whom (in March) he moved on to Brussels. What games he got up to with Smithers in the Belgian capital are not recorded; but his amiable and disreputable publisher, himself obliged to head back for London, left a very sick young man behind him.

The condition of the lungs (referred to by Dowson, non-medically, as a 'congestion') was very serious indeed.[30] From remarks made later by the artist himself we know that Aubrey came to regard those hideous days and nights at the Hôtel de Saxe as the fateful turning-point of his life. In fact, from that time on (he arrived in Brussels early in April 1896 and left early in May) his physical decline would be rapid. Ellen wrote to Ross an anguished letter on 20 April:

> I have been so utterly wretched about Aubrey, doubly so because I can do nothing for him. My only consolation has been to have him prayed for at St Barnabas. At least I thought it was going to console me, but when I heard his name I was heartbroken.[31]

To add to Aubrey's other discomforts in Brussels, the Belgian doctor had blistered him. 'I am utterly furious at my treatment here,' he told Smithers, a few days after Ellen's letter to Ross. 'The last blister has done nothing but give me dreadful pain in the spine so that the least sudden change in position gives me beans.'[32] One can read about the artificial inducement of blistering and its efficacy as a counter-irritant in contemporary English as well as Continental *Materia Medica*; and it could equally well have been prescribed by Dr Symes-Thompson as by the physician attending

Aubrey at the Hôtel de Saxe. The longer the skin remained broken, so the theory went, the better; and Symes-Thompson (editing his father Theophilus's *Clinical Lectures on Pulmonary Consumption*) chills our spines with the case of a lady who made a perfect recovery from the last stage of phthisis through keeping a blister open uninterruptedly for twenty months.[33]

By late April Aubrey could walk without a stick, but realized that when he got back to London he would have 'some little difficulty as to logement'.[34] Stairs were the devil, now that he was so short of breath. If only he could afford a room on the top floor of an hotel with a lift! The breathlessness of which he here complains would point to a new and sinister shrinkage in active lung-tissue. Many problems (among them, who was to come out to Brussels to pack up for him and see him home) delayed his departure for a week or so after he had first begun to hobble round the city again. This enabled the doctor to give him a thorough 'clean-out' with creosote; after which acetate of lead, regarded as useful in checking expectoration, was administered!

It was Ellen, finally, on whom Aubrey had to call to bring him back to England. Mabel, then on the stage, could not get the necessary leave of absence from her employers, the Bourchiers. Ellen had appealed to Ross to perform this service for the family: '*Do* if you possibly can. Will you kindly answer as soon as possible because someone must go. Failing every one *I* must go but fear to be ill myself.'[35] Ross, unfortunately, had to say no. Ellen arrived in Brussels on 3 May, but was so exhausted that the return journey was postponed till the day following. Mother and son crawled back together, and immediately they reached London Aubrey went round to Cavendish Square, where Dr Symes-Thompson pronounced 'very unfavourably' on his condition.

The artist took new rooms at 17 Campden Grove, Kensington, but later the same month he was sent to recuperate, all drawing forbidden, to Crowborough. His stay at the many-gabled Victorian villa called Twyford lasted about a fortnight; to be followed—with a few days' grace in London, always very dear to him—by a further period of exile in Epsom. In the 1890s the Spread Eagle Hotel, standing at the central crossroads, was as familiar a landmark to race-goers as it is now. Aubrey seems to have been happier there than in Crowborough, approving his 'two palatial rooms' and a pretty little 'restaurantish' dining-room; and it was at the Spread Eagle that he busied himself with the *Lysistrata* illustrations: a strange exercise in home-therapy (Figs. 50 and 51).

Seven

Epsom, indeed, proved on the whole the least unendurable, as we might put it, of his English country retreats: not that it failed to witness some recurrence of the ever-menacing disease, but the attacks did not frighten him, since at the same time he received assurances (how unsubstantial!) that he was making good progress. He had also to report—for Smithers's ear only—a little trouble that was 'not venereal'. I have referred earlier to the bravado, the bantering commentary on his sex life, which marks Aubrey's letters to his publisher, who would be spared no details. It is probable, however, that the unwelcome discharge was non-tuberculous, or it would not, as Smithers was to learn later, have so obligingly 'dried up'.[36]

On the other hand, early in August 1896, the haemorrhage returned with a vengeance. Epsom lost favour with Dr Symes-Thompson, who now advised a move to the coast. The resort chosen was Boscombe, in Hampshire. Aubrey himself would have preferred the gay, picturesque Brighton of his childhood; but, more than one physician thinking differently, Boscombe it had to be.

Poor Aubrey! Hither, with the descending equinox, came the retired, the lonely and the decrepit. Beyond the mean, redbrick vernacular of the shops, debouched Sea Road, past villas bearing names like Lucerne, Dil-Aram and Engelhorne, till finally, after Bracknell and Restmore, there rose on its hummock (or anticipated a minor declivity towards the pebbled strand) Pier View (Fig. 52). Somewhere close by—a lodge gave on to Sea Road—lived Lady Shelley, widow of the third Baronet. It may have been a consolation to Aubrey to know that there still existed in Boscombe Manor, slipped between the pages of *Adonais*, a silk bag containing the shrunken ashes of the poet's heart, but he was not invited to the house nor, probably, had he been asked, would his state of health have permitted an evening out. From their seaward-facing windows

LYSISTRATA.

50 Lysistrata shielding her Coynte: frontispiece from *The Lysistrata of Aristophanes*, published (for private distribution) 1896.

in the boarding-house, the artist and his mother might have been able to catch a glimpse of a small thatched building immediately inside one of the entrances to Boscombe Gardens. Had not Symes-Thompson and Grindrod compared the arsenical waters of Mont Dore and Bournemouth? Spa water, perhaps of the same character, could be obtained free on application at this diminutive pavilion. Only once, and then involuntarily as we shall see, did Aubrey take advantage of its resources (a humble fountain); nor did Boscombe's aim to rival Bournemouth in this field ever come to anything, and the thatched building is now a gardener's hut. 'I am beginning to feel that I shall be an exile from all nice places for the rest of my days,' the artist wrote to Raffalovich, not long after arrival. 'Boscombe is only tolerable, I am so disappointed with it.'[37]

He worked when he could. He saw a friend or two. But time dragged, and the fear of blood darkened his boredom. Joined by Mabel and the Smitherses for the initial moving-in, he was soon alone with his mother and would virtually remain so till his death. The sea air did something for his breathing, but while he struggled on with the *Juvenal* drawings (Fig. 95), deriving some pleasure, too, from planning a selection of fifty of his subjects which Smithers was to make up into a book for the following year, the cough persisted.

Late in October, Ellen informed Ross: 'Aubrey has only just recovered from a long and severe illness . . . I watched him day and night for five weeks, and during the whole of that time I only went to bed three times.'[38] But the reappearance of the dreaded haemorrhage had already occurred in late August, and Aubrey gloomily predicted that he would not pull through the winter. It is with astonishment that we hear of his labours at this time as, sitting up in bed, his handkerchiefs stained with blood, he completed the *Frontispiece to Chopin's 3rd Ballade* and an *Atalanta in Calydon* (Fig. 96). If Smithers himself failed to appreciate the finer points of the latter drawing, we at any rate can marvel at such powerful work from the hand of a desperately ill man.

As day by day the sun went down behind the dull line of sea, his nervousness increased. It was in the face now, it seemed, of imminent death that he gave rein to his 'genius for work' (the phrase

51 Two Athenian Women in Distress, from *The Lysistrata of Aristophanes*, published 1896.

is his own): and the *Rheingold* designs were the result. However, a bad attack upset this routine in late September; and it must have been from that time when, as he told Smithers, he was 'laid out like a corpse', that Ellen's vigil had begun in earnest.

Eight

The Beardsleys' financial circumstances are difficult to fathom. And it is typical of the reserve adopted by Aubrey in matters of business that Ellen was never allowed to know from him just how his affairs stood.* Some time in November 1896, she appears to have become alarmed. How regularly the subsidy from Raffalovich was arriving, we do not know, and Smithers's cheques came hedged about with complicated instructions as to when, and not till when, to cash them. Aubrey, in one of his blackest moods, appeared to be nursing some special anxiety, which Ellen put down to shortage of funds. Much frightened, she wrote to Ross: and then, with the discovery that she had misjudged the situation, experienced deep remorse. Ross, always ready to offer help of a practical kind, must have responded at once with a sum to tide them over. Ellen replied:

> I am deeply touched by your kindness and because I cannot accept it, do not for one moment think I am ungrateful. I simply dare not tell Aubrey, my conscience pricks me that I should have mentioned a temporary difficulty that he was in; if he knew I had done so we should have to part, he would think me treacherous and never trust me again. I was unhappy about him because for many days he had been silent and depressed, but it turned out that he was having haemorrhage all that time and wouldn't tell me as he knew it would prevent my going up to town to see Mabel. I beg of you never to betray me as I am sure that it was through me indirectly that you heard the report. And I must also tell you that things are rather better and that I know for certain that Aubrey is not in immediate anxiety. He always speaks in affectionate terms of his publisher, and I think

*It is interesting, in this connexion, to note that at his death sixteen months later his estate was valued at a very little over one thousand pounds (£836. 17. 10 net).

with cause; of course to every one in business there come times
of strain in money matters. You will never I am sure let it be
known that I spoke of these things.[39]

Ellen was obviously afraid that some criticism of Smithers, on
whom (however unsatisfactorily) they were so dependent, would
get back to him. As I have pointed out, Aubrey had good reason
to be anxious about Smithers and the fate of the drawings which
had become his property. That Ellen endorsed his suspicions we
can guess from the character she gave Smithers after the publisher's
death, when her dislike no longer had to remain hidden. No
doubt she had let slip an occasional remark on the subject by
Aubrey, on one of her rare absences from Boscombe: as, for
instance, most recently, in order to help Mabel pack for her tour
with the Bourchiers' company in the United States.
    Aubrey had seemed better again, when this letter was written.
Ross came down to stay a few days with them (it was always kept
a secret that Ellen and he corresponded). But soon afterwards, on
10 December, he received bad news of his friend:

Aubrey had a sudden burst of haemorrhage this morning—we
were out and nearly at the top of the hill leading on to the cliff
(Fig. 52). You might have tracked our path down, the bleeding
was so profuse. I got him to the summer house at the bottom
of the hill where there is a fountain [just referred to], and
got him some water and a lady and gentleman who were
sitting near took charge of him till I got a chair and took him
home. He has had shivering fits, but now he is sleeping quietly
and I hope the haemorrhage has stopped. He has been painfully
dejected since you left and the very afternoon you went away,
he was suffering so much from toothache that he insisted on
going to the dentist, taking gas and having his tooth out. He was
much shaken after it, and I daresay this is the result. I do not
know what is to be done if the depression gets worse, and
indeed I am not sure how long I shall keep up myself.[40]

Aubrey was still in bed when Christmas came, and his spirits
were as low as ever. What, he wondered, did the doctors really
make of him? For his part, he felt certain that it would kill him to

52 Contemporary photograph of the scene of Aubrey's alarming
haemorrhage of 10 December 1896. On the extreme left is Pier View.
'We were out and nearly at the top of the hill leading on to the cliff,'
Ellen told Ross. 'You might have tracked our path down, the bleeding
was so profuse.' She managed to get her son to the small thatched building (near centre) where there was a fountain. Then she took him back in
an invalid-chair to Pier View.

stay on at Boscombe. So, summoning up strength scarcely credible
in one recently at death's door, he had himself transported in a
closed, heated carriage, his mother at his side, the couple of miles
into Bournemouth.

Nine

This was towards the close of January 1897. Their destination, the
house called Muriel, in Exeter Road, is evidence of how strongly
he must have grown to dislike Pier View. Exeter Road curves
down to another pier: no more beautiful than Boscombe's—and
four hundred feet longer. Yet in his eyes the mean little boarding-
house squeezed in between Exeter and Terrace Roads was infinitely preferable (Fig. 53). He delighted especially in the busier
neighbourhood, and dreamed of attending symphony concerts in
the Winter Gardens Pavilion nearby.[41]

He learned from his new doctor, moreover, that Pier View had
been quite the wrong place for him, and that the move just

53 Muriel, Exeter Road, Bournemouth, where Aubrey and Ellen stayed from late January till early April 1897. The engraver's misspelling of the name would have added insult to injury for Aubrey, since the address as it stood embarrassed him.

undertaken would probably save his life. Why, then, had Dr Symes-Thompson and Aubrey's other advisers recommended what Dr Harsant now regarded as an almost fatal move? It has to be remembered, once more, that in the treatment of tuberculosis the profession could offer at this time neither an effective cure nor even an effective palliative. If the symptoms could not be held in abeyance by any single drug (oxide of zinc, bismuth, spermaceti, acetate of lead), the physician hoped to discover an antidote by experimenting with a combination of them. In the same way, hoping for the best, he would try out the climate of Kreuznach and Soden, Bagnères-de-Bigorre or Luchon, or, nearer home, Buxton, Tunbridge Wells—and Bournemouth. But, as we shall see, Bournemouth, 'embosomed in its pine-woods' (so Baedeker described it) proved no more alleviatory in Aubrey's case than damp, despised Boscombe (Fig. 54).

For, sure enough, in March 1897 came another haemorrhage. Muriel's dark corridors stirred a little too sympathetically to the bitter wind blowing across the bay. As well as ill, Aubrey was often

54   Ellen Beardsley said of a pair of photographs,
of which this was one: 'Both are good, I hardly know
which is best.' They were taken in the sitting-room
of the Bournemouth boarding-house, early in 1897.

chilled to the marrow, his hands blue. Once more he retired to bed,
where even sitting up was forbidden: 'What an ignoble existence!'
he groaned to Smithers.[42]

His desire now was all for London: it helped him, in his banish-
ment, to debate with Raffalovich where exactly in that sacred
territory he might finally live and have his being. But Dr Harsant
was against such ideas. He spoke of the necessity of a long, long
rest under a sun less fitful than Bloomsbury's. The north coast of
France he specially recommended. Under the Bournemouth
doctor's direction, Aubrey was now trying Gallic Acid and Ergotine, but, unchecked by these styptics, the haemorrhage continued.
Out of the sickness and loneliness, every now and then, a drawing
would emerge, as, for instance, one March day, a delicate portrait
of Théophile Gautier's heroine: that is to say, the frontispiece for
Smithers's ill-fated *Mademoiselle de Maupin* (Fig. 55).

When the weather improved, the invalid could shake off his
fears for a moment. On 12 March, Dr Harsant made a thorough
examination of his chest, concluding that, whatever the situation

in the left lung, the right had not further deteriorated. Yet no sooner did Aubrey begin to feel reassured than the blood made its appearance again, this time, as Smithers would be informed, 'via the bum'.[43] Dr Harsant's suggestion that it came from the liver would surprise a physician today: blood recognizable as such by the patient must have flowed from the lower bowel. If tuberculous infection of the liver seems unlikely anyway (though there may have been congestion and enlargement through early heart failure), and the symptom's disappearance rules out tuberculous ulceration of the bowel, we are left with one possible, and very simple, explanation: that in addition to his other troubles, Aubrey had begun to suffer from haemorrhoids.

Slowly he recovered from what had been one of his worst

55 Frontispiece   (Mademoiselle   de Maupin) from *Six Drawings illustrating Théophile Gautier's Romance Mademoiselle de Maupin*, published 1898.

frights. By early April (almost entirely through the prospect of financial aid from Raffalovich), escape from Bournemouth was becoming a certainty. Aubrey and Ellen were to travel to Paris, in the first place, stopping a night in London on the way.

At the last moment the journey had to be postponed because of another haemorrhage; but, when finally embarked upon under the supervision of Dr Phillips (Raffalovich's own physician), its inevitable exertions passed off with hardly an ill effect. The glimpse of London (it was to be his last) did Aubrey a great deal of good, raising his spirits wonderfully; and the exquisite pleasure of being in Paris again, after a year of misery, gave him back for the moment an energy he had not enjoyed since the Brussels breakdown.

Ten

Ellen wrote as follows to Ross, on 22 April 1897:

> Paris is doing wonders for Aubrey, I can't believe my eyes seeing him prancing about as if he had never been ill. How long it will last I don't know—of course he took cold 3 days ago and has had to be in bed one day and indoors the other two, but there has been no sign of haemorrhage and he moves about like his old self—in short he is a miracle. I daresay you know this old hotel [Hôtel Voltaire, Quai Voltaire], but if you don't, it is exactly opposite the Louvre and overlooking the river, which is lively for him, and when the weather gets hotter and if we are still here, we shall find the advantage of this open situation. There is of course no lift—so he has to be carried upstairs for fear of haemorrhage, and this is rather a nuisance, or will be, when he wants to go in and out—at present he manages to keep downstairs and only be carried up at night.[44]

Wonderful it was, but with each 'catching cold', the process of softening, or tuberculous cavitation, recommenced, and the case assumed a more unfavourable aspect. There came a return of haemorrhage in May, and with it some of the old fear and depression. When Smithers visited Paris, Aubrey was wise, or ill, enough to decline an invitation to spend the evening with him. Paris— what a wretched confession to be driven to!—had begun to fatigue him.

Accordingly, before May was out, mother and son removed to St-Germain, on the western outskirts of the capital. Here Aubrey saw a well-respected consultant, Dr Lamarre. Fresh hopes were raised, the doctor assuring him that he had only to take care of himself to expect complete recovery! Mountains were what he needed. He must keep clear of the Riviera—for him, the south of France would be more dangerous than Bournemouth. Meanwhile forest air could not be bettered. And Aubrey had orders to rise every day at 4 a.m. and walk for two hours in the charming Forest of St-Germain, which was just on his doorstep.

He complied once or twice; but, since it was between the hours of four and six in the morning that he got his best sleep, soon weakened and the practice lapsed. June was not without its crisis. In July, a Dr Prendergast, to whom he had been briefly introduced, made a thorough investigation of the lungs. Dr Prendergast, too, advised bracing air—but mountains, never. Egypt was discussed as a winter resort, and rejected. If the Beardsleys were to remain in France, Trouville would be just the place. Dr Prendergast left Aubrey with the assurance that he had a right lung in 'very fair working order', but a left that had 'consolidated generally'. His low spirits and feebleness must be attributed in large measure to the deterioration of the liver.

In the end, Dieppe was substituted for Trouville. With the welcome change of scene (Aubrey had soon found himself growing dull in St-Germain),[45] came the deceptive improvement his mother was getting to know so well. It lasted into September, when Raffalovich's Dr Phillips saw him again and expressed his astonished delight at how splendidly things were going. Aubrey might now look forward in confidence to a 'new life'.

The immediate problem was where to spend the winter. Following Dr Phillips's advice, the Beardsleys took the initial step of leaving Dieppe for Paris, where Aubrey consulted a Dr Dupuy. The trouble on this occasion, as reported in his letters, was neuralgia (though that might be a 'cover'-word to certain correspondents). Dr Dupuy, on auscultation, declared the lung condition very serious, but still quite curable. Buoyed up by these recent opinions, Aubrey could comment exultantly: 'I may not only have several years of life before me, but perhaps even a long life.' All the same, a cold caught on arrival at the Hôtel Foyot had pulled him down considerably and in October Dupuy, like his predecessors, introduced counter-irritants. One form they took on this occasion was what the patient refers to as 'turpentine-baths', a term strange in modern medicine, but one that can only mean baths with turpentine added to augment the effect of the hot water.[46]

The year closed in: it was November now. It would be out of the question for Aubrey to spend the winter in Paris. Disregarding Dr Lamarre's objection to the south of France, Dr Dupuy and the Beardsleys between them decided upon Menton. After a journey which just avoided total disaster, they arrived in the lemon-groves of the Côte d'Azur in December 1897. Whether advised by Dr Phillips or by Dr Dupuy, they seem to have acted unwisely in booking rooms at the Hôtel Cosmopolitan, exposed to the mistral as it was.

In Menton, a Dr Campbell attended Aubrey, as the old year went out in a 'pitiless drench of rain'. The artist worked on his Initials for *Volpone* (Fig. 56), if with increasing difficulty, with

56 Initial V (Elephant), from *Ben Jonson his Volpone: or The Foxe*, published 1898.

much of his old enthusiasm, an enthusiasm rekindled as late as mid-February 1898 when Smithers sent him pulls of the blocks. From 26 January he never again left his room and the massed Mantegna prints on the wall. Through the window, the long line of the Mediterranean and the dreary suburbs of the Western Bay constituted his last glimpse of the world.

'He used to be better some days and able to move about his room a little, and read a little, and then the haemorrhage would recur,' wrote Ellen, when all this was still painfully fresh in her mind. 'But it was more slight oozing from one lung and then the other than any one bad attack till ten days before his death when there was a very dreadful attack, the disease had touched an artery and it was tragic.'[47] This proved the terminal point of his long illness: and his mother, forced to recognize it as such, sent a telegram to Mabel summoning her to the bedside. Under the influence of morphia, and thus spared the fit of suffocation which would have been the alternative, Aubrey died (according to whether we reject or accept his sister's account) just before or just after midnight preceding 16 March 1898.

Eleven

It must always remain a cause of astonishment that the artist thus beset with physical problems went on producing drawings of the highest quality, both in conception and execution. In particular, the exacting and triumphant 'Volpone adoring his Treasure' shows what strength of will an all-absorbing concern for his art can stimulate in a dying man. Some of the last letters of all have as their sole preoccupation the methods by which the quality of these drawings was to escape spoiling in the photo-mechanical process; and one of Aubrey's bitterest regrets had been that he must leave so many delicate matters to technicians he could never personally supervise. So what we marvel at is not just the wit and the grandeur of his most successful works, it is the battle against odds that each entailed. And, though painful, it seems to me necessary, to understand the nature of these odds.

For a distressing footnote has to be added to the medical history of Aubrey Beardsley. Anxious as Symes-Thompson and all the other doctors were to help him, devotedly as his mother watched over and nursed him, brave as he was himself and strong as a determination to win the approval of posterity (there was not much else in view) could make him, he had never had it in his power at any time to arrest the fateful advance of his disease. The infection from which he suffered was of the typical, progressive, cavitating kind. He ought to have taken greater care of himself. But it was the inexorable (yet still arbitrary) multiplication of the cavities in the lung-tissue that hastened or protracted the crisis. And had Aubrey burned the candle at neither end, and lived like a vegetable, over those vital five or six years, there is no telling but that he might still have died at the same hour, on the same day, not yet twenty-six years old.

Twelve

Ellen Beardsley dwells in the memories of some still living as 'sad' and 'gentle',[48] for age altered almost out of recognition Ross's lively correspondent and Aubrey's characterful mother. And just as Ellen's later references to her son contribute, naturally enough, towards an ideal portrait, that of a 'dear, beautiful soul, of whom the world was not worthy',[49] so in retrospect the relationship between them acquired new mysteries ('Aubrey and I never quite grew up') and an indestructible solidarity ('Aubrey and I were one') far from apparent during the artist's own lifetime.[50]

On the contrary, what we have found is anything but a Fauntleroy–Dearest courtship. The father's ignoble role did not drive the son into his mother's arms. There is more of stress and strain than mutual trust and affection in the situation thus revealed. The boy seems to have grown up, when health permitted, obdurate; Ellen, by no means blind to his faults, was concerned to retain the mastery. A conflict became inevitable. Frustrated in his petty clerkship, Aubrey must have been difficult enough to manage: having gained his freedom, he expected to have his own way entirely. It was then that Ellen invoked the help of Ross: 'You know, if he were only small enough to whip, I shouldn't trouble you!'[51] No doubt, with the aid of this ally, she scored quite a few diplomatic victories. But there was something else before which she experienced total defeat: that mood of bitter hopelessness which at times overwhelmed her son, those 'blue devils' which he seemed to have inherited in full measure from Vigny's Stello.

She was defeated by his 'dreadful depression', because, while these bouts continued, she could not reach him in any way. It became impossible to know what dangers threatened, what anxieties tormented him. Even at the best of times, Ellen's account of their life together is that of hopes and conjectures, for she was harshly excluded from all decision-making. No doubt in the particular boarding-house at which they happened to be staying they were regarded, when he was well enough to appear, as a devoted couple. And the mild raillery of such terms as 'my revered Mother', or 'my Ma', suggests the same. But the truth, obscured by Aubrey's growing physical reliance on her, was something different.

Mesmerized as we are by the spectacle of the dying artist, we can easily overlook the anguish this sense of separation, felt even at his bedside, meant to Ellen. Only on a second reading do the tell-tale admissions make their point. She must have been very deeply wounded, for instance, when, sick with anxiety, she heard nothing from Brussels at the time of his severest attack: 'I am not worthy to receive news direct.' That her 'darling boy' could irritate his mother as well, is evident from a letter in which she begged Ross to induce him to remain in Crowborough and not come flying back to Town: 'As to his scorning the conversation of various good ladies I haven't patience with such affectation, you don't expect "a feast of reason and a flow of soul" in a boarding-house. . . .' And she continued: 'Enlarge upon the beauties of the place and its many advantages, he thinks a great deal of your opinion, *and naturally doesn't think much of mine.*'[52] This and similar expressions of how little she counts in her son's eyes echo like a refrain through the correspondence with Ross.

Sadder still, in a different way, is her role of onlooker, as described on their arrival at Muriel in a letter of 1 February 1897: 'The change has roused him from his depression, and one by one I see little things being put out, pens, pencils, etc., and I shouldn't be surprised any day to see him start drawing.'[53] No word of his intentions has been given to *her*—nor acknowledgment, presumably, of the dreadful strain to which she had so recently been put (the professional nurse, to whom he took an immediate dislike, having been petulantly dismissed).

That he ever at any time discussed his precious work with her is quite improbable. She merely watched the pen in motion. If her opinion on the virtues of Crowborough was not valued, it can hardly be supposed that he would condescend to discuss more important matters. And—when one has sympathized with Ellen—his case was not much jollier. To be tied forever to this slighted lady of the lamp, denied the company of his friends and a proper share of youthful laughter, to have his nerves perpetually set on edge by one kind of entreaty or another; to endure the unspoken disgust he knew she felt for certain of his drawings; not to be free, not to be able to sit in a café with the gay world busy around him. Instead—the silence, the dismal crying of the gulls, the senseless chatter of the fire that still did not keep him warm enough. A mildly indecent joke at his mother's expense does not seem such a crime, when we begin to appreciate what pent-up misery exploded with it; though Ellen would scarcely have thanked her son for sharing his amusement with Smithers.[54]

Then, contrasting with the delight he himself felt on his return to Paris in April 1897, he had to be kept aware of his mother's disapproval: 'I don't like Paris,' she confessed to Ross, 'and feel like a fish out of water here, I'm afraid I'm dreadfully British!'[55] Aubrey exactly echoes her statement—or was not hers an echo of his? 'Mother cannot abide Paris,' he told Mabel, 'and is utterly British over everything.'[56] She must have made a poor companion at such a moment for her son, to whom the mere smell of Paris was 'such a blessed treat'.

Dependence and incompatability: nurse and patient were bound together by hoops of steel, yet saw eye to eye on nothing. The torment of this life together—as Aubrey saw the precious sights and sounds of Paris and Dieppe flow by him, never perhaps to be enjoyed again—may have subsided a little under the influence of the books of devotion sent by Raffalovich, or brought to him by priests of the neighbourhood entrusted with this errand by his good Brother. Though Ellen had not yet entered the Roman Catholic Church (her son's conversion, of course, had already taken place), there were moments when, at Raffalovich's prompting, they both sought spiritual consolation at the same time: she in the

Maxims of St Thomas Aquinas and Aubrey in Faber's *Heavenly Promises*, though the traditional artist's companion, Ribadaneyra's *Flos Sanctorum* was probably more to the latter's taste, and he had a special affection for the autobiography of St Teresa. In October 1897, when concerned with the disposal of his library, he instructed Smithers to keep, of the profane works, only Wagner: otherwise, he was content to exist on the two volumes of the *Flos Sanctorum*, the three-volume St Teresa and John Gray's *Spiritual Poems*.

More often, as he confessed to Raffalovich, Aubrey found consolation difficult and his heart stony. As the last two months dragged by, his agony must have been terrible on finding himself finally and hopelessly unequal to the effort of resuming work. The bitterest moment of all, perhaps, is that to be found in a document apparently dictated by Ellen, a copy of which has been very kindly supplied me by Mr Reade:

> Some two or three weeks before he died, I was just going out when he asked me to put his drawing board, pen and other materials beside his bed. I think he wanted, when he was by himself, to see if he could draw, but he had not the strength. When I came in I found him lying with his face to the wall and he would not speak. After he was dead I found the pen [called the 'gold' pen] sticking into the floor. I think he must have thrown it away, finding he could not draw.[57]

Then the origins and real authorship of the last letter, discussed earlier, demanding destruction of '*all* obscene drawings', must still remain a matter of speculation. Are we to see in it a reversal of the long-established relationship between mother and son? For years Aubrey had retained the upper hand. Now, helpless at last, the final knell sounded, he was obliged to accept defeat. Ellen's horror of the *Lysistrata* and similar drawings, her deep resentment at the part played by Smithers, found an outlet. She it was, surely, on whose advice that last letter was written—if she did not (as I think more probable) actually draft or dictate it herself. At all events, Ellen addressed the envelope and saw the document posted.[58] One can say, therefore, that in the battle of wills, the victory, melancholy as it was, passed to the mother in the end.

A Flutter of Frilled Things

One

Though the way to the centre of the artist's being, the real Aubrey, must begin somewhere in the work itself, we have not even embarked yet upon that mysterious path. We have talked of satire (scarcely understanding, nevertheless, at what or whom the artist mocked); and of an emphasis upon sexual appetites and appetizers (yet finding in the drawings no ecstatic, Wildean celebration of the fleshly). When we studied him among his friends, we were left uncertain how he regarded, or was regarded by, those whose own love-objects are well enough attested. Nor, on any posthumous acquaintance we can strike up with her, does Ellen Beardsley seem to qualify as one of psychiatry's 'close-binding intimate' mothers, with all the consequences that may follow from a Fauntleroy in hair-curlers. The pretendedly all-revealing letters to Smithers are little more communicative than much of the church-chatter reserved for Raffalovich. Never as banal a correspondent as Dowson, Aubrey of the epistles is still a world away from the inspired decorator of *Salome* and the visionary of the fragments for *Mademoiselle de Maupin*. There is a whole area unknown to us, obviously, which we must now explore.

The way to it, as I have said, will be through the work. At least we shall find the beginning of the path there. There have been many studies of Aubrey's drawings as works of art, and I myself have already made use of these drawings in tracing the artist's relations with his friends and patrons and with Ellen. But their most curious feature, their choice of subject, no one (to my knowledge) has seriously set out to explain. That this choice lay with the artist in almost every undertaking and was not dictated by the nature of the theme to be illustrated must be obvious enough by now; but a typical example is provided by the pen-and-wash drawing, 'The Lady with Monkey' (Fig. 57), originally intended by Aubrey for *Mademoiselle de Maupin*—and then later, in December 1897, requested back from Smithers to serve as one

116

57   The Lady with the Monkey, from *Six Drawings illustrating . . . Mademoiselle de Maupin*, published 1898.

of the initials for *Volpone*. Why the Lady and why the Monkey? This, translated into more general terms, is the question we now ask.

Two

A simple analysis of five hundred of Aubrey's drawings will show that a clear fifth of that number (it could be more, but certainly not less) present female attire or toilette as their actual—whatever their ostensible—subject. Stated baldly, this will take nobody's breath away. Pick out at random three artists, say, practising with great success in the late 1880s, when Aubrey was growing up, and you might find the proportion higher. Alma-Tadema, Albert Moore, Marcus Stone, for instance, applied themselves to paint woman sensually revealed in the peplum or coquettishly smothered in the spencer and pelisse. Indeed, the interest in historic costume has probably never been as intense as it was during the 1880s and 1890s, when solemn committees (with some prodding from the more enterprising mercers) assembled to debate how the medieval belt and the Roman mantle could be combined into one harmonious whole.[1] Adelaide Duchess of Teck and Messrs Boughton and James Sant, both full members of the Royal Academy, would not have studied *La Vie Parisienne*: yet there, too, in the skilled hands of visual journalists like Gerbault and 'Sahib', the clothed and half-clothed siren sang to Ulysses from the Normandy beaches, distinguishable from her Burlington House sisters only by a degree of provocativeness.

But Aubrey on women's clothes is quite a different commentator, never academic, never frivolous. He did not, like Devéria and Gavarni, graduate from the fashion-plate; nor, coming nearer to period, hold both his sides at the vagaries of the wimple and liripipe, in the manner of George Du Maurier. The only instances of straightforward reporting occur early and are rare even then: such may be reckoned the little girl in a party-frock and the Spanish dancer, arms akimbo, two of the sketches from the *Bon-Mots* series, published in 1893 and 1894 (Fig. 58). Aubrey

58   Two vignettes from *Bon-Mots* (Lamb and Jerrold; Foote and Hook), showing conventionally treated costume.

59 a, b A reminder that some of the extravagances of Aubrey's costume-designing reflect the exuberance of the period: two gowns from Worth's 'Robes de Bal, 1895–1901', a manuscript and photographic record of this fashion house's creations. a. Evening dress in white satin with tulle and *boules de neige*. b. Velvet evening dress with flowers reminiscent of the *Morte* designs.

did not get into his stride as *couturier fantastique* till the *Salome* drawings gave him that unique opportunity of self-realization—and self-revelation. For the sartorial element, with the beautiful, the sensual and the cruel, seems (most oddly) to reach back into the artist's very *penetralia mentis*. These drawings, dating from the same year as the later *Bon-Mots* devilries and so infinitely superior to them, nevertheless regurgitate somewhat the borrowings we have discussed earlier: in dress, the Burne-Jones studio-weeds, the peacockian decoration from Whistler and, of course, the Japanese kimono. What surprises is the contemporaneity achieved. The splendid creature in 'The Black Cape' (while hardly Herodian) suggests Lady Chiltern or Mrs Arbuthnot quite as readily as the reigning geisha from Mogami's tea-house.

Aubrey's white-on-black decoration does not drop from the clouds. Nor are his *frappé* and frosted flowers unique inventions of his own. It is well worth while consulting that bible of fashion in many books, the manuscript records of the House of Worth (whose founder became in time couturier to nine queens).[2] Among them will be found a black satin gown sprinkled with constellations of white embroidery, the seamstresses employed on which might have been working under Aubrey's express instructions. Again, the delicate tidal froth of the corsage in 'The Toilet of Salome' (Fig. 20) has its origin in many an actual swathing of tulle-misted satin, set round with bows and buckled velvet streamers. To whatever lengths the artist may then proceed, the first inspiration comes from what he saw around him.

There was a period between 1893 and 1896 when the costume of his own day seemed to exercise the strongest spell over him. The gigot sleeve and the bustle enchanted him. He produced close approximations to the millinery of the moment. If he had pictured them at Ascot rather than on the links, the ladies in his Golf Club Invitation Card would scarcely have seemed strange at all. He brilliantly evoked the feminine world of dress-shops and boudoir, from the minor decorations for *The Idler* of 1894, only one of which was actually used, to that grandest of climaxes, the cover for No. 2 of *The Savoy*, entitled 'Choosing the New Hat'. Even the flower-loaded gown worn by the figure in the illustration to *A London Garland*, published in 1895, derives from *robes de bal* currently embellished with every species of tag and shoulder-knot, a dress as thick with tulle roses as a June pergola with real ones.

In another connexion, as we have already noted, from the era of *The Rape of the Lock* onwards (it was published in May 1896), Aubrey became more and more attached to the Rococo and Baroque (in that order). 'Choosing the New Hat' is at least ninety-nine per cent a mélange of his favourite French engravers, and thus leaves Victorian London far behind. A few references to contemporary dress survive in these earlier issues of *The Savoy*, but if one takes the drawing, 'The Bathers', from No. 1 (an illustration to Symons's 1895 article on Dieppe, for which it is easy to believe that the artist's eyes never wandered to the beach), the eighteenth century is still the foremost influence at work. The majority of *The Rape of the Lock* designs are straightforward period-pieces and, whatever their anachronisms, these do not include (as, for Aubrey, they very well might have done in earlier days) Turkey chintz dressing-gowns or hats with Impeyan wings. *Lysistrata*, his aggressive romp with nudity, provides a lavish display of stockings, but they are not of the kind his mother and sister could have bought in Victoria Street (Fig. 51). All the same, one leaves the *Lysistrata* much impressed by Aubrey the haberdasher, the connoisseur of every kind of ribbon, lute, galloon and Coventry frilling.

Three

More and more aware of the singular charm women's clothes must have held for him, we go on to remark the comparatively high incidence of a related subject, the activities of the dressing-table, not quantitatively to be compared with the first, yet equally striking since it turns up so often among the very finest works.

Traditional art, of course, abounds in *toilettes*. The first thing one recalls is the purring Venetian courtesan, mirror in hand, by Giorgione, Palma and Titian. Then follow Pre-Raphaelite memories of more introspective poses wearily maintained by Mrs Morris and Miss Siddal with a hairbrush or string of beads as simple accessory. This was not how Aubrey saw the grooming of

his Marianas. For them—not without wit and fancy—he provided
the full paraphernalia. In his 'Toilet of Salome' (both versions)
(Figs. 20, 22) are exquisitely rendered jars, phials, powder-box and
puff, scissors and a glass ring-stand made in the form of a miniature
tree, such as some readers may remember on their mothers'
dressing-tables. The life of the Beardsley Woman is less protected,
her literary tastes range wider, than in Venice or Gower Street:
the last shelf of Salome's table supports volumes by Zola,
Prévost, Verlaine, Apuleius and the Marquis de Sade. The
presence of these 'sinister' spirits below gives a new significance
to the articles of beautification, by the time the eye is ready to
travel up to them again.

    The dressing-table reappears in that very beautiful drawing,
'La Dame aux Camélias' (formerly, 'Girl at her Toilet') (Fig.

60 La Dame aux Camélias (originally,
Girl at her Toilet), published in *St Paul's*
and in Volume III of *The Yellow Book*,
1894.

60). Though draperies hide all but the table-surface and the array of jars and boxes is thus limited, a sufficient opulence remains, suggested by the pair of attenuated candles in their elaborate sticks lighting the mirror. The longer I consider this drawing and the rapt mystique it hymns, the more sure I am that Aubrey had the novel, not the play, of Dumas *fils* in mind.* With Symons, he paid a visit to the writer in the summer of 1895 over a year after the publication of this drawing. Receiving a copy of the novel as a gift from Dumas, he made a charming little pencil and water-colour sketch of the lady on its flyleaf. Aubrey would have been deeply moved by Jules Janin's masterly essay, which is bound up with the true story of the beautiful victim of consumption.[3] Janin, at pains to identify Marguerite Gautier with her real-life prototype, Marie Duplessis, supplies a graphic account of the courtesan's death and the opening to the public of her luxurious apartment at Spa, where the stool beside the bed still bore the impress of the knees of the priest who had closed her eyes. This essay goes on to describe how the most respectable ladies of fashion competed with each other to buy the Gautier personal property at auction: her gloves, her boots, her combs, her brushes—even her hair![4] It was with something like the same thrilled reverence that Aubrey assembled these intimate still-lifes of his.

In its most concentrated form, the dressing-table subject is used again for Volume III of *The Yellow Book*'s front-cover (our title page). Here the candles are ironically replaced by miniature street-lamps with gas-burners. The dressing-table in 'The Toilet' from *The Rape of the Lock* is as finely accoutred as any in Aubrey's *oeuvre*, with a greater attention than elsewhere to the texture of glass and enamel (Fig. 43). The title-page design for the first number of *The Savoy* is centred upon a most elaborate and fanciful table, whose surface holds only a fan and a mask (Fig. 61). Infinite in its complications—by contrast—is the *Toilette* scene from *The Savoy*'s selection of the illustrations to what is there called 'Under the Hill', Aubrey's little romance to which we shall soon proceed. One guesses that the clock beside

*Alexandre Dumas *fils* (1824–95) published the novel *La Dame aux camélias* in 1848; the stage version appeared in 1852.

61   Title page, *The Savoy*, No. 1, January 1896, and repeated in No. 2, April 1896.

the labyrinthic candelabra is Marie Duplessis's, that *chef-d'oeuvre* of horology (a pun the artist would not have despised) 'qui avait sonné l'heure' for Mme de Pompadour and Mme du Barry as well. And dressing-tables still play their part in three of his penultimate productions, the wash-drawings, 'Lady at the Dressing-Table', 'Lady with the Rose' and 'Arbuscula' (Figs. 62,

62 The Lady with the Rose, from *Six Drawings illustrating . . . Mademoiselle de Maupin*, published 1898.

63 Arbuscula, from *A History of Dancing from the Earliest Ages to our own Times*, 1898.

63). It was a conception, therefore, that never lost its attraction for him.

In a sense these assemblages upon the mahogany below the mirror, or upon the figured muslins or Victoria lawns which interposed themselves between a woman's hand and the polished surface of the wood, are the counterpart of glittering inventories one comes across in Huysmans, in Pater, in Wilde. Visually, they could be matched perhaps by the boudoir scenes of Boucher, Lancret and J.-M. Moreau *le jeune*. But we are left with the conviction that here was something personal to Aubrey, for which precedents in literature and art were not required. Building with the aid of his sharp observation, his haunting of shops and of museums, he could extemporize indefinitely on the subject of cut-glass, filigrane, glass encrusted with gypsic, *vitra da trina*, and that entrancing manipulation of the substance by which tiny blue and pink rods, themselves of glass, are imprisoned within it. On the other hand, what significance would the form alone possess, if one forgot the purpose of these stoppered flasks? Each no doubt represented its particular perfume, its Bouquet Mogador, its Jasmin d'Espagne, Opoponax, Ylang-Ylang. This little box contains Circassian Rose Opiate—for the teeth. Another, powder, scented Wood Violet or Maréchal. I fear to bore the reader with recitals of more of these articles—diamond- or cane-cut; silver-mounted vessels containing hair-washes, pomades; restorers of all kinds; smelling-bottles; pin-trays in ruby, opaline, amberina; fan-cases, silk-covered, silk-lined. They would not have bored Aubrey!

Four

Less immediately obvious than the preoccupation with women's clothes and the ceremony of their *toilette*, but with an incidence as high or higher, is the artist's ambiguous delineation of sex. One may note that the theme of the hermaphrodite is hardest worked in the early *Morte Darthur*, before Aubrey could have been fully exposed to the moral and cultural ideas of the *Cénacle* (Fig. 15). The point is of interest since the existence of a 'third sex', neither man nor woman, provides the starting-point of Aristophanes' argument in the most memorable speech in the *Symposium*.[5] If Platonic sanctioning of their deviation flattered the *Cénacle*, here it was at its grandest: for the conclusion Aristophanes reaches (by however roundabout a route) makes plain that, as far as perfect love can ever come our way, it will be homosexual.

    I do not believe we need credit Aubrey with such an association of ideas. Nor need we assume that the re-populating of Arthurian England with creatures dually mammiferous and testicled was a mischief wrought in tedium, a way of revenging himself on Dent and the bourgeois reader for the intolerable *longueurs* of the task in hand. For one thing, no one was shocked. By the year 1892, Malory had been so flattened out by Burne-Jones and the soft-furnishing trade, that the sex of the knights and ladies of the Table Round was no longer substantial matter for discussion. No, Aubrey must have proclaimed from the housetops his interest in the hermaphrodite, together with a long series of narcissistic beings almost equally ambiguous, because the unnaturalness of creating them was second nature to him.

In doing so, he often irritated his employers: Smithers, for instance; and inconvenienced his friends—even Raffalovich. In 1895 his dear André's *The Thread and the Path* was published by David Nutt without Aubrey's frontispiece (Fig. 64): 'Whatever you may say,' Nutt had written to the author, concerning the design called 'The Mirror of Love' (now in the Victoria and Albert Museum), 'the figure is hermaphrodite'; and he would have nothing to do with it. Of course, with some clients the situation was reversed, and the watercolour-drawing actually entitled 'Hermaphrodite' may well have been specially commissioned by Julian Sampson, who lost it in the fire referred to that destroyed

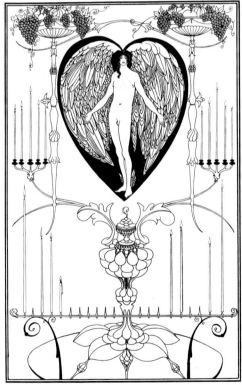

64   The Mirror of Love, intended as frontispiece for Raffalovich's *The Thread and the Path*, of 1895, but rejected by the publisher. First appeared in Symons's *Aubrey Beardsley*, 1898.

the eighth original illustration to the *Lysistrata*.

One can say, therefore, that the genderlessness of Aubrey's character-drawing, which runs right through his work, must have a deeper significance than practical joking. Having considered the physical torments he had to endure in order to complete these designs, aware as we must be of his faith in the importance of his work and anxiety that it should see the light of day in the only way it could, are we really to suppose that he sexually confused or emasculated his figures for the purpose of cocking a snook at a faceless public and catching out the publisher on whom he was wholly dependent? And I am not, of course, talking about the more obvious sexual innuendos of his drawings which secured for them, it hardly needs saying, their *succès de scandale* and constituted their hard-selling feature. It is what underlies the obvious that counts.

One may be further struck by the persistence of the gender confusion in Aubrey's work. It reappears, indeed, very near the end of his life with the greatest flourish of all. I refer to the illustrations for *Mademoiselle de Maupin* (Fig. 65). The project was first mentioned in a letter to Smithers of 11 February 1897, and the drawings continued jerkily under stress of ill-health almost to the end of the year. In late March he was reassuring Smithers: 'I have made up my mind to illustrate *Mddle de Maupin*, come what may.'[6] In August, this became: '*Mddle de Maupin* occupies my spirit enormously.'[7] However, the first doubts made their appearance in late September, when Pollitt was informed about another project, 'The Daughters of Rhenus', which would be embarked upon 'when the Maupin is over'.[8] One remembers, too, Smithers's fear, expressed to Wilde, that Aubrey had tired of *Mademoiselle de Maupin* (as early as 2 September 1897); the same fear, perhaps in the form of a reproach, must now have been addressed by Smithers to the artist himself, for a suspiciously reassuring letter was sent to the publisher from the Hôtel Foyot: 'I am at work this very morning as ever is at the Maupin; and love the book as heretofore.'[9]

In truth, Aubrey had become restless and nervous. The magnitude of the *Maupin* commission alarmed him, in the first place. He wrote suggesting a reduction in the number of full-plates,

65   The Lady at the Dressing-Table, from *Six Drawings illustrating . . .*
Mademoiselle de Maupin, published 1898.

agreed as four to each of the eight parts in which the book was
first to appear. His ambition kept hysterically on the move by the
approach of death, he returned to an earlier enthusiasm and
explored fresh Wagnerian themes. Then, to cover his retreat, he
raised with Smithers a fundamental anxiety in connexion with
Gautier's novel: could any illustrations worthy of such a work be
either adequate *or pass the censor?*[10] That Aubrey should be quib-
bling about 'indecency' must have warned Smithers of the coming
about-face, which occurred in a letter written early in November.

To be fair to the artist—as another letter to his sister, in the same month, makes plain—he was genuinely worried about Smithers's ability to underwrite such an ambitious venture as the *Mademoiselle de Maupin*, particularly on account of the heavy cost of so many half-tone—indeed, photogravure—reproductions. What would be the fate of all these little masterpieces proposed, when the publisher's affairs were causing him, it was generally understood, serious embarrassment?

That they were little masterpieces, all six of them actually completed, their creator had no doubt. Up till three months before his death, he was passing proofs of them, torn between anxiety and delight. On 17 December 1897 a last word is spoken on the subject, when he begged back, as already noted, 'The Lady with the Monkey'.

Five

We can judge, then, of the impetus given by *Mademoiselle de Maupin* to the image-maker in Aubrey. He could well have been introduced to the book by Wilde, as we have seen, an earlier admirer of Gautier. The connexion, indeed, between the Greek view of art (as Wilde understood it) and that of the irresistible Théo is closer than one might suppose. 'Greek art is of the sun and deals directly with things,' Wilde wrote from HM Prison, Reading, in 1897; and, for him, 'merely to look at the world will be always lovely.'[11] Théophile Gautier, whom Wilde had imagined regaling himself with a copy of *Dorian Gray* in the Elysian Fields, expressed in the mid-1830s an exactly similar sentiment: 'If I am worth anything at all . . . it is as a man for whom the visible world exists.

Yet Aubrey, I believe, as in another instance just remarked upon, was not attracted to Gautier for the kind of reasons that appealed to a dilettantish classical scholar and disciple of Pater. A chance word from Wilde may have directed him to *Mademoiselle de Maupin* in the first place, but thereafter the pickings would have been all his own. With its dandyism, its capricious improvisation and its amorality, it might have been written for Aubrey. So much else, too, Gautier and he had in common: their habit, for instance, of inventing modern variations on a seventeenth-

or eighteenth-century theme—for the real Mlle de Maupin, though in the book she might be one of Gautier's own generation, died about the year 1707. It would be like Aubrey to have discovered the facts (such as are available) about this actress and duellist who pursued men and women with equally insatiable appetite, and to have enjoyed the more Gautier's re-creation of the ogress as a kind of Rosalind, daughter of the banished Duke in *As You Like It*, a mirror of grace and delicacy, with whom, in her cavalier-impersonation, both Rosette and d'Albert fall in love.

Since the author steers his way along so amusingly and yet with such skilful decorum, appealing only on two or three occasions, as Sainte-Beuve says, 'trop complaisamment aux sens', it is surprising that Aubrey should have entered that caveat about indecency. Was there something in this book that bade him beware of his own reactions? I think so.

Were *Mademoiselle de Maupin* never to have existed, we should still have the clue to Gautier's own means of sex-arousal in a poem of his, the remarkable 'A une robe rose'.[12] When we turn to the novel, quite apart from the fact that the plot has to do with cross-dressing, certain scenes and passages re-affirm very strongly the particular gratification expressed by this poem. I need refer only to the account of d'Albert's mock rape of Rosette in the fully-lit salon, when he strips her of every ring, feather and garment, commencing with her new and elaborate evening-gown, to show in what direction the carnally-glutted libido of Gautier's hero (oddly autobiographical: they shared, among other things, the name Albert) would take him.[13] A page or two later, indeed, he is already longing to reverse the sex roles.[14] It puts him quite out of patience to be denied the true gust of his own prowess. In a complicated manner—and it is made to seem a great deal more complicated than the machinations of the Forest of Arden—d'Albert could be said to achieve his wish with the arrival of the mysterious Théodore. Like a woman, he falls in love with a charming creature who is, to all intents and purposes, a man, and even becomes the rival of his own mistress for Théodore's affections. What a syndrome for the Viennese consulting-room! And Gautier's tale can be enjoyed at many levels. It is by turns homosexual (male and female), violently heterosexual, transvestist and transsexual. One remarks that the ingenious Frederick Rolfe* did not disdain, some years later, to make use of the same device whereby the fascinating boy with whom the hero's lot is cast providentially, and at the last moment, turns out to be a girl.[15] It was therefore something that could be accepted as a device—in the supra-fictional sense—by the homosexual reader, too: as, for example, by Wilde, one of *Mademoiselle de Maupin*'s greatest admirers; and thus everybody was made happy by this most agreeable of all authors and one with a special claim on Aubrey's sympathy, as an artist who became a writer and as a writer who never ceased to remember he had been an artist.

Six

And we come now, by the natural processes of investigation, to Aubrey's own ambitious attempt to combine art and letters; emerging from the path we have taken through the drawings and finding ourselves on the windy uplands of the 'Hörselberg, near Eisenach' where Wagner—as some critics think, too confidently— sited his operatic Court of Venus. For Aubrey's *The Story of Venus and Tannhäuser*, as its title suggests, was born out of Wagner's music—and even preserves a clear reference to the score. But it is only very briefly Wagnerian. After the opening page or two the Tannhäuser machinery comes to a halt. Aubrey's tenor never gets as far as the cello's entry, with:

O, sag', wie lange hört' ich's doch nicht mehr?

He never reaches the point of regretting anything, least of all the passage of time. Aubrey's admiration for Wagner did not oblige him to swallow the libretto whole. And the reader may see what the artist himself proposed printed on the title-page of poor Smithers's sackcloth-and-ashes edition of 1907: '*The Story of/ Venus and Tannhäuser/* in which is set forth an exact account of the manner of/ State held by Madam Venus, Goddess and Meretrix, under/ the famous Hörselberg, and containing the Adventures of/ Tannhäuser in that Place, his Repentance, his Journeying to/ Rome and Return to the Loving Mountain./ A

---

*Baron Corvo (1860–1913), of homosexual tastes.

Romantic Novel/ by/ Aubrey Beardsley/ Now first printed from the Original Maunuscript/ London/ For Private Circulation/ MCMVII.'

The divergences from Wagner—that is, the omissions of Venus's ultimate defeat, of the repeal of the curse put upon Tannhäuser and of his last dying invocation to the saintly Elisabeth which shows he has returned to the Christian faith—are very important, if they are Aubrey's. While it could be that we see here Smithers's handiwork (arising from the view he may have held that a finally repentant Tannhäuser would be out of key with such a book), we ought not to forget that, when Aubrey explored this theme in his drawings, he himself never got beyond the rejected pilgrim's initial re-acceptance of the Loving Mountain. A design representing 'The Return of Tannhäuser to the Venusberg' (Fig. 66)

66   The Return of Tannhäuser to the Venusberg, *c.* 1894–5.

was among those announced for the story by Lane in 1894: but publication was abandoned. The original drawing for the same design was afterwards (September 1896) presented by the artist to Dent. No work by Aubrey expresses so acutely the crisis of sexual desire.

What makes it particularly interesting, in relation to the synopsis of his own story, is that this drawing virtually repeats the subject and composition of an earlier 'Tannhäuser', dated 1891. As the early drawing must precede the manuscript, then it seems to confirm that, from the beginning, Aubrey had intended the triumph to be, not Christ's, but Venus's. Tannhäuser would see out Eternity in the stews of the accursed mountain.

Seven

I have no doubt at all that *The Story of Venus and Tannhäuser* is the most valuable document we have in an investigation of the kind undertaken here. For Aubrey himself, it was as important as (more important than, Symons thought) any of his drawings, or sets of drawings. Success as an artist had come easily; success as a writer he toiled after. Adverse opinions of his art barely ruffled him; Symons's rejection of the first version of *The Ballad of a Barber* hurt him terribly.[16] In fact, from something he once said, we can infer that he regarded his prose more highly than his poetry. Modest about neither, he was certainly right in this judgment. The opening chapter of *The Story of Venus and Tannhäuser* is, in its *genre*, impeccable.

Commencing this 'big long thing of the revels in act I of *Tannhäuser*' in the early summer of 1894 (a letter to Evans, soon after, marks the moment),[17] Aubrey took it up again while resting at Valewood Farm, and in October was still carrying on 'tortoise fashion'. That the drawings were in his head concurrently is proved by the artist's report to the editor of Hazell's Annual in the same month: 'At present engaged in making a large number of illustrations for *The Story of Venus and Tannhäuser*, written by myself and to appear early in 1895.'[18] (In the event, it was not till 1896 that the first expurgated chapters appeared in *The Savoy*, and the artist did not, of course, survive to see the privately printed edition of the work as he had written it.) So I shall here consider text and illustrations together, in the manner in which they were originally conceived and carried out.

Chapter I, 'How the Chevalier Tannhäuser entered into the Hill of Venus', conveys the impression of having been (as is, indeed, likely) the most anxiously, as well as lovingly, elaborated, paragraph by paragraph, of any sequence of the story. Aubrey was, after all, proving himself to the reader, inclined to prejudice against an artist straying from his accepted speciality into quite a new one. The whole chapter is an explicit allegory of the sexual act. The plumed hero, finally entitled 'the Chevalier Tannhäuser', but arriving at this nomenclature by easy stages from the 'Abbé Fanfreluche' and the 'Abbé Aubrey', is an eighteenth-century dandy whom mention of Mme du Deffand in the second sentence seems to consign to the age of the *philosophes*, but who becomes in the first superb illustration ('Tannhäuser before the Hill of Venus' or 'The Abbé') (Fig. 67), more of an English Regency buck. Much that I have said already will suggest how great a part dress of one period or another must play in any literary (as artistic) production of Aubrey's. Thus it is the author's initial concern to show us how exquisitely the Chevalier has been groomed for his expedition to the Court of Love. And the hour of dusk, the hour of his arrival before the 'ombre gateway', is essentially that when other dandies are dressing for dinner. The Brummell note, once sounded, is sustained:

'Would to heaven,' he sighed, 'I might receive the assurance of a looking-glass before I make my début! However, as she is a goddess, I doubt not her eyes are a little sated with perfection, and may not be displeased to see it crowned with a tiny fault.'

A wild rose had caught upon the trimmings of his muff, and in the first flush of displeasure he would have struck it brusquely away, and most severely punished the offending flower. But the ruffled mood lasted only a moment, for there was something so deliciously incongruous in the hardy petal's invasion of so delicate a thing, that Tannhäuser withheld the finger of resentment, and vowed that the wild rose should stay where it had clung—a passport, as it were, from the upper to the under world.[19]

67   The Abbé (illustration to *Under the Hill*, expurgated version of *The Story of Venus and Tannhäuser*), from *The Savoy*, No. 1, January 1896.

And his last action, as he steps off to his destination, is to undo a 'tangle in the tassel of his stick'. However, one wouldn't wish to give the impression that this dwelling upon cravat and ruffle becomes in any way obtrusive. Others, besides myself, who enjoy the first scene, Act I, of Wagner's opera will find how subtly Aubrey's polished sentences convey, at one moment a brass-based sonority, as when he describes the tapestry-gorged moths, at another—Vespers of Venus, the Chevalier calls them—the haunting trebles and altos of the stage-sirens: 'faint music as strange and distant as sea-legends that are heard in shells'.

Yet in spite of all this, we do not share the Chevalier's obvious confidence in himself as the Great Lover nor rate very highly his chances of satisfying the Queen of Love herself, as he enters the 'shadowy corridor that ran into the bosom of the wan hill' with the 'admirable aplomb and unwrinkled suavity of Don John', wonderful euphemisms for the vaginal vestibule and spongy, erectile tissue Aubrey had in mind.

Eight

What should we expect to discover, as the coulisse opens out into another world? The reader will have foreseen the Goddess's preoccupation and the article of furniture on four legs so necessary to it, whether one's back hair is being combed in Paris or in Pimlico. 'Before a toilet that shone like the altar of Nôtre [sic] Dame des Victoires, Venus was seated in a little dressing-gown of black and heliotrope': thus the second chapter opens.[20] The passage that follows is like the putting of all those silent pen-and-ink *toilettes* into words. The formerly immovable jars, boxes, flasks, rings, ribbons, slippers and gloves are opened, sniffed, smoothed, or slipped into, and all expatiated upon. Borne along by the rise and fall of phrases soft as nainsook and Silesias, words woven to weight (gauze, fine, superior, heavy) yet always flocculent, we can imagine ourselves for a moment being attended to by a Mr Beardsley behind his brass-ruled counter in a draper's shop. Then something terrible happens: the obsequious young man in the tortoiseshell fringe suddenly straightens himself up, utters that neighing laugh remembered by Max Beerbohm in a post-war broadcast, and lets fly with a hail of indecencies. The chandelier explodes, the electric-telegraph is short-circuited, the walls of the drapery establishment cave in!

I hope this impression will be thought neither too general nor too fanciful, but it is Aubrey's approach to the theme rather than the material involved—every fetish the boudoir can provide—which we are concerned with here. The drawing for 'The Toilet' is full of equivalent touches, and felicitous ones, though it cannot equal artistically the portrait of the Chevalier. The masked coiffeur of *Salome* reappears, symbolizing more excitedly the fetish of braid-cutting, and the Mistress of her Queen's Pleasures, Mrs Marsuple, adds ballast with a hint of all the other items in the *Psychopathia Sexualis*. 'How Venus supped and thereafter was mightily amused by the curious Pranks of her Entourage,' Chapter Three, is as much concerned with the dress of those who sup as with the scene around them. Venus herself attends bare-bosomed, while Tannhäuser is at ease in ruffled shirt, black silk stockings with 'pretty garters' and a 'wonderful dressing-gown'. 'As for the rest of the company, it boasted some very noticeable dresses, and whole tables of quite delightful coiffures': and another vast inventory is embarked upon, including veils, fans, masks, wigs, collars, feathers, tights, tunics, drawers, stockings, petticoats, skin-dyeing and skin-painting.[21]

As there has been plenty of titillation, so now, in succeeding short chapter after chapter, follows performance. Tirelessly, Aubrey works through the clinical varieties of perversion—at the risk of tiring himself and ultimately (how could he avoid it?) tiring the reader. This is not to overlook many brilliantly decorative passages and much mischief that amuses. But the disadvantages inherent in the undertaking soon make themselves apparent. The complete freedom he never allowed himself in his drawings approximates to chaos here. Would he have learned this lesson, had he lived longer? Since it is the fashion to round on Symons and Ross and Haldane Macfall,* because they would not accept what was then called *Under the Hill* as a huge success, I feel bound to record my own entire agreement with them. On the other hand, its short first chapter will survive as one of the most brilliant prose-poems in our language; and as the illustration that goes with it (of the Chevalier, troubled by his wild rose) is peerless among pen-drawings, it has a double claim to immortality.

*Author of *Aubrey Beardsley: the Man and his Work*, 1928.

Nine

But are the extravagances of *The Story of Venus and Tannhäuser* only fetishist? I must break off in mid-argument to follow a new train of thought for which the third of Aubrey's illustrations inter-leaved with his romance, 'The Fruit Bearers' (Fig. 68), could provide a convenient point of departure.

The richly-inventive drawing named shows two servants at the feast attended by Venus and Tannhäuser: the leading one, a satyr, bearing the fruit of the picture's title. The huge weight of sagging grapes on the splendid dish continues up pyramidally, its apex blurring into a mass of trellised roses very similar in form, which in turn are repeated in the smaller rose-patterns on the satyr's bloomer-suit and on the upper garment of the second, following, servant. The mass effect of the small round shapes staring at us with their simulated eyes (simulated, that is, by the dark heart of the rose and the shadow on each grape) borders on the hypnotic.

An observer interested in ocularly-acquired memories might find himself comparing this 'way of seeing' with the visions (medically described for the first time in a celebrated paper by D. W. Prentiss and Francis P. Morgan in September 1895, when Aubrey was still at work on his story and its illustrations (induced) by mescaline.[22] On the other hand, it must be made clear from the start that there is no direct evidence associating the artist's imagery with trances brought about in this way. In 1891, James Mooney of the US Bureau of Ethnology had brought back to Washington from a visit south a supply of mescal, which he handed over to Prentiss and Morgan. Their concern with the drug was overridingly therapeutic; but a Scottish specialist, Dr S. Weir Mitchell, after trying out a dose on 24 May 1896, discussed his experiences in a much broader context.[23] They began with minute stars or flashes of light, followed by visions of great splendour. The most remarkable and memorable of these, in the doctor's own opinion, consisted of 'clusters of what seemed to be huge precious stones, but uncut, some being more like masses of transparent fruit'; and, he adds, 'I constantly carried for days a quite vivid image of one of these jewel clusters.'[24] His paper, published in *The British Medical Journal* on 5 December 1896, ended by

68   The Fruit Bearers (illustration to *Under the Hill*), from *The Savoy*, No. 1, January 1896.

predicting a 'perilous reign of the mescal habit when this agent becomes obtainable.'

How easily obtainable by the layman was it? A small quantity came into the possession of Havelock Ellis,* and on Good Friday 1897, in the rooms he shared with Arthur Symons, Aubrey's colleague on *The Savoy*, he brewed a 'tea' from three mescal 'buttons' (the dried, flowering tops of this peyote cactus) and proceeded to sip it between 2.30 and 4.30 in the afternoon. Ellis was a romantically-minded man, the experiment highly self-conscious. And he had read the papers both of Prentiss and Morgan and of Weir Mitchell. On the other hand, the editor of the 'Mermaid' series of Elizabethan dramatists had perhaps a greater understanding than his predecessors of the subtleties of language and the matching of visual with verbal image.

As might be anticipated, Ellis's account (it appeared in *The Contemporary Review* for January 1898)[25] is wholly aesthetic, a positive glutting of that inward eye that is the bliss—he had waited till Symons was away—of solitude: indeed, he suggested that Wordsworth would be the mescal-drinker's favourite poet. Sitting in his rooms alone, then, in the deserted Temple, he first became aware of pale violet shadow floating over his point of vision. His hands, holding a book, took on a monstrous appearance. Now, though coyly, the splendour approached. What form did it adopt? That of 'golden jewels, red and green stones, ever changing'. They remained visible for a while, these 'glorious fields of jewels, solitary or clustered, sometimes brilliant and sparkling, sometimes with a dull, rich glow'.

> Then they would spring up into flowerlike shapes beneath my gaze, and then seem to turn into gorgeous butterfly forms or endless folds of glistening, iridescent, fibrous wings of wonderful insects. . . But, in spite of this immense profusion, there was always a certain parsimony and aesthetic value in the colours presented. They were usually associated with form and never appeared in large masses, or if so, the colour was very delicate. I was further impressed, not only by the brilliance, delicacy and variety of the colours, but even more by their lovely and various textures—fibrous, woven, polished, glowing, dull, veined, semi-transparent.[26]

*Henry Havelock Ellis (1859–1939), best known for his *Studies in the Psychology of Sex* (1897–1928).

I may be forgiven, I think, for being reminded of Aubrey's 'The Fruit Bearers', when, with slightly shaking hand, Ellis notes down those heaped jewels which for Weir Mitchell had also suggested 'masses of transparent fruit'. Even more interesting is his reference to the 'fibrous wings of wonderful insects', and a later remark to the effect that 'perhaps the most prevalent' visions had been the 'glowing effects, as of jewels, and the fibrous, as of insects' wings'. For that inevitably sends us back to Aubrey again, and the first chapter of *The Story of Venus and Tannhäuser*:

> Huge moths, so richly winged they must have banqueted upon tapestries and royal stuffs, slept on the pillars that flanked either side of the gateway, and the eyes of all the moths remained open, and were burning and bursting with a mesh of veins.[27]

Still in connexion with the first chapter of Aubrey's story, we may strike another similarity between the immediate environment of Tannhäuser and the architectural fantasy recorded by Weir Mitchell, the doctor's virtuosity in description on this occasion actually eclipsing Ellis's:

> A white spear of grey stone grew up to a huge height, and became a tall, richly finished Gothic tower of very elaborate and definite design, with many rather worn statues standing in the doorways or on stone brackets;[28]

though Ellis, too, had the satisfaction of watching his finger-tips 'grow into ribs of vaulting or dome-shaped roof'.[29]

Compare with this autopsically-rendered architecture Aubrey's own pillars flanking (by overt symbolism) the gateway of the Mons Veneris, which were:

> fashioned in some pale stone, and rose up like hymns in praise of Venus, for, from cap to base, each one was carved with loving sculptures, showing such a cunning invention and such a curious knowledge that Tannhäuser lingered not a little in reviewing them.[30]

One does not forget, either, the resemblance noted by Dr Weir Mitchell between effects of mescaline and those produced in some forms of ophthalmic megrims, on which he had reported in 1887:

for one of the hallucinations noted by another contemporary inquirer into the megrim phenomena, Dr de Schweinitz, took shape, much in the manner of the background to 'The Fruit Bearers', as a 'trellis of silver covered with vines and flowers'.[31]

Additional points may be considered: the recurrence right through Aubrey's work of massed jewels and massed fruit, two of the last drawings, 'Volpone adoring his Treasure' and the Initial V, for *Volpone* (an elephant bearing fruit and loaded with jewels and having, one must remember, not the remotest connexion with Jonson's play) (Fig. 56), providing as good examples as any; and, while bearing in mind the influence of Mantegna, particularly his 'Triumph of Caesar' at Hampton Court, the connotations with mescaline are still uncanny. Though for Dr Weir Mitchell it was 'mainly a colour experience', for Ellis, on the contrary, the passage I have already quoted makes clear that form and texture (Aubrey's *forte*) predominated. And if Aubrey really did get his best ideas by candlelight in a darkened room, it links up with Ellis's experience that the visions required, for their best effect, a dark room in flickering firelight.

Ellis got as far as seeing figures as well as the form-constants noted by others (in modern times, by Klüver)—spirals, cones, lattice-work, carpet-like patterns, etc.—and in this his experience seems to have been unique:

> All sorts of odd and grotesque images passed in succession through my mind during part of the first night [after dosage]. . . . I would see figures with prodigious limbs, or strangely dwarfed and curtailed, or impossible combinations such as five or six fish, the colour of canaries, floating about in air in a gold wire cage.[32]

But these, he hastens to add, were mental images, not visions. And when this witness actually cites Aubrey's drawings in the same breath as the mental images—'They might have been the dreams of a Baudelaire or of an Aubrey Beardsley'[33]—I think it is time to exercise caution. For Ellis, as a fellow *Savoy* contributor, would have known the drawings under discussion like the back of his hand. On 'mental images', therefore, he might all too easily be leading us into a circular argument.

Ten

The thing to do, it had seemed to me, following the threads of Aubrey's fetishism, was to make the acquaintance of a psychiatrist willing to read and report on the unexpurgated *Story of Venus and Tannhäuser*, not as it would have been approached by Ellis or the encyclopedically cultured Aldous Huxley, but with robust objectiveness. I was lucky enough to find such a helper.

It happens that in 1953, just about the time when Huxley, as related in *The Doors of Perception*, was following Ellis and testing his aesthetic response to mescaline, my helper, Dr X., with a group of colleagues, had himself been planning experiments with the same drug for medical purposes (connected with the psychotic state which, it is claimed, mescaline and lysergic acid can produce). Throughout his reading of Aubrey's story, Dr X. was first and foremost struck by the similarity between Aubrey's 'visions' and those he himself had experienced under mescaline. Among the points he listed were an overall complexity, richness, plurality and repetitiveness; the constant syncretic linkage and conjunction of opposites; ordinarily immobile surfaces which shifted like sand; the covering of surfaces with spots, reminding him of red blood-corpuscles; surface networks and arborizations; the obsession with masks (Dr X. had seen a Rorschach card as a mask, when under the drug, and it is common for mescaline subjects to see faces as masks). Some instances, in particular, of the abrupt adoption and discarding of topics appeared to Dr X. as 'pure mescaline'.

This, of course, offers no definite proof. From Prentiss and Morgan to Huxley, it has always been understood that mescaline is not a drug that can safely be used by invalid subjects. It seems unlikely that Aubrey, with so sensitive a stomach (the buttons, then taken orally, produced unpleasant gastro-intestinal sensation), would have risked regular dosage, even had sufficient quantities of the drug been available. On the other hand, as late as 1894 and 1895 he could still behave rashly when the spirit moved him, and in March 1896 what may have been his last spree of all occurred in Paris, in the company of Dowson, Smithers and Gabriel de Lautrec,* not long before the disastrous trip to Brussels. About

*1867–1938, French man of letters.

15 March, Dowson wrote to Henry Davray,* a mutual friend:

> Have you seen Beardsley? I hear he has returned to Paris and
> will stay there for two or three months. . . . He was very
> amusing on my last Sunday in Paris. We went to see Lautrec,
> and Beardsley took some haschish for the first time. There was
> no result for some hours; then suddenly, while we were dining
> with Smithers at Margery's the haschish began to work very
> powerfully. Luckily we were in a *cabinet* or I think we would
> have been turned out—for Beardsley's laughter was so tumul-
> tuous that it infected the rest of us—who had not taken haschish
> —and we all behaved like imbeciles.[34]

One wonders what made Aubrey laugh (under mescaline,
Aldous Huxley found Berg's *Lyric Suite* 'rather funny', but not
riotously so).[35] When J. Redwood Anderson—Hull poet and
friend of Walter de la Mare—experimented with three-and-a-half
grains of *cannabis indica* (hashish), the horrors he went through
appalled him.[36] Indeed, variety is the spice of drug-assaying. We
should have to exercise the greatest caution about the type of
visions Aubrey might have had, supposing he ever tried out
mescaline for release or inspiration. For instance, though both
Weir Mitchell and Ellis saw the clustered forms I was reminded
of in 'The Fruit Bearers', Aldous Huxley—though expecting to do
so—did not.[37] I don't want to pursue vain speculation, nor dally
with Redwood Anderson's specific reference to Aubrey's work in
connexion with effects (under cannabis) of *elongation*.[38] It is true
that the artist (besides his passion for dwarfs) regularly elongated
other figures. The servants in 'The Fruit Bearers' (Fig. 68), for
example, are respectively seven-and-a-half and eight feet in height.
But elongation has its own artistic pedigree; and I think I have
remarked before that Aubrey was a Mannerist.

Just two medical points may be made. First, in March 1897
Dr Harsant prescribed for his patient ergotine, which is the active
principle of ergot of rye, itself the plant's diseased seed employed
as a medicine.[39] (*D-* lysergic acid diethyamide, an alkaloid of ergot,
is better-known to us today as LSD.) Had Aubrey been con-

---

*1873–1944. He wrote an enthusiastic notice on Aubrey in *L'Hermitage* in 1897.

tinuously and injudiciously dosed with ergotine, hallucination and depersonalization would have resulted. But we cannot for a minute suppose it happened. Secondly, and this, of course would supply the likeliest answer, could it be proved: tuberculosis has been thought in some quarters to potentiate visual disturbances similar to those induced by both mescaline and lysergic acid. It might therefore be that the 'cluster'-type image and elongated-architectural image are capable of hysterical reproduction in the absence of the toxin. Any assessment of the hallucinatory origins of Aubrey's imagery must clearly wait on further discoveries in this field.

Eleven

The matter just discussed does not, of course, bear upon the fetish images which had been concerning us earlier. I cannot discover that Hofmann, Mayer-Gross or Hoch encountered patients suffering from *delusions* about women's underclothes.

Let us return, then, to our imaginary draper's shop or, rather, let us take the lift from the department with which Aubrey has proved himself so familiar to an imaginary, but still related, Department of Psychological Medicine many floors up. Turning from the subject of mescaline, Dr X., too, doubted the splendid Tannhäuser's stamina as Great Lover. Aubrey's hero preens too long before the portals of the Venusberg. As the 'story' staggers on, the extended preparation for his grand sexual encounter with the Goddess bids fair to spoil the actuality. Love, for the Chevalier, is at least three-parts dalliance. He seems almost reluctant to leave these fore-pleasures and take the ultimate plunge.

And though he takes it in conventional style:

Tannhäuser, pale and speechless with excitement, passed his gem-girt fingers brutally over the divine limbs, tearing away smock and pantalon and stocking, and then, stripping himself of his own few things, fell upon the splendid lady with a deep-drawn breath,

the author must immediately confess:

It is, I know, the custom of all romancers to paint heroes who can give a lady proof of their valliance at least twenty times a night. Now Tannhäuser had no such Gargantuan felicity, and was rather relieved when, an hour later, Priapusa and Doricourt and some others burst drunkenly into the room and claimed Venus for themselves.[40]

Would not 'smock and pantalon and stocking' have been good enough substitutes for Venus herself? A passage from a letter to Smithers, of 23 December 1896, suggests that a 'pantalon' alone could satisfactorily perform the office. And in confirmation of the impression Aubrey gives his reader, that only those passages describing clothing made of the most delicate fabrics display (among so much that is coldly, calculatedly there to shock) a genuinely heightened emotion on the part of the author, one remembers Richard Le Gallienne's 'interesting talk' with Aubrey about the story. 'I recall,' says Le Gallienne, 'the excitement with which he told me of some of the illustrations he proposed making, notably one of the wardrobe of Venus, with all its provocative garments. In such feminine matters he was as abnormally learned as he was in the curious by-ways of French and other classical literature.'[41]

That he had been 'learning' for a long time, is made clear from a correction of some importance in the original manuscript, now in the Rosenbach Collection at Philadelphia, occurring on leaves 57 and 58. In the rejected passage can be be made out, among other first thoughts: 'Heavens how many times have I lingered eagerly improperly upon the sea shore Brighton beach watching the little girls young girls pull up tuck up their [illegible] petticoats and drawers and slip into the water. The [?] loves why do they ever grow up?' One is reminded here, of course, of the identification of the writer with his hero that existed from the beginning. *It was a Tannhäuser doing duty for Aubrey* whose emotions led to the expunged passage.

Any point, therefore, at which the writer forgets that he is supposed to be inventing a tale about a reveller at the Court of Venus—precisely as happens in the erasure above—may supply us with a valuable, if fleeting, glimpse of the real Aubrey. Such a point occurs, surely, on leaf 27 verso of the manuscript, where it is

Aubrey ('a little grisé') *not Tannhäuser*, who 'lay down on the cushions and let Julia do what she liked'. Mr Brian Reade, to whom I am indebted for a transcript of both passages, has not, of course, failed to note the evidence this seems to offer of the artist's own sexual passivity.

Corroborating the unaggressive role is an increasing effeminacy in Tannhäuser's choice of clothing for himself, from a 'dainty night-dress' to 'trousers of black lace in flounces, falling—almost like a petticoat—as far as the knee; and a delicate chemise of white muslin, spangled with gold and profusely pleated'.[42] A line or two before the manuscript ends, and not unpredictably, Tannhäuser appears dressed as a woman.

Twelve

'I am going to Jimmie's on Thursday night dressed up as a tart and mean to have a regular spree': thus Aubrey expressed himself to Lane, in a letter postmarked 12 September 1893.[43] The tone of this communication is somewhat ironic—the writer apotheosizing his publisher as 'Dear and Reverend Sir'—but not so ironic as to imply that the proposal quoted was not going to be carried out. 'Jimmie's' stood for the St James's Restaurant and Tavern, between Air Street and the Circus, then Piccadilly Place, and provided a regular port of call for prostitutes. Yet if Aubrey really did dress up as a tart and spend the evening of 14 September 1893 at this establishment, he would have found himself in more venturesome, not to say dangerous, company.

It had been at the St James's bar, only a few months previously, that Alfred Taylor, who pimped for Wilde, picked up for his uses the brothers William and Charles Parker. He had opened the conversation, so Mr Gill elicited from Charles Parker at the Old Bailey, by waving his hand at some female street-walkers and saying: 'I can't understand sensible men wasting their money on painted trash like that. Many do, though. But there are a few who know better.'[44] And on the following night there had been a dinner for four at the Solferino, with red-shaded candles, champagne and brandy, Wilde playing host. After this, the Parkers, ex-valet and ex-groom, regularly attended Taylor's perpetually-curtained premises over a closed baker's shop in Little College

Street. The landlady of No. 13, satisfying the same Counsel for the Crown on 26 April 1895, gave a description of the rooms as revealed internally by coloured lamps and candles: the sumptuous furnishings, the incense burners and the oriental-style mattress on the floor. There were also as part of the general wardrobe— and much was made of them at the trial—a woman's wig and shoes and stockings. 'I never saw any dress,' added the landlady. But under rigorous cross-examination, Taylor was obliged to admit to the existence of one.[45] Nothing the prosecution had laid at his door would be more damning: in a dress, one of his boys could walk the streets at night and lure back to the brothel the easiest of blackmail victims for the plucking. Taylor, with his long experience of embarrassing situations (after one of which he had been expelled from Marlborough), well understood the drift of Gill's questioning; as did Frederick Atkins, when pressed on the very same point by Wilde's counsel, Sir Edward Clarke, himself engaged in discrediting (for what that was worth) the young male prostitutes put up against his client by the Crown.

Without doubt, cross-dressing for one purpose or another did take place in, and on excursions to and from, Taylor's various nests of ill-fame. There was talk of a mock-wedding between Taylor and Charles Mason, the latter in bridal white;[46] but the strongest evidence is provided by a number of arrests made on 20 August 1894.[47] Among a group of men charged with assembling and associating together in Fitzroy Street for felonious purposes were Charles Parker and Alfred Taylor themselves. What had led the police to enter the premises on the occasion of a riotous party with piano-playing, dancing and singing was the presence of two men dressed as women, one of whom was the notorious Arthur Marley (not 'Marling', as Montgomery Hyde calls him), a theatrical—the distinction is perhaps necessary here—'female impersonator'. The more serious charges came to nothing, however. Marley and an associate paid fines. Five other men were bound over and the rest, Parker and Taylor among them, went free. Over-precipitate action by the police on this occasion reflects, I think, besides the widespread existence of the blackmail and official anxiety to come to grips with it, the strength of public feeling, much of it erotic, roused by such male-as-female masquerades.

In the memories of many magistrates, divisional-inspectors and, particularly, police surgeons, would still have rankled the Boulton and Park case of 1870.[48] Boulton dressed the part of 'juvenile', Park that of 'matron', but they would also appear, their faces painted and powdered, in masculine attire with ladies' boots. The bewildered beadle of the Burlington Arcade and a score of West End front-of-house managers did not know whether they were at the mercy of men pretending to be women or women pretending to be men. The law found itself similarly at a loss, though when, in high feather, Boulton and Park took a brougham to the Boat Race and picked up two city gentlemen, it got ready to pounce. Like Marley, later, 'Lady Arthur (or Stella) Clinton'—as Boulton called himself, when for some while the house-guest of Lord Arthur—and 'Fanny Winifred Park' (who occupied the dressing-room in the Clinton ménage), played a few walk-on parts at The Egyptian Hall and at the little theatres of the time, half-professional, half-amateur: it was a useful cover, sometimes a hard-and-fast alibi.

Another such occasional performer was Amos Gibbings, Old Reptonian and man of fortune, who gave a transvestist ball at Haxell's Hotel in the Strand. At this ball, rendered more piquant by the attendance of a few women of easy virtue, Boulton sang 'Fading Away' with a sensibility that led the band-leader to congratulate him on the most wonderful woman's voice he had ever listened to. When Boulton was ultimately stripped of his finery at the House of Detention, the police took possession of a scarlet silk 'body', three petticoats, a green gauze dress, a bodice, a pair of drawers and stockings sewn together, two bustles, a pair of bronze boots, a red flannel shirt, and a quantity of wadding. Park had made do with a dress, a crape shawl, a crinoline, a pair of stockings and, in addition to the wadding 'taken from the breast', a pair of white boots. Crowds in the streets rioted in fury at being balked of an opportunity of seeing the prisoners arrive for trial in female dress, a feat Marley himself, grinning in black and gold, actually managed to bring off. And in court Dr Paul, the police surgeon, was not congratulated on his part in the compulsory stripping and examination of the two men: for such, of course, they turned out to be.

Thirteen

It can therefore be established that, if Aubrey travelled up from Pimlico to the West End to play the woman at the St James's Restaurant, on a certain September evening in 1893, the game was an old and risky one. The chief temptation for Boulton and Park had been a gratuitous distribution of winks and smiles: this produced (say, in a box at the theatre, to the great embarrassment of the lessee) frenetic excitement in the public when it perceived—as it usually did—the *ladies'* ambiguity. Alone, or with another masquerader of the same sex, Aubrey himself might well have succumbed to the bestowal of a 'come hither' glance or two and then got into serious trouble in a place where engaging in 'drag' (*dressing-up as a girl*: a term in current use as early as the 1860s) had generally an 'unlawful and abominable' purpose.

Might it have been naïveté on his part? But no, Aubrey was never naïve. By September 1893, Piccadilly would have held few secrets for him. He had already become a pillar of the *Cénacle*, the friend, or friendly enemy, of Wilde and, perhaps even more relevant here, the friend of Ross, whose name went down regularly, night after night, in the notebook of Inspector West of Vine Street. But Robbie seemed to lead a charmed life, even before the Asquiths became his patrons. And there was a difference between open importuning among men and what would be regarded as felonious gender-switching.

If one were asked for a simple answer, it might be that Aubrey took the risk because the pleasure he derived from these antics was greater than his fear of danger; that his behaviour, in fact, was compulsive. Yet we never hear of another instance. This may appear extraordinary; yet if recent clinical findings, such as those of Dr John Randell published in 1970, indicate that frequency of cross-dressing varies considerably, then the element of exhibitionism which undoubtedly goes with it, the equally compulsive need to parade thus before a large gathering of people, will obviously vary, too.[49] Alternatively, the highly narcissistic orientation which *The Story of Venus and Tannhäuser*, in addition to countless letters, indicates as their writer's, might have been better satisfied by a secret shared with a mirror, surmounting, on these occasions, a *table de toilette* piled high with chignons and glittering with costume-jewellery.

Though medical opinion is not unanimous on the aetiology of transvestism, there seems some broad agreement that its origins may be looked for in the home environment. The pattern of absent, or unsympathetic, father and dominant mother produces not only homosexuals. Out of it—or the broken home—emerge, so the sampling shows, a very large proportion of cross-dressers.[50] If you add to this the frailty of the invalid child (the onset of the trans-vestist wish nearly always occurs before the twelfth year), his special need for affection and reassurance, his early leaning, which persists as, again, *The Story of Venus and Tannhäuser* will confirm, towards the soft, the tender and the delicate, and his shunning of the big and the strong, then one appears to have the classic case passed on to the psychiatrist from the endocrine clinic.

But do all the other characteristics of the artist harmonize with this crude diagnosis of his 'condition'? Will Rothenstein remarked, not upon Aubrey's softness, but his *hardness*.[51] If in his drawings he seems to reserve his harshest satire for the strong, sensual woman, he is often little kinder to the effeminate man. And it is salutary at all times, when you are thinking about Aubrey, to listen to the music of Wagner, the composer he continued most to admire throughout his life. For myself, this introduced a difficulty. One can easily imagine 'Lady Arthur Clinton' in mauve satin trimmed with blond lace (one of the evening-gowns from Gibbings's extensive wardrobe in Wakefield Street) singing 'Fading Away' and successfully putting in all the 'feeling'. What we might well think beyond visualizing is a fellow drag-addict (however in-tellectually the other's superior, still femininely orientated) listening, rapt as do the girls in Aubrey's drawing, 'The Repetition', to the love-and-death duets of *Tristan and Isolde*, surely the most highly-charged avowal, anywhere in music, of hetero-sexual love?

This was a far cry from the transvestist carolling at Haxell's Hotel. But fraught also with possibilities of another kind. In a roundabout way, Wagner's own favourite and most subtle and complicated opera may help us, when puzzled by Aubrey's rash appearance at the St James's Restaurant and Tavern in women's clothes, to a solution. Operatic principals are commonly cast as star-crossed: this is proper to the *genre*. Yet it is difficult to think of a story, acted and sung on the stage, in which the passion of hero for heroine is at once so irresistible and so irrevocably damned by convention (in terms of Isolde's loyalty to her Irish knight, whom Tristan has killed, as well as of Tristan's fealty to King Mark). Nothing is left them but a hopeless determination endlessly to prolong the night of loving and put off the day of retribution, or so to enter into one another's beings that their punishment, when it falls, will find them completely and eternally one. Desire and the doom of that desire have been at the core of the music from the opening phrase of the Prelude which Aubrey, as it happens, gave orders to be printed alongside his 'Repetition' in *The Savoy*.

The question we ask ourselves now is, could the artist, latently homosexual, fetishist, transvestist, nevertheless experience genuine passion for a woman?

I suggested that such considerations might bring us back to the St James's Restaurant. It seems to me that they do.

We may wonder why Lane should have been confided in. Then we recall that the publisher was in Paris when Aubrey wrote to him of an event which would take place *before his return*. The dressing-up 'as a tart' might have been included as an item in keeping with the generally mischievous intention of the whole letter: to shock, or mildly alarm, his 'Dear and Reverend Sir', that far from impressive personality whom Rolfe once described as looking as if he had been 'suckled on bad beer'. Again, the need to confide—while, at the same time, bowing to an elementary caution—may have been as compulsive as the exhibitionism itself. None of the *Cénacle* seems to have been informed and invited to share in the fun. We may be sure, otherwise, that the garrulous Dowson, always interested in Aubrey's doings, would have passed the story on. Wouldn't Max have instantly enlarged on it to Reggie Turner? But not a word. This, if it was not a private venture, could have been strictly a family one.

Fourteen
Aubrey had a sister. Up till now, I have deliberately made no more than a passing reference to Mabel.

No one could better have played up to Aubrey's impersonation. She was just about to become a professional actress, but was as yet unknown and unlikely to be recognized in a place like 'Jimmie's'. She and her brother, moreover, were old partners in illusion: for three or four years they had organized those little 'home entertainments' for which Aubrey designed the programme-covers, acting, singing and dancing together for the amusement of their parents (on Ellen's evidence, Mr Beardsley would sometimes watch, too) and themselves. The two children must have enjoyed their elaborate make-believe as 'M. and A. Beardsley, sole lessees and managers of The Cambridge Theatre of Varieties', so designated because they lived then in lodgings at 32 Cambridge Street.[52] Aubrey sang 'Eighteenpence' and 'The Little Stowaway', Mabel, 'Quite English'. In a sketch, 'Man of Honour', Aubrey played the Man, while Mabel gave an excellently-documented interpretation, no doubt, of his Landlady.

But for their entertainment called 'The Jolly Mashers' Mabel became second Jolly Masher to her brother's No. 1. And in a note dated 12 January 1921, the elderly Mrs Beardsley recalled a wonderful three-hour performance which the children gave of Marlowe's *Tragical History of Doctor Faustus*. In this play, Mabel took the part of Faustus and Aubrey that of Margaret. 'He had,' Ellen tells us, 'long straw plaits fastened on each side of his head.'[53] One should not make too much of that. But long, long after the evening at the St James's Restaurant (whatever actually happened there), and after Aubrey's death, Mabel had her portrait painted by Walford Graham Robertson (Fig. 100). It is a picture that presents a double problem and I shall be returning to its other aspect later. But we may note that Robertson has depicted Mabel, with hair only 'a little longer than short', as a slim, conventional, well-groomed man in the very style that had been Aubrey's. There is no panache about it, no Vesta-Tilleyism, no burlesque. It is, indeed (through the kindness of Mr W. G. Good, I know it well), a sad, serious, straightforward likeness of a woman masquerading as a man, an eonist, as Havelock Ellis, going back to the Chevalier d'Eon, called such persons.

Bearing in mind the light-hearted theatrical partnership that had preceded it and this anything but light-hearted glimpse of what would follow, can we continue to think a double cross-dressing for the evening of 14 September beyond the bounds of possibility? And did brother and sister, dressed in each other's clothes (the likeliest situation) take possession of each other's souls, too, and echo Wagner's ultimate bliss:

> Du Tristan, Isolde ich . . .
> Du Isolde, Tristan ich . . . ;

—or: 'Myself I have ceased to be: now, and for eternity, *I am you*'?

We reach here, I think, the climax of one interpretation of the relationship between brother and sister, a relationship we shall be exploring in detail in the chapter that follows. If it were not a matter of great interest and importance in the study of Aubrey's work to attempt to reach a conclusion one way or the other, the difficulties—not to speak of the unpleasantness, as it will appear to many people—of dealing with such themes as mutual transvestism, incest and, ultimately, transsexualism, would counsel us to abandon the attempt forthwith.

Implicit in Wagner's music are the sublime certainties of High Romance, so notably lacking in a workaday world. The composer enjoyed the advantages of being able to prescribe magic potions and (not without divine assistance) to construct the neatest, irreversible chains of cause and effect. We are concerned with a wholly human situation, where contradictions, changes of heart and mixed motives are the order of the day. Above all, the historian of Beardsley family life and, in particular, of this relationship between brother and sister, has to perform his task with the most miserly handful of facts to help him. If there were not, as I have said, a riddle worth the solving, he would throw up the sponge at once. But the riddle merits a determined attack since, as I see it, we may have here not just a sexual conundrum but the unrevealed matrix of Aubrey's art.

With these reservations endemic to the human condition, therefore, let us turn now from the full-throated, splendid crescendo of *Tristan*'s love-duet, and go back twenty years, to a time when, if the theme is to be heard at all, it is as yet no more than a faint, ingratiating murmur upon the strings.

Aubrey and Mabel

One

The earliest world of these twin souls had been Brighton. There, in 1871 and 1872, Mabel and Aubrey were born. And there, no doubt, they spent their happy summers between the sea and the Surgeon-Major's ugly but substantial house in Buckingham Road (Figs. 69, 70). Then, in 1884, when Aubrey was just turning twelve and his sister a year older, the children came back to Brighton for a longer period to stay with a great-aunt in Lower Rock Gardens.

'She had peculiar notions about children,' recalled Ellen, of this great-aunt, 'and would not let them have any toys. She thought them too precocious, though she always pretended they were backward children. My father went in to see them one day (it was when I was very ill in London, in a nursing-home, in fact) and found them sitting on their little high-backed chairs with nothing in the world to do. "The children can't be happy like that," he

69 Brighton in the early 1880s: the West Pier, opened in 1866, where Ellen met her future husband, father of the artist. As young children, Mabel and Aubrey would have found this section of front and beach the most readily accessible from their grandfather's house in Buckingham Road. Lower Rock Gardens lies not far to the east (or left) of the scene shown.

156

70 Aubrey and Mabel as young children.

said. My aunt assured him that they were as happy as birds. "Then all I can say is," he retorted, "that they have damned contented minds." '1

One can accept the queerness of the old aunt, yet still think it not extraordinary that she found the pair precocious. It was long before this that Mabel, confronted with a portrait of Gladstone at a friend's house and asked who it represented, turned haughtily away, saying: 'These are not my mother's politics.'2 She recited a good deal now in the drawing-rooms of Ellen's well-to-do employers and their friends: the skating scene from *Pickwick*, for instance. Ellen's reminiscences continue: 'Her father used to take her for a walk in the Park sometimes on Sunday mornings and on one occasion a strange gentleman lifted his hat and asked if he might speak to the little girl who had pleased them all so much with her recitations.'3 Aubrey copied Kate Greenaway drawings, but excelled at the piano and played duets with Mabel. Sometimes the houses were rather grand, and Ellen remembered the children performing in St James's Square, when there was at least one duchess present. It is not surprising, therefore, to learn that, on being taken to Westminster Abbey, Aubrey asked his mother: 'Shall I have a bust or a stained-glass window when I am dead? For I may be a great man one day.' 'Which would you like, darling?' asked his mother. He considered: 'A bust, I think, because I am rather good-looking.'[4]

In reality, Aubrey was less handsome than sensitive in appearance, his sleek red hair still short-fringed enough to reveal a too capacious brow. The thin cheeks and slight bowing of the shoulders suggest the invalid; but the gaze is steady, amused and assured. Mabel's round face draws the eye to a perfect, pouting Cupid's-bow of a mouth, yet is more serious (Fig. 71). Of the

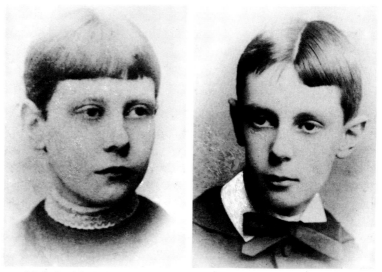

71 Mabel and Aubrey in the early 1880s: about the time of their stay at their great-aunt's house in Lower Rock Gardens, Brighton.

two, we are told, Mabel's ambition soared the higher: she had set her heart on becoming a great actress. Unfortunately (and Ellen remained obstinately of this opinion) the necessary temperament was lacking. 'Aubrey used to encourage her,' she went on, 'but I used to tell her the truth about herself.'[5]

These were the charming, gifted children seated on their 'little high-backed chairs,' on the occasion of the Surgeon-Major's visit to Lower Rock Gardens. Bright, grave, seraphic presences, blandly unoccupied: do they not strike a faint literary echo? In 1904, Henry James was glad to have 'three or four definite recollections' of Aubrey, and he could speak with affection of 'dear Mabel'.[6] Is it possible that some odd tale about them came to his ears, something typically scandalous from Frank Harris, say, inspiring the creation of Miles and Flora in *The Turn of the Screw*? Certainly, none of the Bensons ever believed that James got that story from their father, the Archbishop, whether specifically on 10 January 1895, as the novelist averred, or at any other time.[7] The thought is as fascinating as it is incapable of substantiation.

Two

Miles and Flora had to be taken to church by their terrified governess. Aubrey and Mabel, at twelve and thirteen, were old enough to take themselves. Ellen Beardsley is again our authority: 'Their chief interest [during the five months, August 1884 until January 1885] was in going to church, a very high church, "The Annunciation", in Washington Street.'[8]

Brighton, viewed through a bow-window, with its pleasant terraces and limpid sea, seems a haven of peace, physical and spiritual. But throughout the second half of the nineteenth century the town was one of the bastions of the Catholic Revival. The Revd Arthur Douglas Wagner, the turbulent priest concerned, was Vicar of the church attended by Ellen and her future husband during their engagement, and a good friend of Ellen's family. The flèche of this church, St Paul's, is in its way as remarkable as the cloud-castling domes of the Royal Pavilion: it was raised with Wagner money, like the romantic flint walls and dusky timbering, and the appeal of the church's bold return to ritual soon began to drive the last proprietary chapels out of business. One of Wagner's curates was Alfred Gurney,* another friend of Ellen's family, afterwards to be Aubrey's earliest patron, and we shall come back to him later when the scene changes to London, where Gurney

---

*The Revd Alfred Gurney (barely mentioned in my Introduction) was born in 1845. After his education at Oxford and entry into Holy Orders, he published numerous trifles in prose and verse and, like Aubrey (whom he may have influenced in this respect), became a devoted Wagnerite. He died at Roehampton in 1898.

was appointed Vicar of St Barnabas, Pimlico, in 1879.

Arthur Douglas Wagner's father, a former Vicar of Brighton, had built two new churches at his own expense; the son, inheriting further fortunes, built more than any other private gentleman in England before his death in 1902. The tale of these achievements is remarkable. No wonder he could present petitions, question the oath of the Royal Supremacy, flaunt Eucharistic vestments and adopt the Eastward Position. In Brighton he founded and built St Bartholomew's, the Church of St Mary and St Mary Magdalene, the Church of the Resurrection. In addition, he founded a Community of the Blessed Virgin Mary, for whom he made premises available in Queen Square. Outside Brighton, he built St Mary's, Buxted, near Uckfield. And in Brighton itself, again, he established a little outpost of empire in remote Washington Street, the Church of The Annnunciation, of which Ellen Beardsley was speaking.

It is instructive to follow today, and on foot, the route by which sister and brother would have reached Washington Street from Lower Rock Gardens. *Friend's Almanack*, I note, makes no mention of public transport on a Sunday in 1884; and even in 1886 the Sunday horse-buses served only the cemeteries.[9] The children must have walked. Beardsley students should undertake the return journey, morning and evening, the more keenly to appreciate what a powerful incentive dragged two children, one with respiratory trouble and by no means strong on his legs, up the old Brighton Downs to the last vestiges of chalk path and market-garden twice every Sabbath and back again (the declivity, some of it, far from comfortable, too). But The Annunciation was not so cursorily attended by its devout: they probably made the journey more often than twice on certain feast-days and festivals. On Good Friday, for instance, at this period of the church's history, there were eleven services in all, starting at seven in the morning and ending at about ten at night, thus: a Memorial of the Passion; the Stations of the Cross; the Penitential Psalms and Meditation; Matins; Ante-Communion and Sermon; the Three Hours' Devotion; a Children's Service; the Litany; Evensong; the Mission Service and Sermon; and the Preparation for Death and Address.

These rigours and submissions prepare one for a portrait of
Father George Chapman, priest-in-charge at the time. Says one
of the Sisters of Mary: 'I remember him going round the church
before Mass, his tall, gaunt figure passing along while he peered
anxiously among the congregation to see if any who ought had not
made his confession before coming to Communion. He would
draw them out quietly to his confessional where they went
reluctantly but came back with radiant looks to go to the altar.'[10]
Making a spearhead of The Annunciation, Wagner had no doubt
selected a fanatical Ritualist whom, in case of trouble, he would
have delighted in backing against his Bishop. A curious note by
the Brighton Grammar School master, Fred Carr, in the Lane
papers, suggests George Chapman was just such a man; and,
at the same time, that there was a very close relationship between
the priest and Aubrey. In January 1885 the boy became a boarder
at the Grammar School, and Carr must have been kind enough to
make it possible for Aubrey to go on attending his favourite church
during term-time.

'I remember on one or two occasions,' said the retired school-
master, in 1920, 'taking him to Sunday Evensong to The Church
of The Annunciation in Washington Street, Brighton, of which
church the Revd Father Chapman was vicar [the church was not,
in fact, assigned its own parish till 1888]. Father Chapman was, I
believe, Beardsley's guardian, a man of what were then considered
most advanced views which then appealed strongly to Beardsley.'[11]

While the enemies of the Anglo-Catholics saw in the latter's
interpretation of the Ornaments Rubric a way of showing sympathy with Popish doctrines about the Holy Eucharist, for the
High Church party the return to a more colourful ceremonial was
an acknowledgment of a growing taste for Art and Beauty. Wagner
himself felt such admiration for the picture of Our Lady *Salus
Populi Romani* in Santa Maria Maggiore, in Rome, that all his
churches had to display a copy of it. Father Chapman, too, no
doubt, however austere his personal life, regarded The Annunciation's east window, with its Rossetti panel flanked by a couple
of Burne-Joneses and executed by Morris, as one of those
'necessary luxuries', provided inimitably by Art to the greater
Glory of God. And since he must have been aware of Aubrey's

medical history, he would have felt especially sympathetic towards the young artist in his congregation: for Father Chapman was also a consumptive, his span of years severely limited.

There, then, under the red-tiled spire high on the hill, knelt the two children, eyes riveted upon their sick but splendidly-apparelled friend the priest, hearing (like Sir James Stephen) the 'chant of some ancient liturgy, floating down the fretted aisle'. Their early acquaintance with the Vicar of St Paul's, as well as with Alfred Gurney's Catholic-minded community in Pimlico, had prepared Aubrey and Mabel for devotions to the Madonna of an intensity that, had he learned of them from an exultant Wagner, would have made Archbishop Tait's hair stand on end. Who can speak, therefore, of any unexpected change of faith when, one by one, the entire Beardsley family, including the dour Vincent Paul himself, sought ultimate refuge in Rome? Or regard it as extraordinary that it was the children who anticipated their parents in this? From Aubrey's sending her a little French prayer-book from Paris in March 1896, we assume that month (about the 12th) to have witnessed Mabel's reception.[12] The artist's own took place, as I have had reason to point out more than once, just over a year later.

The majority of Aubrey's admirers have expressed scepticism concerning the sincerity of his faith. In fact, it is nonsense to suggest that Raffalovich dragged him, sneering and blaspheming, across some vast divide; that it was a need to keep in with his paymaster that did the trick. For my own part, I see no incompatibility between backsliding and belief. The more heinous the sin, the more desperate may be the sinner's sense of the punishing presence of God. Beardsley students, having undertaken the trapes up Brighton Downs in the worst imaginable weather, should now turn to the standard 1840 three-volume edition of the sermons of Bourdaloue like the one before me (*e libris Edv. Bouverie Pusey, STP*), comprising some three thousand pages of double-columned pearl type and latterly forming part of Aubrey's favourite reading: they will find this Jesuit, dialectically, just as tough going as the Washington Street ascent and equally indicative of a passionate desire on the part of the artist to sustain his belief.

Three

I do not wish to infer that there isn't an ambiguous and even a comic side to the hectic of highest 'High' in the 1880s, as it brought the converts streaming down the Brompton Road and into the Oratory during the prefecture of Father Bowden. When Bishops in Convocation squabble over cope and chasuble, this must tempt the playwright to create an hilarious Ritualist actually called Dr Chasuble, as Wilde did in *The Importance of Being Earnest*. Dr Chasuble accepts the idea of matrimony very late in life and Miss Prism's warning that 'by persistently remaining single, a man converts himself into a permanent public temptation' could, historically, be taken in another way.

If the religious enthusiasm which produced Newman and Faber was masculine in ethos, celibate and male-seeking, then (in the aesthetic archiepiscopacy of Walter Pater) priests from the Anglo-Catholic ranks who set out to Beautify Worship—capital-letters are forced upon one in such discussions—appear in their thinking indistinguishable at times from the author of the essay on *Winckelmann*, even to that bombshell of a passage which reads: 'I have noticed that those who are observant of beauty only in women, and are moved little or not at all by the beauty of men, seldom have an impartial, vital, inborn instinct for beauty in art.' This explains, I believe, the remarkable ascendancy, among a number of wealthy and aesthetically-inclined High Churchmen of the day, of Burne-Jones, who had succeeded in creating, as well as the bloodless woman, the undemanding male. In 1889, Burne-Jones was deeply shocked by the poverty of ritual with which Browning's funeral service was conducted in Westminster Abbey —and ceremonially-minded men of God felt hot shame and were themselves deeply shocked that our national arbiter of taste (though no longer a practising churchman) was deeply shocked; and they returned to palace and deanery determined to do better.

Characteristic of the wealthy, cultured clergyman in no doubt at all about the important role that beauty must play in his religion, was Alfred Gurney, as we have seen, one who had had his sense of independence fostered by Wagner at St Paul's, Brighton. But whereas Wagner, shy and short-sighted, had entertained little, Father Gurney received the great world in style at his Parsonage of St Barnabas, Pimlico, within easy walking distance of the Beardsleys, whether they lived in Cambridge Street or Charlwood Street. This is confirmed by the recollection of Sir Ninian Comper, who, in unpublished papers Mr Anthony Symondson has kindly transcribed for me, mentions his calling to dine at Gurney's in 1882: 'It was in response to an invitation from Alfred Gurney to "one who combined the love of Cowley with the love of art". A fear I held that evening dress might be out of place was reversed when the Parsonage door was flung open by two footmen.'[13]

Advancing far beyond reverence to one beloved image (Wagner had carried photographic reproductions of the Santa Maria Maggiore picture in his pockets, to distribute to the poor), Father Gurney cast an appreciative eye over the whole field of mystical and religious painting. On the occasion of his visit referred to above, Comper notes: 'Rossetti had just died and the conversation of a select company at dinner was devoted to descriptions of his last hours, and of his habitual fear of being alone; he would keep a friend with him to the small hours of the morning and rise before noon to stretch out his brush languidly from his couch to touch his canvas. To everything, the guests murmured "How beautiful!" '[14]

It was a remarkable coincidence that brought the Beardsleys into such close touch with the former curate of St Paul's, and a fortunate one for Aubrey and Mabel. If at the Church of The Annunciation in Brighton they revelled in the missionary zeal of Father Chapman, at St Barnabas they found in their parish church one of the most stimulating centres of Anglo-Catholic worship London had to offer them. The incense-laden air vibrated to Gregorian chants; for after a silence of three centuries, the ancient ecclesiastical music was being restored, and the beauty of the singing under Helmore, a champion of Plainsong, had become, in the words of Lord Halifax, one of Gurney's warmest supporters, 'unsurpassed and unsurpassable'. The choir was trained in Helmore's own *The Psalter Noted*, and G. H. Palmer, priest-organist and a special friend of Aubrey's, had himself edited a celebrated collection of Office Hymns and Sequences. Another curate made St Barnabas's Chapel-of-Ease in the Pimlico Road his special care, supervising its Devotion of the Rosary, its blessing of red roses on the altar every St George's Day, and its solemn processions organized throughout the year.[15]

Alfred Gurney, with his long, cleft beard and dreamy blue eyes was a most attractive personality. One can imagine the sudden transitions of his energetic daily life: the cassock exchanged for riding-cords as he leapt into the saddle for his canter down Rotten Row; a visit to a Wagner concert with Richter conducting, followed by an aesthetic party, and back to the Parsonage to be called in time to say six o'clock Mass the next morning.[16] To read his letters to children (Miss Alleyne, who was much at his house, has shown me hers), is to enter into a world of blissful confidence in God and human goodness where sin can never rear its ugly head.

This combination of natural interest in the young, great wealth, valuable connexions *and* an enthusiasm for art made the Vicar of St Barnabas a patron heaven-sent for his young parishioner still engrossing insurance policies in Lombard Street. The name Gurney occurs several times in early lists of Beardsley ownership.[17] Alfred was evidently buyer-in-chief. On the Vicar's death in 1898, some of the drawings passed to his elder son Hampden. Another member of the family who took great interest in Aubrey's work was Mrs Russell Gurney, widow of the Recorder of London. And where the name Gurney occurs as owner, the drawing is religious in subject. Modern taste prefers to turn a blind eye to this regrettable preoccupation with Madonnas and angels holding flaming hearts, with lyres and lilies (Figs. 72, 73). It has even been suggested that Aubrey's straightforward devotional subjects were mere potboilers produced for this wealthy clergyman. But the designs did not come into existence quite like that. Aubrey and Mabel thought as naturally in terms of Thrones, Dominations, Princedoms, Virtues, Powers (with their appropriately-coloured wings, their aureoles, globes, sceptres, wands) as, on other occasions and in other terms, of the different liveries of the coachmen waiting for their mistresses on the steps outside the Army and Navy Co-Operative Society's store.

It is likely that Alfred Gurney made as agreeable an impression upon Mabel as upon Aubrey. I had an opportunity of opening,

72 Angel with a flaming heart: 73 Adoramus Te: early work commissioned by the
early work commissioned by the Revd Alfred Gurney.
Revd Alfred Gurney.

not long ago, a copy of one of the Vicar's little volumes of devotional verse for children, entitled *A Christmas Faggot*, inscribed in
his own graceful hand: 'Mabel Beardsley, Christmas 1885, from
the author'; and turned the end-paper to find his likeness, serene
and beautiful, in an old photograph pasted over the book's first
blank leaf—no doubt, by the thirteen-year-old recipient herself
(Fig. 74).

Four

In November 1891 the busy priest found time to write to Ellen
(from the Junior Carlton Club):

> It is so good of you to let me share your pleasure in Edward
> Burne-Jones's appreciation of Aubrey. It is most encouraging
> and delightful. Tell Aubrey that Shields* also, though he
> brooded so silently over the pictures, expressed himself warmly
> to my Aunt afterwards about the talent revealed in them.[18]

*Frederick James Shields (1833–1911).

74   The Revd Alfred Gurney (1845–1898), Vicar of
St Barnabas, Pimlico, and formerly a curate at St
Paul's, Brighton, where he first became friendly with
the artist's mother. From a photograph pasted into
a volume of his devotional verse, inscribed: 'Mabel
Beardsley, Christmas 1885, from the author'.

Before I proceed to the main point of the letter, it is of interest
to note that the artist who 'brooded' a little inauspiciously at first
over Aubrey's drawings (early works like 'The Litany of Mary
Magdalen' and 'Hamlet Patris Manem Sequitur'), was himself
patronized by Alfred Gurney's aunt, Mrs Russell Gurney. Introduced to her by Lady Mount Temple in 1889, Frederick Shields
had been commissioned to decorate in its entirety the Chapel of
the Ascension in the Bayswater Road: a twenty-year task that
illustrates the kind of wealth the Gurney family could devote to
art.

   Father Gurney would have taken particular pleasure in news of
the ripening acquaintance with Burne-Jones, since it had been over
Sunday luncheon at the Parsonage that Aubrey's inaugural visit to
the famous painter had first been mooted. I mentioned this
important event much earlier, but have reason now to return to it.
Aubrey wrote to King on 13 July:

Yesterday (Sunday) I and my sister went to see the Studio of Burne-Jones, as I had heard that admittance might be gained to see the pictures by sending in one's visiting card. When we arrived however we were told that the Studio had not been open for some years and that we could not see Mr Burne-Jones without a special appointment. So we left somewhat disconsolately.

I had hardly turned the corner when I heard a quick step behind me, and a voice which said, 'Pray come back, I couldn't think of letting you go away without seeing the pictures on a hot day like this.' The voice was that of Burne-Jones, who escorted us back to his house and took us into the studio, showing and explaining everything. His kindness was wonderful as we were perfect strangers, he not even knowing our names.[19]

I need not relate the rest in detail: how Aubrey's own drawings, which he 'happened' to have with him, were examined and lauded by the Master; and how they had tea together with several other persons, including Oscar and Constance Wilde (with the former of whom, as I have said, this brief meeting led for the moment to no closer acquaintance), before boy and girl returned to Charlwood Street in triumph.

For Mabel, I believe, the visit had been as important as for her brother. In the little sketch of Aubrey which Ellen and Mabel wrote between them, Burne-Jones is represented as saying that he could not see a *lady* turned away on a hot afternoon without tea.[20] On another occasion Ellen, hardly—as we have seen—in the habit of flattering her daughter, stated that it was not conscience but a glimpse of Mabel's glowing hair that changed the Master's mind at the last moment.[21] It must have been most gratifying to Aubrey, when the artist whom he so much admired drew him back into the shady garden of the Grange, where the roses bloomed and the peaches ripened on the wall and the soft pink of the lavender-hedge was just beginning to attract the bees. But here was a triumph, too, for Mabel. Instinct would have disclosed to her the flattering cause of Burne-Jones's change of mind. She it was who had brought about this swift, unexpected and even inconvenient offer of hospitality on the part of London's leading Beauty-fancier.

It could well have been on Sunday 12 July 1891, precisely, that Mabel, not quite come of age, formed as strong a determination as her brother to see their present circumstances altered for the better.

And what were these circumstances? The facts are maddeningly few and far between. What school had she attended as a child? If convenient proximity to the grandparents' house governed the choice of Brighton Grammar School for Aubrey (why, otherwise, was he not sent to Brighton College?), then similar considerations may have resulted in Mabel's going to a 'ladies' school' at 7 Alexandra Villas, only a few minutes' walk from the Surgeon-Major's house. In 1884–5, when Aubrey was still a day-boy in Buckingham Road and he and Mabel were staying with their aunt, the arrangement would have permitted him, during the early winter evenings, to escort his sister back to Lower Rock Gardens on the other side of the town. While a boarder at the Grammar School, Aubrey wrote two disagreeably facetious 'love-letters' to a girl called Miss Felton. One of them concludes, in verse-form:

Whilst this letter is flying
With rapture I'm crying;
Don't show this, I beg you, to dear Betsy Topp.[22]

We now discover that a Miss (Mary) Topp was Headmistress of the Alexandra Villas school at the time. As unmarried sisters commonly joined forces in such ventures, what is more likely than that 'Betsy' was the disciplinarian of the two? Where does Mabel come into this? It is easier for a boy to strike up acquaintance with a girl at his sister's school. The letters themselves could well be a joke, inflicted on the innocent Miss Felton by Aubrey and Mabel, tormentors working in concert.

But if Mabel commenced her education as a pupil of Miss Topp's, it seems probable that she went on to some more sophisticated establishment; for she succeeded ultimately in winning a fifth place in all England in the Cambridge University 'Local' Examination. When Miss Gladstone offered her a scholarship at Newnham, however, she declined it.[23] Money was tight, no doubt, and for the time being she shelved her ambition to become an actress and took up teaching.

Five

It happens that one of her colleagues at the rather dismal Polytechnic School for Girls in Langham Place was Netta Syrett.
Mabel, in Miss Syrett's eyes, promised little out of the ordinary:
'She was a rather big girl, with a good erect figure. She held
herself well, but she could scarcely be called pretty. Her hair was
red, the kind of red usually described as "ginger", and she had a
nice pink-and-white, slightly freckled complexion.'[24] A pink-and-
white complexion, *freckles*—these were attributes hardly suited to
Aubrey's sister in her future role as consort of the 'Fra Angelico
of Satanism'!*

Still, the Polytechnic's Second Mistress goes on to concede, one
was always struck by Mabel's 'charming courtesy' of manner. The
pupils, daughters of the small shopkeepers of Regent Street and
Oxford Circus, were certainly impressed; yet had their reservations, too. As one of them explained to Miss Syrett: 'Miss
Beardsley is awfully nice to us. But you like to teach us, and she
doesn't.'[25] Mabel's colleague lived in the Victoria area and often
found herself travelling to and from Langham Place on the same
omnibus. Occasionally she was invited to 59 Charlwood Street,
where she met Aubrey, then in his eighteenth or nineteenth year,
'a very slight, thin youth, with the most curious face I have ever
seen.' He was still drooping on a stool at the Fire Office, and the
name Beardsley meant nothing as yet. Though Netta Syrett would
herself soon be contributing to the lighter literature of the time in
a spirit mildly *fin de siècle*, she was obviously less well acquainted
with the vagaries of love than Mabel. Her feelings towards the
Headmistress of the Polytechnic School for Girls, for instance, had
'held more than a tinge of repulsion', though she was the object of
much solicitude from that quarter. Miss Syrett's worries about this
relationship were only relieved when 'Mabel gave me a reason for
it'.[26]

Spending a great deal of time with her brilliant, restless brother
and sharing his exalted notion of their destiny, Mabel could
hardly be expected to have derived full or permanent satisfaction from teaching. She had by no means given up the idea of a

*Roger Fry in *The Athenaeum*, 1904: the article was reprinted in *Vision and Design*.

career in the theatre, but that was not yet a practical proposition. For the moment she made do with taking prayers: 'It gives me an opportunity to practise my stage walk and diction.'[27] Some undeniable affectation seems to have been part of Mabel's character from very early days, a 'grand manner' no sooner smiled at than forgiven by her admirers, but not much to the taste of the more philistine. That she was briefed to lecture Netta Syrett, herself in many respects quite an emancipated girl, on the topic of lesbianism suggests that at Charlwood Street few subjects were taboo between herself and her brother; and the imparting of such information to her girl friends seems much of a piece with Aubrey's own lordly views on woman as one's willing prey.

Six

Nothing of this, all the same, prepares us for the anecdote concerning Aubrey and Mabel related by Frank Harris in *My Life and Loves*. Like Raffalovich, Harris is supposed to have met Mabel before he encountered her brother, on whom he comments with some severity in another work, his entertaining and unreliable *Oscar Wilde*. Lord Alfred Douglas once reproved this author for falsifying with many a circumstantial flourish a conversation he had not heard, in a club he had never entered. Harris's inventive 'verbatim', as sounder witnesses than the estranged Douglas have confirmed, is least to be trusted when given something like an exact date, time and place. The passage in *My Life and Loves* runs as follows:

One afternoon about 1890, Aubrey Beardsley and his sister Mabel, a very pretty girl, had been lunching with me in Park Lane. Afterwards we went into the Park, and I accompanied them as far as Hyde Park Corner. For some reason or other I elaborated the theme that men of thirty or forty usually corrupted young girls, and women of thirty or forty corrupted youths.

'I don't agree with you,' Aubrey remarked. 'It's usually a fellow's sister who gives him his first lessons in sex. I know it was Mabel here who first taught me.'

I was amazed at his outspokenness. Mabel flushed crimson and I hastened to add:

'In childhood girls are far more precocious. But these little lessons are usually too early to matter.' He wouldn't have it, but I changed the subject resolutely and Mabel told me some time afterwards that she was very grateful to me for cutting short the discussion. 'Aubrey,' she said, 'loves all sex things and doesn't care what he says or does.'

Harris goes on:

I had seen before that Mabel was pretty. I realized that day when she stooped over a flower that her figure was beautifully slight and round. Aubrey caught my eye at the moment and remarked maliciously, 'Mabel was my first model, weren't you, Mabs? I was in love with her figure,' he went on judicially. 'Her breasts were so high and firm and round that I took her as my ideal.' She laughed, blushing a little, and rejoined, 'Your figures, Aubrey, are not exactly ideal.'[28]

As I have been at pains to remind the reader, Harris was a congenital liar (Shaw had reasons of his own for calling him unpalatably outspoken, rather than untruthful), and it is, of course, very much open to doubt whether any such conversation ever took place. The text is suspect, to say the least. The stooping Mabel ('slight and round' at just about the time Miss Syrett found her 'rather big') strikes one as an image straight from the pierhead slot-machine. Aubrey, to judge by the evidence, never talked in this manner, nor called his sister 'Mabs', though in some of the letters she becomes 'Ma', (pronounced 'May'). No: it is Harris's voice, breezy or stilted, that booms throughout. His are the clichés and the semi-jocular thrust of the elbow in one's ribs.

The author of *My Life and Loves* (1923–1927) appears to have begun by working out his theme—the sexual impulse, from first glimmer to final refinement—in the abstract, as it were; then gone on to select suitable exponents of the listed practice. At this stage (early in Volume I) something startling in the way of incest was required. What better pair to act the part than the precocious Beardsleys? Both were safely dead and could enter no protest, exact no retribution. As for the public, it would not fail to accept this flouting of the Levitical decree as a natural preamble to the disturbing art of *The Yellow Book*. Indeed, even though Aubrey's 'confession'—if it were ever made—might refer to some childish escapade in a very distant past, and though the source is in a dozen ways disreputable, the seed of suspicion has been planted in our minds. *Pas de fumé sans feu.* In a letter to Reggie Turner, Max Beerbohm once wrote: 'The Beardsleys are becoming suspect.'[29] What did he mean? I have put the question to Lord David Cecil, who must be as sensitive to Maxian nuances as anyone, and to Mr Henry Maas, who has plunged deepest into the Beardsleys' own correspondence. But as the word 'suspect' never recurs in this or any related context, no definite answer is forthcoming. Rumour, all the same, is not easily scotched.

Seven

How likely or unlikely is the idea of incest in itself?

If there is a fact we can establish, it is that, precocious in most things, both young people were also sexually curious beyond their years. Consider Miss Syrett's Mabel, readily proffering advice on a subject never discussed among girls of their (or perhaps any) class in late-Victorian England; while Aubrey, not long from school, adopted among his callower peers the somewhat similar role of sexual sophisticate. It is not much, but a step in the direction—of what exactly? *Wish, situation, or complex and actual performance?*—I borrow the phraseology from Eugen Kahn. The literature on the subject is neither considerable nor particularly helpful. Parties to incest have never had any inclination to rush into print—nor, in the main, have they been equipped to do so. Scientific papers suffer from the restricted social groups studied, in which overcrowding, low intelligence and alcoholism play too decisive a part. Of the cases investigated, the clinical majority involve father and daughter relationships. Since Oedipus tore his eyes out, few of us have risked marital-type partnerships with our mothers, though, following Freud's experience in a Vienna hotel, we have not been allowed to forget that this was a passion we were ready to succumb to at the earliest stage. Let us be warned further by one of Dr Legrand du Saulle's cases, a son whose mother became his mistress: the young man, in close confinement at Bicêtre, hanged himself.[30]

With siblings, we are told, the situation is altogether more relaxed. For when young, it appears, they are no more dismayed by *Inzest-Scheu* than by other adult anxieties. What was good enough for the Greek gods and the Ptolemaic dynasty in Egypt is good enough for them. A writer in *The Psychiatric Quarterly*, in 1963, confessed that he had known 'a good many incestuous brothers and sisters. None ever committed suicide. Few even knew they were supposed to be bothered by feelings of guilt. No doubt some are. They are also bothered by other things—such as cockroaches.'[31] All the same, 1963 is not 1883, nor even 1893, and environment is as likely to be the deciding factor in incest as it is in other deviations from the norm. One has to bear in mind the difference between life in a modern American slum and that in seedy, but still middle-class, end-of-the-century Pimlico.

Another problem is presented by the Biblical clause. Leviticus excuses no misunderstanding on this particular statute, in which the children of Israel are to walk: 'The nakedness of thy sister, the daughter of thy father, or the daughter of thy mother, whether born at home, or born abroad, even their nakedness thou shalt not uncover.' The young Beardsleys knew their Bible—and their prayer-book, which contains, of course, its own table of consanguinity. Whereas in the teeming, moronic, alcoholic ambience of the slum such niceties might get overlooked, in Charlwood Street, within sobering earshot of the bells of St Barnabas and its Chapel-of-Ease, there could have been no forgetting the judgments of the Lord.

We have seen the protective influence of religion at hand throughout the growing-up of Aubrey and Mabel. Now on quiet pavements between Ebury Bridge and St George's Drive they could hardly stroll two hundred yards without running into a friendly, cassocked figure—Becker's, D'Arcy's, Maturin's, Blacker's—hurrying about his godly business. In a photograph, I count no less than nine assistant clergymen gathered round the short, yet commanding person of their Vicar, where a Glastonbury thorn enwreathes the sunny porch of the Parsonage. And in Alfred Gurney, brother and sister possessed, surely, a spiritual father— unlike the defaulting Vincent Paul Beardsley—really strong to save. Or can it be that his aesthetic sympathies had somehow enfeebled the man of God? Had he sufficient of the rude energy of one of those Knights Templar, in whose expensive, shining armour he once appeared at a children's party?[32] Perhaps St Francis was right to fear lest art, through wealth, drive out religion. One can end by failing to see the Cross for the elaborately jewelled and painted crucifix. Too much lingering in the rarified air of the Uffizi and the Grange, Fulham; too much, too splendid, music; altogether an overplus of symbols, visual, auditory, even olfactory, of the Divine: the logic, alas, of Matthew XIX, 23, 24, is remorseless. To Father Gurney, well protected against the harsher facts of life himself, the young Beardsleys must have seemed a pair of cherubs.

Eight

These close companions had been brought closer still by the excitement of the *Morte Darthur* commission in the autumn of 1892. We have it on Ross's authority that Aubrey did not discuss his withdrawal from the Fire Office with either parent.[33] It was Mabel who advised him to launch out on his own: Aubrey took her advice, and a new life began for both of them, since before long Mabel was to give up her humdrum job for a career in the theatre.

Aubrey's affection for Mabel may have been brotherly and nothing more. I have myself passed through a stage when a suggestion to the contrary seemed ludicrous. Since 1966, however, anyone discussing Aubrey's life and art must take account of the possibility of incest. It was in that year that Mr Brian Reade staged his splendid Beardsley exhibition at the Victoria and Albert Museum, and the question came up of the identity of a certain portrait.[34] According to the late Lord Tredegar,* the sitter's name was Watkins, a young man born about 1892 who had spent his life in Paris. Lord Tredegar appears to have been mistaken, but it was in connexion with the supposed portrait of 'Mr Watkins' that 'some probability of intimacy between Mabel and Aubrey Beardsley' was first officially put forward.[35] 'There is also,' and I quote Mr Reade again, in a letter on the subject addressed to me, 'a legend, still maintained in the hearsay of living persons, that

*The fourth Baron (1893–1949).

Aubrey was fully incestuous; also that he boasted of this.' In Mr Reade's view: 'What is beyond doubt, I would say, is that there is enough internal evidence to suggest at the least subjective incest (so to speak), and from a psychological viewpoint this should not be ignored.'[36]

The fact is, there are several problems requiring a solution, and I propose to take them chronologically. In 1893 and 1894 Dent published three volumes of *Bon-Mots* (by Sydney Smith and Sheridan; Lamb and Douglas Jerrold; and Samuel Foote and Theodore Hook), for which Aubrey provided the illustrations. This was one of the commissions which enabled him to give up his insurance post, and he was in process of finishing sixty of these little grotesques by the autumn of 1892. The publisher allowed him every liberty. He could decorate the page as he wished. This makes the more remarkable his constant harping upon one particular and unexpected theme. Original in so much, Aubrey seems to have been the first artist to single out and elaborate the subject of the unborn—unborn or aborted?—child. Embryos appear in the drawings projected for *Lucian's True History*, which Lawrence and Bullen gave him to illustrate on the 9 December 1892 (Fig. 75). They continue over 1893, both in the Lucian work and in further *Bon-Mots* designs (Fig. 76). And, perhaps the most remarkable example of all, 'Incipit Vita Nova' (Fig. 77), has been given an estimated date of *c*. 1893. Embryonic subjects which appear in the magazine *St Paul's* in 1895 are from drawings actually made in 1893, and Aubrey's creative interest in the theme—though an echo of it occurs in the front cover for *The Savoy*, No. 2, as late as March 1896 ('The little creature handing hats', he tells Smithers, 'is *not* an infant but a strangled abortion')[37] —seems to have been exhausted by the end of that year.

Wherever it might lead us, we should, I think, find ourselves obliged to regard this recurring embryo-motif as a clue not to be neglected. Why did Aubrey lavish such attention on it? Why was that attention concentrated into the short period from late 1892 to mid(?)-1893? I return once more to the pioneer study Mr Reade has made of this particular subject, which he had an opportunity of developing further in his book, *Aubrey Beardsley*, published in the year following the Victoria and Albert Museum exhibition of

75 Design for illustration, *Lucian's True History* (published in *An Issue of Five Drawings illustrative of Juvenal and Lucian*, 1906), featuring an embryo.

1966. But, as sometimes happens when one is dealing with comparatively recent events, the historian in this instance found his hands tied. The information came to him that an illegitimate child

76 a, b   Two vignettes from *Bon-Mots* (Smith and Sheridan), published 1893, showing embryos, and including an abortionist.

was born to Mabel: but his informant would allow nothing more than the fact itself to be made public. No evidence as to the nature of the 'birth' is forthcoming. We glean, however, that Aubrey was not the father.[38]

Is the embryo-motif to be connected with the birth of a child to Mabel? The question has been raised, and an answer must at least be hazarded. First, perhaps, some alternatives may be passed in review. A theme that appears startlingly novel and personal in one artist's work may often turn out to be the invention of another. The embryo pictorialized puts us immediately in mind of one of the most distinguished figures in the Symbolist movement, Edvard Munch,* by nearly ten years Aubrey's senior. There are, indeed, some parallels here. Dominant, entangling, vampiric women are common to the work of both, for instance. And it is remarkable that Munch should have produced his first version of 'Madonna', with its representation of an embryo and a border-design of tadpole-like spermatozoa, in 1893 (Fig. 78). The satire—though, as always, gloomier—is quite in Aubrey's vein, too. This is the painting at Göteborg. There is another version, of 1894, in the National Gallery at Oslo, and a black 'key' for the celebrated colour-lithograph of the same subject followed in 1895.

If 'Madonna' had been one of the pictures Munch showed at the Berlin Künstlerverein in 1892, we might have been able to trace some connexion with what Aubrey was currently engaged upon. Ideas are detached and parachuted off on every wind that blows,

*Edvard Munch (1863–1944), again like Aubrey, was influenced by Toulouse-Lautrec.

and there is no knowing but that one of these ideas—from Paris, the Riviera, Italy, Germany, or wherever Munch happened to be during the restless years 1889–92—landed like a passus of the dandelion on the English artist's drawing-table, before he actually

77   Incipit Vita Nova: embryo design *c*. 1893.

dipped his pen in the ink to begin on the first embryo-motif for the *Bon-Mots*. Though, personally, I think the dates are 'wrong', or too speculatively tight for manoeuvre here, let us go on keeping the Norwegian painter in mind. Remarkably enough, Munch was the son, as Aubrey was the grandson, of an Army surgeon. In the houses of both Christian Munch in Oslo and William Pitt in Brighton there must have been a library of standard medical works. Wilhelm His published an engraving of an eight-weeks-old embryo in Vol. III of his *Anatomie menschlicher Embryonen* in 1885: this was later to appear in *Gray's Anatomy* (Fig. 79). I mention it not only as a striking image that might well have caught both Munch's and Aubrey's eye, but because, so a consultant paediatrician assures me, Aubrey's embryos in general approximate to this same length of gestation. Gray's did not take over the German engraving

78   Edvard Munch (1863–1944), 'Madonna'. The
black 'key' for this colour-lithograph was drawn in
1895: it is thus later by a couple of years than
Aubrey's embryo designs. The spermatozoa border,
however, is an original touch Aubrey might have
envied.

till 1909, but wherever Aubrey studied the subject, in whatever
publications between 1885 and 1895, the influence of His would
have been paramount. And we need not quite abandon the more
picturesque fancy of an Aubrey and Mabel let loose in the Surgeon-
Major's library, as children, tracing from the old books there the
formation of the vitelline duct and the first budding of the limbs.
Both had extraordinarily inquisitive and receptive intelligences.
If, as her mother reported of Mabel, one can read and reject
Carlyle for his cavalier treatment of syntax at the age of six, a
textbook of systematic anatomy should not try one too hard at
eleven or twelve. And the images would have impressed themselves indelibly upon Aubrey's imagination, to be returned to and

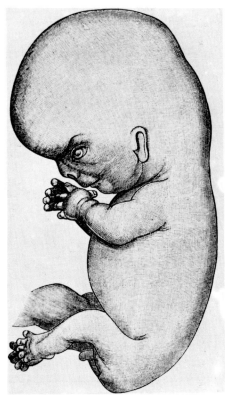

79   Human embryo about 23 mm (head to rump) and about $8\frac{1}{2}$ weeks old. This engraving appeared first in Wilhelm His's *Anatomie menschlicher Embryonen*, 1885, and later in *Gray's Anatomy* (17th edn.). Both Munch and Aubrey could have been influenced by His's important work in embryology, especially as medical books were available to both artists in their early youth.

made use of when, years later, the cathartic moment came.

Another possible explanation for the appearance of the embryo in Aubrey's work has to do with the persistence of certain infantile attitudes into adult life peculiar, so some recent research suggests, to tuberculosis subjects. Saul and Lyons, after a psycho-analytical study of a small series without controls, concluded that the frustration, anger and guilt shown by their patients sprang from a wish to return to a state in which the respiratory tract is not used for breathing, a wish, therefore, to return to the uterus.[39] Would late 1892 have been the time for Aubrey to begin expressing this subconscious yearning for the womb? Certainly, he could write to King on 9 December: 'I've been horribly ill this year.'[40] On the other hand, late 1892 found him in the highest spirits at the thought of having thrown off the yoke of the insurance office. I must add that these alternative considerations are reflected in the conflicting views of experts I have consulted on the point: one enthusiastically espousing the idea of the self-identifying embryo; another, at mention of it, glancing significantly at his wastepaper-basket!

Nine

We come back, then, to the embryo as token of Mabel's indiscretion. Such a theory will plague us with endless knots and knags but, for all that, we must risk splitting our nails on some of them.

The question has been asked: was Aubrey present at his sister's miscarriage or abortion?[41] This would account, it is suggested, for the vivid impression (later translating itself into pen-and-ink renderings) of the eight-weeks embryo gazing accusingly up at him under its formidable, bulging cranium. One might think there is too much of *grand guignol* here: an embryo of that duration reaches a maximum of twenty-three millimetres' growth and Aubrey would have had to bring a magnifying-glass to it. On the other hand, he could have been strong-stomached enough to carry off this inch of gory gristle and drop it into a bottle of formalin, to be *lovingly* (I use the word advisedly: we are talking about a very unusual young man) preserved in a dark corner of his wardrobe, taken out and re-studied as he worked his way through the *Bon-Mots* commission. I could better accept the idea of Aubrey's presence at his sister's miscarriage or abortion, had he been her partner in this particular affair: which we are informed he was not. And whatever strange secrets 59 Charlwood Street may hide, and even if the pen-drawn embryos refer after all to the artist's incest, I still find it easier to believe that their direct inspiration was a plate in a medical work rather than a pickled homuncule.

But much more difficult to accommodate than the petty details is the psychological attitude of the brother. We do not need informants, named or anonymous, to tell us that Aubrey deeply and incontrovertibly loved Mabel from the beginning of his life to its end. If, in 1892 (the favoured date), she gave birth to an illegitimate child, or had a miscarriage, or a child was aborted, would he have wished to draw attention to the event? Is not the satirical treatment of the embryo, supposing this situation obtained, an even unkinder cut? What could the joking achieve but Mabel's unhappiness? The only possible reason for Aubrey's reminding her of her peccadillo would have been to hurt her. We must, then, assume that he himself was hurt, and bitterly hurt, by what had happened: a situation which, given the preternatural closeness of brother to sister, is certainly understandable. He was wreaking his vengeance. Yet it was an indiscreet game to play for a member of the gossipy *Cénacle*. And if hints of Mabel's illegitimate child got round, what about her teaching post? Can this be the same Aubrey who had spoken with pleasurable anticipation of her promotion to headmistress?[42]

Let us look again at the embryos. They do not really accord with the notion of a bitterly rebuking brother. And would not the most natural assumption be that, like the artist, Mabel, too, regarded the little monster of the 'Incipit Vita Nova' with amusement? A comic interpretation certainly seems simpler: and what is simpler is likelier. In 1892–3, Aubrey, then, was most probably sharing a joke about embryos with his sister. Perhaps we can leave it at that for the moment.

Ten

There was assuredly no bad blood between them when, in 1893, Charlwood Street was left behind and they moved to 114 Cambridge Street. It has sometimes been said that Aubrey and Mabel shared the lease of this house: in fact, Aubrey made No. 114 over to Mabel, as sole owner.[43]

His sister played her part in all Aubrey's activities. When, with more commodious premises for it, they began to entertain, Mabel acted as hostess. She was present at that most momentous event at the end of 1893: 'I well remember the occasion when *The Yellow Book* was inaugurated,' she said subsequently. 'There were four of us—Mr and Mrs Harland, Aubrey and myself. It struck us that a new magazine would be a desirable thing, and so we all talked about it; perhaps we talked simultaneously, I am not sure. Should it be daily, monthly or quarterly, and what title? It was the last Sunday of the old year (1893) that this and other momentous matters concerning *The Yellow Book* were decided.'[44] It continued to be a temptation to all who had been friendly with Aubrey to declare their presence at this critical juncture. Lane, according to himself, was there. MacColl speaks of the question being broached in blazing summer at Dieppe. Miss Syrett recollects that the initial discussion (in her presence, of course) whiled away a wet afternoon in the Cromwell Road. Still, there is no doubt that Mabel was very much at the centre of affairs.

The year 1894 held other excitements for her than the appearance in April of *The Yellow Book*. It was at the end of the summer term that she took the plunge and left the Polytechnic School. Her destination, as we have noted, was to be the theatre. It seems that the recitations she gave as a child had continued throughout her teens under the able supervision of her mother. 'Sometimes,' recalled Ellen, 'we would both get so worked up over something that we would cry in each other's arms, and then dry our eyes and go on again.'[45] In 1892 Ida North had created the role of the Moon Maiden in Dowson's *Pierrot of the Minute*, and it was in this piece (afterwards published with Aubrey's illustrations) that Mabel, we are told, first tried out her wings as an actress.

She made her professional début on 3 September 1894, at the Assembly Rooms, Malvern. The piece was a touring company's version of *A Woman of No Importance*, produced originally by Tree at the Haymarket Theatre in 1893. Ellen came home from Woking (following the unhappy stay at Haslemere with Aubrey) in time for Mabel's last rehearsal in London, on which she commented to Ross:

She did her part admirably, but oh! the Company! Such very extraordinary people. I picked up my skirts and sat gingerly on a rather dirty bench at the back of the stage looking on at the performance. Determined to do my duty bravely I beamed with smiles at all of them though I never quite discovered who was who. The man I thought was the carpenter turned out to be the Archdeacon in the piece [T. N. Walter played the Ven. Archdeacon Daubeny, D.D.] and a stout motherly-looking person who I thought would be kind to Mabel and fasten up her frocks and so on, proved to be Lady Somebody [probably Lady Caroline Pontefract, played by Mrs Henry Kitts]. Nothing surprised me by the time it was over, and as the children had given me strict orders not to be depressing before I went, I pretended to be quite charmed with everything and everybody, though it was borne in upon me more than ever that my spirited offspring certainly supply me with a perpetual series of little shocks. I went to Paddington to see Mabel off for Malvern on Saturday, and encountered the Company again, and since then I have had two letters from her, the last telling me of her début on Monday night. She speaks very humbly about herself, says she wasn't nervous and that she thinks she did well. The great thing is that she seems well and happy.[46]

We might be surprised by the condescending manner in which Ellen alludes to one of Beerbohm Tree's* companies, rehearsed by him at The Haymarket, directed on the road by the respectable partnership of Morrell and Mouillot and led by an actor and actress of high standing, H. B. Conway and Miss Lingard. And was there nothing to be said in favour of the play itself? Wilde's *A Woman of No Importance* acts well and is witty enough. In its day, and before disaster overtook the author in April 1895, it was even considered a vehicle of lofty moral purpose: the Revd C. F. Aked, a Liverpool Nonconformist minister, had been sufficiently impressed to write of it: 'I am prepared to greet Mr Oscar Wilde as one of high rank among the foremost preachers of the day.'[47] Yet Ellen could only mock what she makes seem more like a scene from *Roscius Daggerwood* presented by Mr Crummles. Perhaps one may draw two, or even three, conclusions. In the first place, she seems always to have held Wilde in strong dislike (particularly resenting the common notion that Aubrey was his equivalent in the field of art). Secondly, there is apparent, in spite of the rising social status of the 'Profession', some affront to Pitt family pretensions. But the chief reason for her denigration of everything and everybody concerned would have been the great objection she had to her daughter's choosing this particular career.

*Herbert Beerbohm Tree (Herbert Draper Beerbohm 1853–1917), half-brother of Max Beerbohm and the most celebrated actor-manager of his day.

I am only surprised she didn't lament Mabel's initiation in the role of Lady Stutfield. Of all Wilde's walking echoes, this is the most dismal: an extremely ungrateful part to play, the painfully unnatural opposite of 'painfully natural' Hester, a stereotype of fatuity, a prime example of what Lord Illingworth called the 'triumph of matter over mind'. Was this unfortunate casting of Mabel as the shallow, twittering woman of fashion in drawing-room comedy, so frequent from now on, an unconscious recognition by Tree and others of the tinsel in her off-stage personality?

Eleven

Towards the end of 1894, when she was varying three-night stands in the provinces with periods as understudy and 'extra lady' under Tree at The Haymarket, Aubrey produced a particularly beautiful drawing entitled 'The Mysterious Rose Garden' (Fig. 80). It began as a straightforward Annunciation: for the flowered trellis clearly represents the garden enclosed by a hedge of roses, the *hortus conclusus* of the Canticles, whither the Celestial Messenger has arrived to inform Mary of her destiny.

Although the variations to which this theme has been susceptible, even in the Age of Faith, are well-nigh countless (by some Fathers it was presumed that the Annunciation took place just after sunset, at the tolling of the Angelus; by others, at midnight, to accord with the hour of the Nativity), Aubrey introduced, as we should expect, some remarkable changes of his own. Gabriel, though wearing an ample acolyte's robe and carrying the customary wand, is equipped, not with angel's wings, but with the winged shoes of the pagan Hermes. He bears a lanthorn, whose illusion of glowing light is one of penmanship's historic achievements. Less expectedly, he is moustached like a Knave of Hearts, and appears to whisper behind his hand, rather than proclaim aloud, the *Ave Maria*. The Madonna herself is naked. This, it may have been, led well-wishers to persuade him to exclude the word 'Annunciation' from his title. But there is no immodesty in the nakedness of Mary (if it *is* Mary Virgin); and nothing in the work as a whole, a first glance would suggest, to require for it meanings alien to its own presumed subject.

Obviously, Aubrey's variants on any given topic might be

80 'The Mysterious Rose Garden'. Is there a reference here to Mabel? A card sent by her to Ross, postmarked 1894 (month illegible) and hitherto unpublished, informs him: 'Aubrey has done "The Annunciation" and wants to shew it you before he sends it off. . . .' Symons speaks of 'that terrible annunciation of evil which he [Aubrey] called *The Mysterious Rose-Garden*, where the lantern-bearing angel with winged sandals whispers of more than "pleasant sins".'

infinite—and infinitely astonishing. One interpretation of this work, to which I am coming shortly, is erotic, blasphemous. We must find ourselves asking the question from time to time: is too little account taken of so many long years of devout church-going? For the church-going had not stopped. And I have thought it at least a blasphemy out of the ordinary that the theme selected for the purpose of shocking the faithful should be the Annunciation. The central panel of the little Brighton church's east window, wherein is set the dusky-blue version by Rossetti, could have been often enough in Aubrey's mind. But when this drawing was composed, the Beardsleys were living at 114 Cambridge Street (Fig. 8).

81   114 Cambridge Street, Pimlico: leased in Mabel's name from late 1893 to the early summer of 1895. It was the only real home—as distinct from lodgings or rooms in boarding-houses—that the artist ever knew.

As he stepped out of his front-door, between the free-standing columns of the portico with their quasi-Ionic capitals, he would face directly across the street the Church of St Gabriel's, Pimlico (consecrated 1853). Here was a daily reminder of the respect due to the Angel of the Annunciation.

To throw off light-hearted (if still scandalous) extemporizations on the story of Salome, whose name does not actually occur in the Scriptures, is a different matter from setting out in cold blood to parody one of the two most solemn incidents in the whole Christian story. It is easy for a modern agnostic to relate the Virgin Birth to the routine begetting of bastards: but would this have been an easy thing for Aubrey, the friend of Alfred Gurney, to do? If we accept with some critics that 'The Mysterious Rose Garden' is an intentional parody (it could be an unintentional parody) of the interview between Mary and the Archangel; that it portrays a spoiled virgin suddenly apprised of her awkward situation and stunned by the prospect of all the shame and subterfuge ahead;[48] then, once again, the possibility of a reference to Mabel has to be considered.

We are back, in fact, to the circular discussion of the embryo-motifs of 1892–3. Has Aubrey deeply resented the birth of Mabel's illegitimate child, and once more drawn attention to it? The obstacle to this idea of a resentful Aubrey, when we discussed the embryos, was that no resentment was conveyed—nor, therefore, presumably felt—in the actual drawing of the creatures. And I think that obstacle is still with us, when we examine the charming, dreamy composition of 'The Mysterious Rose Garden'. What conclusions can we come to, if the embryos implicate Mabel and if the Annunciation theme is also dedicated to her, but in both instances without anger? For me, this would be tantamount to assuming a relationship between brother and sister in which the spirit so transcended the body that Aubrey was pleased, rather than displeased, at Mabel's proof of womanhood, that what had occurred with a man unnamed (whose identity is now known to me, but under the same conditions of secrecy which, as I pointed out earlier, governed Mr Reade), failed completely to sever the original bond.

Twelve

One of the reasons that have led critics to identify the naked
figure of the girl in 'The Mysterious Rose Garden' with Mabel is
the existence of another nude, similar in type, now for many years
identified as the artist's sister. This nude occurs in an earlier
design of 1894, the frontispiece to the *Plays* of John Davidson,*
an equally fine example of the artist's work (Fig. 82).

The history of the identification is of interest, offering its own
warnings about the difficulty of making precise statements on such
a matter. On 1 March 1894, Aubrey wrote to the Editor of the
Daily Chronicle:

> In your review of Mr Davidson's plays, I find myself convicted
> of an error of taste, for having introduced portraits into my
> frontispiece to that book. I cannot help feeling that your
> reviewer is unduly severe. One of the gentlemen who form part
> of my decoration is surely beautiful enough to stand the test
> even of portraiture, the other owes me half a crown.[49]

In the paper's issue of the 1st, the reviewer's regrets had been
occasioned by the introduction of 'one or two well-known faces of
the day' into the design. Aubrey himself makes clear that one of
these two well-known persons was Sir Augustus Harris,† the
impresario, with whom he had had a disagreement about a seat at
Covent Garden. This, as may be readily verified from contemporary photographs, is the central figure in dress-clothes. Nor,
with the hint given in his letter and its likeness to the *Salome*
caricatures of Wilde, could there be any doubt about the identification of the vine-wreathed personage to the immediate left of
Augustus Harris. To 'put vine-leaves in one's hair' was besides,
Cénacle slang. Max observed 'rich clusters' in Oscar's hair (when
Aubrey, painfully sober, had been a member of the party) just
three months before this drawing was actually carried out.[50] 'The
subjects of Beardsley's two portraits,' Lane confirms, ten years
later, in his Publisher's Note of 1903, to *Under the Hill*, 'were
Mr Wilde and Sir Augustus Harris.'[51] In his List, published with

*1857–1909, poet who died by his own hand.
†1851–96, knighted as a Sheriff of the City of London. He appears to have been in
management at Covent Garden, when Aubrey failed to get a seat after paying his half-crown.

82 Frontispiece from John Davidson's *Plays*, published in 1894
(drawing completed by November 1893). The nude girl has long
(mistakenly?) been identified as Mabel Beardsley. The other figures,
left to right, are said to represent Henry Harland, Oscar Wilde, Sir
Augustus Harris, Richard Le Gallienne and Adeline Genée.

Ross's *Aubrey Beardsley* in 1909, Aymer Vallance adds, as further
identifiable, Henry Harland (the faun); though Mr Reade thinks
this could be a self-caricature, as indeed the prominent ears might
be intended to suggest. On the other hand, Vallance knew Harland,
so it is difficult to understand why he should have made this claim
without some good reason. But if we follow that line of argument,
why didn't Vallance go further and identify at least the male
figure in the background? Mr Good kindly informs me that this
masked figure was still nameless in Walker's unpublished catalogue and bibliography, compiled mainly during the 1920s, and
in the Tate's 1924 Beardsley Exhibition catalogue, for which
Walker supplied the notes. By 1964, with the publication of the
Tate's Catalogue of *Modern British Paintings, Drawings and
Sculpture*, it is identified unequivocally as Richard Le Gallienne.
Yet surely Le Gallienne, regarded as a bad joke by the *Cénacle*, is
quite miscast as Harlequin? Nor does the man in the drawing bear
any likeness (masked, how can he?) to such photographs of the
poet as survive.

I do not want to weary the reader, but it seems to me important
to examine in some detail the credentials of these 'identified'
persons in a drawing which is held (in the Tate catalogue, as a
statement of fact) to include two more caricatures, one of Adeline
Genée,* the other of Mabel. Adeline Genée did not arrive in this
country till 1897, after Aubrey had ceased going to the theatre:
in 1893, she was still in Stettin and two years younger than Max's
adored Cissie Loftus, the 'child wonder', on *her* first appearance
at the Oxford. Miss Genée receives no mention in Aubrey's
letters, nor is there a direct sketch of her as there was (it perished
in Sampson's fire) of Ada Lundberg, whom Sickert also admired—
at the Marylebone Music-Hall. . . . Somewhat shaken in confidence
by this, let us leave the dancer and turn to the actress, Aubrey's
'sister', the nude girl, that is, linked with Wilde on the extreme
left of the frontispiece.

In his 1924 Tate Exhibition catalogue notes, Walker merely
stated: 'Of the two female figures, the one on the right was a
well-known dancer and that on the left a well-known actress.' But

*Miss Genée was ninety-three at the moment of my writing this.

his entry in his own unpublished catalogue and bibliography includes Mabel's name, added after the original note and in different ink. At some time in the 1920s, therefore, this piece of information came Walker's way, but very understandably he did not make it public, even after the proviso: 'the frontispiece is *supposed* to contain'. Very understandably, since this was during the lifetime of Ellen Beardsley (who survived till 1932); nor was he free to discuss what such an identification implied even as late as 1949, when he published his *Beardsley Miscellany*, for Ellen had been succeeded by Miss Lilian Dash as keeper of the family memorials, and she would not have permitted any theorizing to the discredit of Mabel.

If the theory that Mabel is Mary in 'The Mysterious Rose Garden' depends upon Mabel being the nude girl in the frontispiece to Davidson's *Plays* (because an 'identification' has been rather hastily accepted here, on grounds of physical and facial resemblance), then the artist's purpose is even more difficult to account for in the Davidson drawing than the later one. In 'The Mysterious Rose Garden', the theme, whether or not religious, is unworldly; its treatment delicate, dignified. The frontispiece, on the contrary, is strictly 1893: a world as sensual as Wilde and as vulgar as Augustus Harris can make it. The introduction of a nude, leering Mabel into the frontispiece, a Mabel dancing attendance on Wilde, is a very different affair from the idealized Mabel-if-Mabel of the neo-Annunciation. The story circulates (scandal, historians' after-dinner supposition?) that in the frontispiece Mabel is mocking Wilde, and that this drives home a trick she has played on him in real life: arousing his libido, during one of her transvestist adventures, then spurning him. And that the drawing expresses Aubrey's indignation at Wilde's bidding for Mabel's favours, even *en mascarade*. The legs of the playwright are seen as locked together by some kind of prickly thong: this to represent his heterosexual impotence. A wider range of Mabel's activities is read into Nos. II and III of 'The Comedy Ballet of Marionettes' which were published in July 1894 (in Volume II of *The Yellow Book*), belonging, therefore, to about the same period of composition as the two drawings we have been considering at such length. In 'The Comedy Ballet', the figure thought to represent Mabel shares antics with a lesbian, and between them, in No. III, they deceive the clumsy male lover wearing cuckold's horns (Fig. 83).[52]

What a labyrinth! And these daedalian paths may all originate from that one (suspect) passage in Frank Harris's *My Life and Loves*. Harris remains the single witness to any declaration on

83   The Comedy Ballet of Marionettes, III, from *The Yellow Book*, Volume II, July 1894.

Aubrey's part that he used Mabel as a nude model. That he did so is, even technically, difficult to accept. To my mind, transferring actual studies from life into the eclectic world of his art would have destroyed its scrupulous balance completely. Aubrey's vision, one would say, nourished itself on pictures in books, jointly with pictures stored in his head. There is no evidence that he appreciated or put to good use the life-classes at the Westminster School of Art. Nature was not in Aubrey's line: he preferred Mantegna, Dürer and Burne-Jones. Is it just that we cannot forget that slim piece of evidence passed on by Harris? We may be wholly deceiving ourselves in 'recognizing' Mabel in the expressionless Maid of 'The Mysterious Rose Garden' or the licentious bacchante of the frontispiece, either bodily or facially, quite apart from insisting upon turning two perhaps unrelated female figures into one.

Thirteen

Meanwhile, from late 1894, the subject of all these speculations was making a start in her new profession and bidding fair to become the 'Society beauty' which, according to Miss Syrett, had been her steadfast aim. A former tendency to plumpness gradually gave way to the slim and willowy figure which late-Victorian audiences admired. Her hair, once too pale a red for some people's taste, was helped to a Titian warmth. Even her eyes, the sharp Miss Syrett noted, seemed to grow larger and more brilliant.[53]

Like Aubrey, she had always been an enthusiastic playgoer and now, when not 'walking on' for Tree, enjoyed displaying her assiduously cultivated charms in Mrs Leverson's box or in the stalls. At the first night of Wilde's *An Ideal Husband*, for instance (a glittering occasion at The Haymarket—attended by the Prince of Wales—on 3 January 1895), a fashion correspondent perceived 'with special pleasure and a good deal of curiosity, Miss Beardsley, the sister of the astonishing artist of *The Yellow Book*'. She was, the correspondent added, an 'uncommonly pretty girl'.[54] And not without originality in her predilection for clashing reds, appearing, coppery-haired, in a pale mauve gown trimmed with bunches of pink heliotrope. Later, it would be a scarlet or wine-coloured dress, on the boldest occasions 'shrimp-pink'. Some reports scolded her for her eccentricity, others admired it. But from the first, like her brother, Mabel seems to have understood the importance of being noticed.

Could she, one wonders, have fulfilled the whole of her ambition and actually 'entered Society'? We shall never know, for the scandal that made the name of Wilde for long unmentionable besmirched that of Beardsley, too. Exactly three months after the first night of *An Ideal Husband*, the trial of its author opened at the Old Bailey. On the other hand, apart from dropping Wilde's name from their bills in certain instances, theatrical managers did not panic, and after Wilde's trial and sentence welcomed rather than regretted Mabel's blood-tie with a Decadent almost as notorious. She was kept busy throughout the latter part of the fateful year. And when Aubrey, Symons and Smithers began to plan a successor to *The Yellow Book*, it was Mabel, so she tells us, while spending a holiday with them in Dieppe, who chose *The Savoy* as its title.[55]

As Aubrey worked through his *annus mirabilis* of 1896, Mabel, in her different sphere, made progress, too. Under Arthur Bourchier's* management, she created the part of the flirtatious widow, Mrs Maydew, in *The Queen's Proctor* at The Royalty (Fig. 84); after that she played Edith in *Donna Diana* at The Prince of Wales. When the London theatrical season of 1896 came to an end, she accepted an invitation from Bourchier to go to the States and Canada. In Baltimore, on Violet Vanbrugh's falling sick, she briefly took over the leading role in *The Chili Widow*. Then, when the tour of this play had prematurely ended, she met C. B. Cochran, her brother's school-friend, at a supper party given by the celebrated American actor-manager, Richard Mansfield.† Cochran persuaded Mansfield to engage her, and relates: 'Mansfield was always telling Mabel Beardsley that she could not act; but he liked her, as she made his supper parties very agreeable.'[56] However, she seems to have done her best. In April 1897, in a newspaper review of Mansfield's production of

*Arthur Bourchier (1863–1927) was married to Violet Vanbrugh about the time of Mabel's début.

†1857–1907, known as the Irving of America. His production of *Arms and the Man* was America's first glimpse of Bernard Shaw.

Arms and the Man, we catch a glimpse of her, 'emotionful as Bernhardt'![57]

How did the inseparables face separation? For Aubrey, the pain of parting must have been in some degree alleviated by his hope

84   Mabel as Mrs Maydew in *The Queen's Proctor* at The Royalty Theatre, 1896. From a photograph in the Enthoven Collection, Victoria and Albert Museum.

and belief that the experience would be of value to Mabel in her career. What she meant to him is nowhere made more plain than in the short will he had drawn up on 17 July 1896, when he was staying at The Spread Eagle, Epsom, four months before her departure. In this document, witnessed by the hotel proprietor and Smithers, *everything* was left to Mabel, who was also appointed sole executrix. There is no mention of Ellen; none, more predictably, of his father. Towards the end of his time at Epsom, it was Mabel who went down to Boscombe and booked the rooms for Aubrey and her mother at Pier View. She was with them on their arrival on 12 August and the *List of Visitors and Residents at Bournemouth* (Boscombe supplement) shows that she remained at Pier View for a full month. Brother and sister would never again be able to spend as long together. On 15 November, he told Raffalovich: 'It is sad not to see Mabel before she starts for America. I envy her passage, boat life is so delightful.' And on the 17th: 'In the bay here, the sea is as smooth as a shirt front, so I wish Mabel could have started from Southampton. I do hope her crossing may be quiet and resting after all her hard work.'[58]

Her activities in America (and Canada) were followed by Aubrey, ever expecting great things of his sister as an actress, with intense interest. In his interview for *The Idler* which took place in December 1896, he took the opportunity of speaking about Mabel's part in *The Chili Widow* (by error, the reporter assumed she had been in the London production), and though the magazine had not been intending to offer the artist's sister a free advertisement, Aubrey saw to it that with the reproductions of his own drawings was included her latest photograph.[59] 'Is it not good news about Mabel?' he asked Raffalovich, on 1 February 1897, referring to the transfer to Mansfield's company. 'Though it is sad of course to think one will not see her for so long. Before June [her expected return] my lungs may have done dreadful things. Still I hope with much confidence now to see her again. A fortnight ago I really felt wretched over her delayed return. Dear girl, she would feel it dreadfully if she did not find me here when she came back.'[60]

As the weary days went by in Bournemouth, where Aubrey and his mother now hoped for nothing more than a move back to London, he had Mabel constantly in mind. He must get a little home for her once again. And it worried him that in her anxiety about his health she seemed always on the verge of throwing up her job and returning to England before her contract was completed. He was aghast at the amount of travelling involved in her tour with Mansfield, and this led him to wonder whether, after all,

it would not be better for her to return: she might collapse under
the strain. Her letters were his chief consolation, that March of
1897, when the blood was 'very obstinate' with him; all the more
so since Mabel herself could write of having 'such a good time'
and being a 'great success'. Yet a day or two later, she wired to ask
if she ought not to drop everything and rejoin him. Anxiously, he
assured her she must not give up her engagement on his account.
Soon, however, it was possible to start pencilling the days off the
calendar, as the end of their separation drew near. In April,
Aubrey was wondering whether the three of them might not be
able to share a small furnished house together, in France, for a
couple of months in the summer: he was now writing from the
Hôtel Voltaire. The Beardsleys, mother and son, were in St-
Germain, when Mabel at long last reached Liverpool on 2 June.
Two days later she was with them at the Pavillon Louis XIV.

Fourteen

In the normal course of research, I have read a great many letters
from writers and artists. Faced with another cardboard box, old
tea-chest or (in these scientific days) polythene bag, I regularly
feel hope born anew. Some masterpiece of self-expression,
equivalent to a poem or a painting by the same hand, will at last
reveal itself. It never does. I remember the *Peg's Paper* banality of
one letter written by a painter of high intelligence when he found
his life suddenly in ruins and wished to convey news of the
calamity to the woman for whom he had sacrificed everything.
Rare are the documents exchanged privately that confirm a man's
genius, or even a sensitivity above the average. In this, Aubrey
was no exception. His letters written to impress *are* impressive;
the rest have little to distinguish them beyond an occasional comic
archaism. There are rarely hints of the deepest human emotion:
never—perhaps none of Aubrey's correspondents was deemed
worthy of the privilege—a memorable confidence on the subject
of his love for Mabel. We need not feel surprised, therefore, that
the record of this all-important reunion of 4 June 1897 is set down,
if enthusiastically, in the most commonplace terms: 'Mabel's
arrival this morning was such a great surprise and such a great
pleasure for me. I think she looks wonderfully well considering all

her voyaging; and not changed at all since I saw her last,'—so Aubrey wrote to Raffalovich.[61] Not long after, we learn:

> This morning I communicated with Mabel at the Chapelle of the Pensionnat S. Thomas. It is such a dear little church, and the Mass was sung by the Pensionnaires really very well. The sisters are quite charming and looked after us so kindly. You can imagine how happy the service made both of us. I shall always attend S. Thomas's Chapel in future. The aumonier seems very nice, I believe he is coming to see us. He preached a short sermon this morning with a great deal of style and unction.
>
> Whit Sunday has filled the garden here with breakfasters, and the place looked so gay and pretty, the weather being quite adorable. I hardly ever go into the town but spend my time under the alleys, and amongst the rose trees of the Pavillon. It's so jolly having Mabel here.[62]

On the day she left (11 June) Aubrey wrote in very different vein to Smithers:

> I still continue to be fairly well but also continue to be hugely depressed. I would forgive this abject sort of life if I only made rapid progress towards recovery, but to go on month after month unable to turn my hand to anything is quite loathsome. . . . My sister has been and gone.[63]

If Raffalovich was his main confidant, where Mabel was concerned, there were other matters his dearest Brother was not to know of: when Aubrey decided that Ellen and he must learn German (to be able to read Wagner in the original?), he had to remind Mabel: '*Don't* by the way tell Raf of the lessons.' She could keep an eye on things for him—and call in unexpectedly on Smithers and see how the Royal Arcade shop was doing. For she was much in the West End from July, when she obtained a part in *Four Little Girls* at The Criterion. Now that Ellen and Aubrey were in Dieppe, he looked forward to Mabel's coming over for a week-end, but, afraid that invalid waywardness might prejudice his cause, looked to Raffalovich to put in a good word for him:

> I should much like Mabel to come over when she has time to spare. Still I am afraid she would get dreadfully bored with me

and my ways. Dear Mother I know has been sadly tried these
last few months. But Mabel will tell you how impossible I am
to get on with. And what can *you* think of me with all my
constant grumblings and changes of mind?[64]

Four Little Girls lasted a mere month at The Criterion. It was a
pity the family could not join up again for the rest of August and
September at the Hôtel Sandwich; but the play re-opened at The
Metropole, Denmark Hill. There was another problem: Mabel
had run short of money. Raffalovich explained this to Aubrey,
who replied, with touching humility, that he had not made
himself responsible for the ticket for fear that these visits to a
hopeless invalid might over-tax her nerves. Much relieved on
learning of the true state of affairs, he could now send her a 'little
cheque'.[65] A photograph, a 'small vague one of Mabel wandering
among the trees' was 'surely quite the prettiest thing the camera
has ever done', he wrote to Gray, thanking him for it on 23
August.[66] By then Mabel had already arrived in Dieppe, and
another idyll began. The Beardsleys moved now from the Hôtel
Sandwich to the Hôtel des Etrangers, in the rue d'Aguado, and in
the covered terrace here he was able to sit out most of the day with
his sister, in spite of persistent rain. The days were not long
enough, but there were seven of them, and when she left, Aubrey
had conquered his blue devils for the moment.

In November 1897 Mabel was engaged to take up Miss Annie
Hughes's part in *Oh, Susannah!* at The Royalty. It opened on the
30th, with a curtain-raiser, *A New Leaf*, in which she also played.
Aubrey wrote to her from Menton on the 24th: 'Your part in the
lever de rideau must be trying, but I suppose the piece is not
sufficiently well written to demand a very finished study of the
London tart. I wish I was at your side to give you some grandly
realistic tips.'[67] Facetiousness? Yet a strange echo from the past.
And, had it been badinage, an exclamation-mark was surely called
for. Was he not, half-humorously, half in earnest, hinting at the
specialized adventures they had shared?

The Royalty farce got good notices: 'I knew you would be a
great success,' wrote Aubrey, on 3 December. 'Dear child, she
does deserve to succeed,' he added, with less confidence, to
Raffalovich.[68] Alas, in spite of the good notices, the run of *Oh,*

Susannah! proved to be short-lived. Mabel began to dabble in journalism, applying to her brother for ideas when she was invited to join in a discussion on Bohemianism in *The Idler*. It was a struggle for him to write at all, in late January 1898, but his brief comments have the sound common sense Max admired in him: 'The more society relaxes the less charm and point there is in Bohemianism. Flourishes in France because society is so rigid. Will never quite die in England as it is the refuge and consolation of the unsuccessful. Young writers, painters, etc., in England are in such a hurry to *épater* the bourgeois and to "arrive", to separate themselves from one another rather than to herd together, and to appear quite "sérieux".'[69]

Incredible as it may appear to us, brother and sister were also discussing the foundation of a Catholic quarterly review, with Smithers (not yet approached) as prospective publisher. Interviewed in a journal called *The Rocket*, Mabel spoke of the quarterly's prospects with airy confidence. It is true that Aubrey had got as far as proposing illustrations for Robert Southwell's *Burning Babe*, but one feels that his entering into the idea of a new religious journal (to bear the most unlikely of publisher's imprints) may have been to conceal from her how little chance there was of his seeing out another month, let alone a quarter. In fact, the article in *The Rocket* appeared just eighteen days before her brother's death.[70]

Fifteen

The fateful summons came at last. Mabel was acting in a curtain-raiser, *The Nettle*, and understudying Lottie Venne in *22a Curzon Street*, a double bill which had opened at The Garrick on 2 March. She set off at once on the long journey to Menton.

On 12 March she wrote to Ross:

Dear Aubrey is very very ill, we fear he cannot live many hours. He is touchingly patient and resigned and longs for eternal rest. He holds always his crucifix and rosary. Thank God for some time past he has become more and more fervent.
Pray for him and for us.
Mother is very worn though we have two nurses.[71]

There is no need to dwell upon the relief it must have afforded
Aubrey to have his sister with him. The haemorrhage for a
moment staunched, the ghastly effort of drawing breath eased, the
dying man, not yet stupified by morphia and clutching to his
breast beads and cross, still had one hand free to lie in Mabel's.
These desperately induced meditations on the sacred wounds of
Jesus and endless telling of Aves, Paternosters and Glorias could
only bring them closer together. Now it was as if they were
children again, toiling up the half-made streets to the little Church
of The Annunciation. In religion both had found mystery and
high romance, the colours of a picture (like the east window of
The Annunciation) 'tingled up', 'buzzed around' and 'given
atmosphere' by Rossetti and Morris and Burne-Jones, to use
P.R.B. studio-jargon.

From the bright local colours of the Pre-Raphaelites to the
jingling devotional harness of the black-plumed horses Liguori
drives is no great step—when the box within the hearse is so
shortly to be your own. St Alphonsus Liguori was the Bishop of
Sant' Agata dei Goti who pawned his shoe-buckles to feed the
hungry during the Naples famine of 1764. To Aubrey and Mabel's
Most Blessed Leo XIII (and, no doubt, to the Dubliner who
stamped *nihil obstat* on Aubrey's English translation), the Holy
Ghost moved the soul without difficulty through the pages of *The
Christian Life*, *The Way of Salvation and of Perfection* and *The
Clock of the Passion*. 'My great love', was how the artist described their author, less than a month before he died.[72] Perhaps
he forbore to read the Lives of the Eight Holy Virgins (who
embraced the axe, as their hysterical descendants the syringe)
and the blood-curdling passages on Death and the Pains of Hell;
repeating, instead, those incantations in *The Clock of the Passion*—
intentionally, no doubt, hypnotic. This was a diet of brimstone
and treacle, all the same, that with sounder lungs Aubrey might
have spared himself.

St Teresa of Ávila is another matter. Her autobiography Aubrey
had specially recommended to Mabel: even in London, Hachette
or Dulau would be sure to have a reasonably-priced edition.[73]
Perhaps she brought a copy with her. One can imagine Mabel
reading him the opening chapter, which describes how Teresa

and her brother Rodrigo longed as children for the martyr's crown and then, finding martyrdom impossible in a well-ordered household, took to building hermits' cells in the orchard whose walls always collapsed. Teresa's mixture of humour, good sense and imagination gave her an inevitable first place in Aubrey's affections as long as his critical faculty continued to function. Nor would he have followed contemporary Northern fashion in condemning *en bloc* the works of Bernini. The *Ecstasy* of the Saint, in Santa Maria della Vittoria, he must have known—through engravings or photographic reproduction—as well as his Mantegnas.

Ignorant folk might have laughed at Teresa in her own day: 'What a St Paul she is with her heavenly visions, or another St Jerome!'; and Baedeker's *Guide* now hurried the sightseer past Bernini's monument to her with fulsome apologies for such a show of emotion. But Aubrey and Mabel understood very well those spears, pointed with fire, that plunged into one's entrails and left one utterly intoxicated.

Sixteen

As she sat beside her brother during those last days, that soon became hours, such ideas must have occupied the two with something of the nightmarish inconsequence just suggested. One asks oneself what was left of the obscene and the blasphemous which had played a curious, yet not inconsiderable, part throughout Aubrey's development of his gifts, and from which Mabel herself cannot be wholly excluded. It is impossible to accept that she did not know the *Lysistrata* drawings. Nor can one believe that she was unfamiliar with the manuscript version of *The Story of Venus and Tannhäuser*. And the reader will have understood that, if an explanation involving Mabel has to be found for the *Bon-Mots* embryo-motifs, the Davidson frontispiece and 'The Mysterious Rose Garden', it is that these drawings appeared with her connivance and approval—I was even going to say, at her suggestion: for the sister seems often to have led, rather than followed, her brother.

Aubrey's celebrated last letter, quoted in full at an earlier stage, left Menton before Mabel's arrival. Would it, one wonders, ever have been sent, or composed, if his sister, not Ellen, had been his only companion at the time? The destruction of *all* 'bad drawings' was, if you think of it, an impossibly sweeping command. What, in such a spate of works displaying, or cleverly half-concealing, the indecent, constituted a 'bad' drawing in the sense intended? Such unsophisticated phraseology itself suggests Ellen's dictation. And again I wonder at the absence of any similar entreaty where *The Story of Venus and Tannhäuser* was concerned. If Aubrey's conscience were troubling him so deeply, some of those chapters in the hands of Smithers, hardly a master who sent forth, in Liguori's words, 'the sweet odour of a virtuous life', would have weighed heaviest of all. Nothing easier, when Ellen was out of the room, than to engage his sympathetic sister to send off a note to Bedford Square, extending the pictorial ban to include the written word. But Aubrey didn't do this. If he had, we can depend upon it that Smithers would have given such a letter all the publicity with which he surrounded the one that did reach him.

Another difficulty. Dismiss as one may the bawdiness of *Venus and Tannhäuser*, there remains the curious plan of the book, as set out by Aubrey himself (one must suppose) on the title-page, to the importance of which I have already drawn attention. How could the artist make his peace with God, when he had deliberately denied to Tannhäuser the last-minute reprieve that would have enabled that hero to escape the wiles of Venus? For Aubrey's Abbé (or Abbé Aubrey), the staff would not blossom, his sins would therefore find no forgiveness and he must return to the everlasting defilement of the Venusberg. This makes nonsense of Wagner's solemn musical preparation for the miracle, of Elisabeth's simple and moving prayer:

Allmächt'ge Jungfrau, hör mein Flehen!

And, for that matter, of Wolfram's bitter-sweet invocation to the Evening Star, its magic not then diminished by over-familiarity. Aubrey, while at the same time (as we have seen) adoring and revering the music, seems to have felt impelled to improvise afresh on every Wagner libretto. It is certainly puzzling to understand how, eager to accept consolations rejected by his own Tannhäuser, he ever managed to rest easy with this turn of plot to answer for.

Thanks to the kindness of Mr J.-P. B. Ross and Sir Rupert

Hart-Davis, I have before me, as I write, the original letter from Mabel, in which—through the kindly Robbie—she tells the world of her brother's death, a letter surely among the most touching in the annals of British art (Fig. 85):

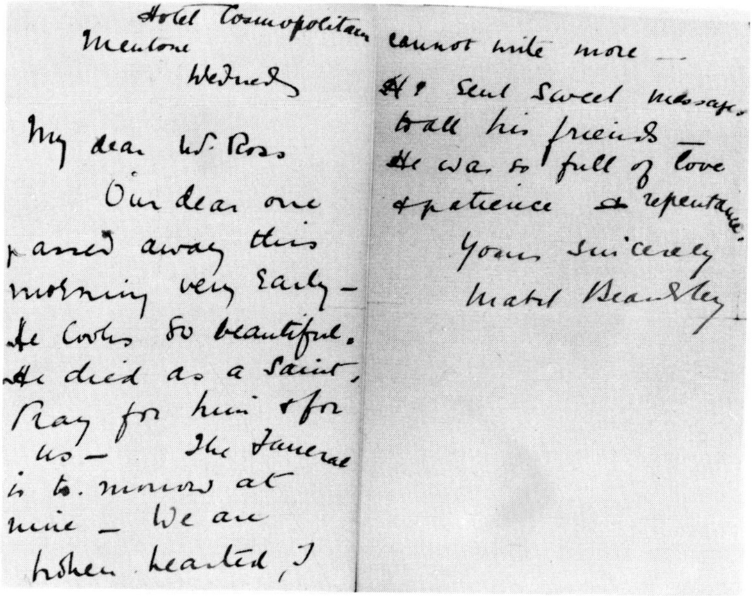

85   Mabel's letter to Ross, of 16 March 1898, announcing the death of her brother.

> Hotel Cosmopolitain
> Menton
> Wednesday [16 March 1898]

My dear Mr Ross

Our dear one passed away this morning very early—He looks so beautiful. He died as a saint. Pray for him and for us—The funeral is to-morrow at nine—We are broken-hearted, I cannot write more—He sent sweet messages to all his friends—He was so full of love and patience and repentance.

> Yours sincerely
> Mabel Beardsley[74]

With Aubrey's passing (whether before or after midnight), his devoted sister was left, we can very well see, stunned and grief-stricken. But this was not the end of her story—nor of Aubrey's mysterious participation in it. Mabel lived on for just over another eighteen years. In these late glimpses of her, now to be gathered together, may be envisaged a kind of apotheosis of the artist himself, one that defies exact analysis yet cannot be ignored.

The Dying Lady

One

When the second Solemn Requiem was over[1] and the last sad
octaves of the Chopin *marche funèbre* died away down the aisles of
the Jesuit Church in Farm Street on 12 May 1898 ('Dear Robbie,
how you have worked to arrange the beautiful service!'),[2] Mabel
collapsed. No name is put to her illness, and recovery was rapid;
at the same time, a note to Ross makes clear that the shock of her
brother's death, on top of the stresses and strains of professional
life, had led to some irreversible physical decline.[3] A pile of rich
red hair had been the most remarkable feature of this strange
beauty: from now on it would be her extreme pallor.

In October, just seven months after Aubrey's death, Mabel
attended a private view at the Grafton Galleries, perhaps her first
appearance in public since the memorial service. A number of
well-known people were to be seen making their tour of the
rooms (Henry Savage Landor,* just back from Tibet, the actress
Gertrude Kingsford, Lord Cork, Lord and Lady Powis), but the
greatest curiosity was reserved for this tall, slight young woman of
twenty-seven. A journalist—absurdly: or was it so absurd?—
noted down a 'pale face in which are the red lips and large eyes
her brother loved to draw'. But Mabel's half-mourning paid the
subtler tribute to Aubrey's art: the eccentrically-cut black velvet
jacket, flecked with white embroidered spots and relieved by a
little ivory lace at the throat, was well set off by the fine greys and
sombre blacks of the Manets and the Whistlers hanging on
Marchant's walls. Even the rather flashy likeness of Mme Réjane†
by Albert Besnard, dominating the first room, reminded one of the
dead artist's particular admiration, from his first days in Paris, for
this *comédienne*.[4]

Gradually, as her health began to pick up through the autumn

---

*Grandson of the poet, and author of *In the Forbidden Land*, 1898.
†1857–1920, frequently seen in London from 1894.

208

and winter of 1898 and in the early months of 1899, Mabel was
seen more often, still wearing costumes of the 'magpie order'
which deliberately emphasized her relationship to the lost genius
of black-and-white. By the summer, she felt strong enough to
accept the part of the Duchess of Strood in Pinero's *The Gay Lord
Quex*, then going into rehearsal at The Globe. But she had over-
estimated her newly-recovered stamina: for the moment, the role
proved too exacting, and she applied for a temporary release,
filling in with lesser parts at the St George's Hall.

Letters to Ross written immediately after Aubrey's mother and
sister returned to England show that they never set up house
together: Ellen went to lodgings in Wellington Square, and Mabel
moved in with Mrs Erskine (her former hostess at Hyde Park
Mansions) to a new flat at the Marylebone Road end of Gloucester
Place.[5] Relations between mother and daughter had never been
entirely happy. On Ellen's side, miserable as he had often made
her, there was no substitute for her brilliant son. His will, cutting
her out in favour of Mabel must have been an embittering factor.
Grief, it seemed, was to be her sole legacy from those two arduous
years when she had borne the heavy burden of the nursing and
faced the menace of death almost daily. Had Lady Burne-Jones
not given her back the late Sir Edward's 'Siegfried' drawing,
a gift from Aubrey, she would have been left with nothing
from his pen to remember him by.[6] On the other hand, there were
some comforting reflections to lighten Ellen's gloom in these first
years. 'Of whom the world was not worthy,' was how she could
think of her son now.[7] It was the little Kate Greenaway copyist
whom the angels had lifted up to Heaven. Aubrey's lost innocence
returned: Smithers, evil and proposing evil, could not pursue him
any longer. The dread disease itself was vanquished at last. Kind
friends (headed by the sympathetic Ross) raised subscriptions and,
a little after the turn of the century, used their influence to obtain
for her a small Civil List pension.[8]

One assumes that Mabel's sense of loss was more complicated,
but it was not easy to penetrate the lavish grandeur of her manner
and the mysterious coruscations of her green eyes. If it was not
easy then, we are at an even greater disadvantage today. In
particular, estimates of her character differed sharply, it seems,

according to the sex of the critic.

The attitude adopted by Faith Compton Mackenzie is of the amused—but undeceived—observer.[9] It was at Mrs Erskine's they met, in the dusty late summer of 1899, while Mabel, twenty-eight years old, nonchalantly fulfilled some simple engagements for George Grossmith and Arthur Playfair at the St George's Hall, and the very youthful Faith Stone (as Lady Mackenzie then was) trembled on the brink of her first stage part. The term 'landlady' will not quite do for Mrs Erskine. No. 6c Bickenhall Mansions was no typical theatrical lodging-house, with Dendy Sadler's 'Thursday' and a framed certificate of the late Mr Erskine's Buffalo membership nailed to the wall. Mrs Erskine was what used to be called 'highly educated', and her daughters attended drama school as her sons, if she had had any, might have attended Cuddesdon. One forgets from what pious homes sprang the Hawtreys and the Vanbrughs, though George Du Maurier had long ago drawn attention to the connexion between gaiters and buskins in his *Punch* cartoons. Faith Stone, whose father, an Eton housemaster, was also a clergyman, would most certainly not have been sent to Gloucester Place if Christian standards had not been strictly maintained there.

One might question Mabel's sincerity in small things, but not her devotion to her brother. Photographs of Aubrey crowded her bedside-table. He seemed to be with her every moment of her mysteriously trivial, and trivially mysterious, day. When Faith Stone was struck down by influenza at Bickenhall Mansions, Mabel came to visit her: not walking, of course, but gliding. 'Are you, dear child, well enough to enjoy a book? I have brought something of my brother's for you. Being just pictures, they will not tire you, as the printed word might.' And the young girl, already in a fever, found herself shut up for the night with the characters from Aubrey's Van Gelder-paper and Japanese-vellum *Lysistrata*![10]

The attitude this gesture illustrates seems to have been wholly characteristic. A year later, when discussing a contemporary edition of Hans Andersen for *The Saturday Review*, Mabel wrote:

For children, everything is alive and has a story, nothing seems

impossible or incredible; no, not even the most daring fantasies
of a certain black-and-white artist which to them are but
delightful friendly creatures seen in dreams, familiar and
amusing. Some day they will grow up and get stupid and per-
plexed by these same drawings and forget that they once knew
and understood them.[11]

Young Faith Stone was evidently not young enough to find
Aubrey's monsters, boiling with lechery and perverse invitation,
'delightful friendly creatures'. If Aubrey had revelled in the forbidden topic, both in conversation and in his drawings, Mabel
herself, once the discreeter of the two, the trembling, blushing
companion Frank Harris remembered (or says he remembered)
during their walk through the Park 'about 1890', grew noticeably
bolder in this respect after her brother's death. His missionary
zeal must live again in her! And just as Aubrey had appeared, in
the eyes of many, to glorify the vice he professed to castigate, so
to the cynical it seemed that a curious note, almost of approval,
marred Mabel's eloquent appeals for greater Christian charity in
our treatment of abnormal sexual relationships.

Thus one man friend recalls her 'sororal compassion for those
who crossed each other in Dante's *Purgatorio*': the male and
female homosexuals who, like dusky clouds of emmets meeting,

Each snatch a hasty kiss, and then away

and whom, says Dante, the mob taunts with cries of 'Sodom and
Gomorrah!' and lively reminders of the shame of Pasiphaë. 'I
have known so many of them,' Mabel sighed, 'I am sorry for
them'[12] (Fig. 86).

Two

In January 1900 she felt strong enough to return to the cast of
The Gay Lord Quex, taking up again the part of the Duchess of
Strood. Time certainly plays havoc with what entertained our
fathers and grandfathers. Vainly one peruses—in cold print—
this drama set in a New Bond Street manicurist's saloon, in
search of some reason why it should have run at The Globe for
three hundred nights in 1899. 'It is a page torn from the book of

86   Mabel felt particularly at home with sexual misfits. 'I have known so many of them, I feel sorry for them,' she told Raffalovich.
a. Katharine Bradley and Edith Cooper (1846–1914 and 1862–1913), literary collaborators under the pseudonym of 'Michael Field' and her close friends.
b. Charles Shannon and Charles Ricketts (1863–1937 and 1866–1931), artists, who played a leading part in the Christmas ceremonies of 1912 as recorded in Yeats's 'Upon a Dying Lady'.

life,' wrote *The Times* of Irene Vanbrugh's big scene with John Hare, when the tables are turned again and again between Little Miss Nobody and the well-seasoned roué. In almost all pages 'torn from the book of life' by Pinero about this time there was a well-seasoned roué, who ended up by enjoying the best of both worlds: and Hare, though somewhat stricken in years, regularly reappeared in that guise.

In *The Gay Lord Quex* the acting plums are reserved for the Marquess himself and the manicurist. Only in consideration of her social position does the Duchess head the list of ladies in the cast. All the same, the role was the most important Mabel had so far undertaken, and even if it was to be on tour only, she had the honour of being rehearsed in London by Pinero himself. There was one good scene when, as Quex's former mistress, the Duchess strikes a bargain with him: it was a scene thought by some to verge upon the offensive, but Mabel played it with generally acknowledged skill and tact.

If a certain desolation has settled on the play itself, Mabel's album of press-notices offers an even gloomier remembrance that all flesh is grass.[13] We have seen the actress in her lodgings. Now observe her in her dressing-room at The Opera House, Manchester, through the eyes of a provincial reporter. Miss Beardsley he found a 'conversationalist of conspicuous individuality', hardly knowing which to admire more, 'her charm and grace of manner, or her keen insight into art, literature and the stage'. Of her brother Miss Beardsley said much, but it was not for publication: 'There are some things which are sacred even to an interviewer.' The story of her stage career, up to and including *The Gay Lord Quex*, having been related at length, the reporter concluded: 'The remainder of our talk was upon art, and a book of her brother's wonderful drawings was kindly lent me by Miss Beardsley.' And then, as 'even an interviewer recognizes that there are limits to a lady's patience and goodness, I said good-bye after one of the pleasantest conversations I have been privileged to enjoy. Miss Beardsley is as artistic as she is charming.'[14]

One turns from this grateful naïveté to the more sophisticated prose of 'The Candid Friend', a year later, in August 1901:

You may tell her without insulting her that she is not an actress: in the first place, because any distinguished part comes naturally to her and, secondly, because she has none of the narrowness or Bohemianism which we connect with a stage career. She knows everybody and shines everywhere, but it is always with her own original light, as a star among moths.

She is one of the few living women who possess a lucid mind and, if she were not so sensible, she might persuade you to accept almost any impossible heresy. Her intuitions are marvellously sharp and clear: she reads a character like a book, and her golden voice illuminates every utterance. A century ago, she would have held a *salon*, dictated politics, baffled electorates. Today she is content to direct men and women with a velvet glove, and her sympathetic temperament is the secret of her autocracy.

She is original enough to accomplish anything, from leading a fashion to inaugurating a White Rose rebellion. She is a Catholic, not only in religion, but by temperament; and in everything she does or says there lingers an aroma of chivalry and quixotic fancy. My only regret about her is that Watteau did not live to paint her portrait on the terrace of Saint-Germain.[15]

A photographer, however, stepped into the breach, with a picture quite as romantic as the little character-sketch we have just been reading (Fig. 87). The *Gay Lord Quex* tour had long ended, and in 1901 she was playing in *The Degenerates*. There is certainly something of the 'terrace of Saint-Germain' about this corner of the photographer's studio. Conder-like clouds pile up in the background, silhouetted against which is an avenue of noble trees. Mabel emerges from a corsage of tulle and silk, threaded through with sprays of hydrangea, the striped, gossamer swathings of the dress spiralling out like ectoplasm. But she is strangely different from the Mabel of *The Queen's Proctor*. What has happened to the breadth of features from cheekbone to cheekbone, inherited from Vincent Paul Beardsley; to the pouting, rosebud mouth? Mabel's face is hollower, has lengthened. Did her nose have this tip-tilt, so Aubreian, before? Her eyes, one would judge, no longer glitter.

87 Mabel shortly after a revival of *The Degenerates* at the Imperial Theatre in 1902. A marked change in appearance, leading to a much closer resemblance to her brother, is a noticeable feature of this photograph.

For all his compliments, the *Theatre World*'s correspondent had dropped a number of hints which, when taken together, add up to the reason why Mabel, in spite of a remarkable personality and a multitude of friends in high places, never became the successful actress she had aspired to be (and still aspired to be, while parading alibis in the field of letters). It was simply—as her mother, as Richard Mansfield and as, no doubt, English actor-managers had impressed upon her—that she could not act well enough. Perhaps, with her intelligence and natural style and some tears, she might have taught herself what humbler mummers enjoy as a gift from God. An impulse, however, persuaded her to take a different line. Identifying herself with Aubrey meant, in this instance, that she adopted a cult of anti-professionalism. As her brother boasted that he had pursued his art only to please himself, so she was fond of declaring that she acted only to please herself. It was not a maxim calculated to enhance its holder's prospects in the world of the theatre, and Mabel paid the price for it.

Three

There has probably never been seen on the stage a more brilliant combination of artifice and illusion than marked the last years of the Victorian era and the first of Edward's reign. It was as if a dining-room had been moved lock, stock and barrel from the Albany for the first act of *The Second Mrs Tanqueray*. The hill-and-heather landscape in *Mrs Lessingham*, the first act set in *Ravenswood*, the ballroom in *Derby Winner* exemplified further marvels of the naturalistic school of scene-painting, dazzling a front-stall audience whose names would form as important a part of the critics' first-night account of the production as those of the actors themselves. Before the footlights, and immediately behind them, all was vulgar splendour.

Back-stage told another story. And if, like Mabel, you spent the greater proportion of your working life playing the provinces, the contrast grew. Never strong, she must have found her Hulls and Halifaxes trying, as she made up before cracked mirrors, and the rats scampered over the old pantomime-masks and tarnished gilt furniture on the other side of the dressing-room wall.[16] So much one gathers from a glance through Mabel's album, which contains every equivalent of those long bills of benefits, 'Important Engagement!', 'Direct from the Criterion!', 'Society Success of the Period!', 'Full London Cast!' (which, of course, it never was), pasted long ago into the scrap-book of Dickens's Miss Snevellicci.

By September 1901, the tour of *The Gay Lord Quex* was over and Mabel 'resting'. How better memorialize the past than by crossing to Dieppe in the gold of autumn? Here she had stayed with Aubrey in health and sickness; and here Aubrey had conceived the wonders of *The Savoy*. Yet a 'gas-plot' suited her better than crude sun, and her limes were not lindens. There is that about nature, undirected, unadorned, by man, which was at variance with the Beardsleys, brother and sister. If Aubrey turned his back on the sea, so, very likely, did Mabel. And notice was as important to her as to him. Her eccentricities proliferated.

'She creates a great sensation,' wrote Max, to his still faithful Reggie Turner.[17]

A Dieppe snapshot of two years later shows Max himself and Constance Collier* (suitably chaperoned) chatting together in the neighbourhood of the Établissement des Bains against a sparkling Channel background; but if there is one thing we note about the women on this sunny September day in 1903—and Miss Collier was also an actress, much better known and more successful than Mabel—it is how well wrapped-up they are.[18] Mabel, on the contrary, dispensed entirely with hat, veil, long gloves and parasol: 'She trails about all day,' Max reports, in 1901, 'in evening dress—low neck, no sleeves, and a train as long as the Rue de l'Hôtel de Ville, which she carries swathed over her arm.'[19] Walking with this exotic Mabel on the terrace (reserved for subscribers) to seaward of the Casino, Max met Mrs Horace Nevill, daughter-in-law of Lady Dorothy Nevill, with whom he was on the friendliest terms. He took off his hat. Mrs Nevill cut him dead.[20]

One asks oneself whether it was the dress alone that led to Max's momentary rebuff. 'Let the good women who are tempted and resist have a chance of some stage canonization also!' cried Clement Scott, professional Jeremiah and execrable poet, dismayed by the decline in dramatic morality, a decline made more

*1878–1955, one of Beerbohm Tree's leading ladies.

alluring by the bending to its service of the dark beauty of Olga
Nethersole, the daring décolleté of Mrs Pat Campbell, the adorable,
wide-eyed 'innocence' of Miss Baird—and the charms of such
barely sparkling luminaries as Mabel Beardsley. We have already
noted the superficial, worldly parts habitually allotted her. She
seems to have been as natural a choice for the *risqué*. The Duchess
of Strood not only (delightful phrase) 'burned a good deal of red
fire': she 'overstepped the mark'. Like part, like player, once
again? How did Mabel conduct her own affairs of the heart,
whatever category they might come into? It was at least curious
that such a striking woman, so fond of men and so admired by
them, should elect to remain single. At the height of *The Yellow
Book* success, when Mabel entertained weekly at 114 Cambridge
Street, Count Stenbock* (loosely attached to the *Cénacle*) composed a skit on the amours of Aymer Vallance. These doggerel
verses, which begin (they can scarcely be said to have an ending),

> '*He loved me once,*' said Emily,
>   *And then he took to Maisie.*
>   *But now he loves that minx Elise*
>   *And Mabel with her Thursday teas*
>   *And Cycle-loving Daisy,*'[21]

are quite absurd.
Something comes across, nevertheless, of the 1893–5 Mabel, gay,
flirtatious, filling the cups with tea—and her idle hours with girlish
scheming. But the Mabel who, in September 1901, swept along the
rue d'Aguado, like Sara Bernhardt playing the Princess Lointaine,
was no longer a girl.

Four

On 8 May 1902, she appeared in *The Finding of Nancy*, put on at
The St James's Theatre for a matinée performance only. The
circumstances of her being asked to undertake a part in this
production have been related by Netta Syrett, *Nancy*'s author.
George Alexander† objected to one of the play's characters who
had some harsh things to say about the heroine. The offending

*1860–95, of Swedish origin and a desultory author.
†Sir George Alexander (1858–1918), manager of the St James's Theatre from 1891.

lines must be cut, he told Miss Syrett: no nice woman would say such things. 'But she isn't meant to be a nice woman.' 'Then,' replied the actor-manager, 'I don't think Miss So-and-So can play the part.' 'Mabel Beardsley would probably be very glad to do so,' said Miss Syrett. And Alexander's final word was a sharp: 'Very well, get Mabel Beardsley!'[22]

A pasteboard peeress, a stop-gap, a last-minute volunteer for the 'not quite nice': this was hardly a glorious situation. But it was Mabel who amused the men, and made the suppers sparkle. And occasional journalism preserved her modest reputation as a blue-stocking. What are the elements of tragedy, she asks? 'It is the hopeless agony of exceptional souls, the torture of the fully equipped mind in the extremity of human misery, the closing of adverse powers round the passionate strength that would carve its way freely to satisfaction; the foretaste of hell for the guilty whose imagination can conjure up a possible retribution.'[23] On another occasion, she inquires: 'Does the pursuit of art absolve from moral obligation?'; but leaves us, this time, without an answer.[24]

Another role was presently found for her in *The Lion Hunters* at Terry's Theatre, (famous for its earlier run of *Sweet Lavender*). If the part did not amount to very much, her evening-gown eclipsed all others. It was in a new kind of shot taffetas, in shades of pink and blue, producing an effect that subtly flattered her complexion. She was thirty-one, and had never looked lovelier.[25] The young actor in the cast who fell in love with her was George Bealby Wright:* twenty-five years old and, notes Walker approvingly, of her own social position (Fig. 88). Mr Wright senior might have thought differently. He managed great estates near Melton Mowbray, and his daughters Julie and Daisy were famous horse-women in the Shires. On leaving Eton, George Wright had pursued a variety of interests. He read the classical authors for pleasure, and wrote poetry. In the garden at Saxelby, the family home, a workshop was built for him where he experimented with a machine to reclaim oil from cotton-waste. When old Mr Wright died, George, like many another ex-luminary of the Eton Society,

---

*George Edward Wright, as he was born, adopted the name George Bealby on the stage and so became known in private life as George Bealby Wright.

88   Mabel's husband, George Bealby Wright, the actor (1877–1931):
a photograph taken about the time of their engagement in 1902, when he
was twenty-five and she thirty-one.

'Pop', turned to acting; and it was in *The Lion Hunters* that he
and Mabel first met.

Ellen welcomed the idea of her daughter settling down at last,
when Bealby Wright proposed marriage. She and her future
son-in-law were friends from the first. 'I am looking forward to
my marble,' she wrote to him in Rome, in July 1903, 'it will be
of value to me as a good catholic.'[26] He had evidently given her
news of some *objet d'art*, religious in subject, which he was
acquiring for her; and from this acknowledgement we learn that,
like her children before her, she too had been received into the
Roman Church. Mabel, meanwhile, was in South Africa, touring
in a London success, *The Marriage of Kitty*. It did not promise
well. Ellen feared that at any moment the company would find
itself stranded and penniless. Her opinion of Mabel, that she lacked

both temperament and natural talent, had never changed. And without either, in spite of today's flattery in the gossip-column or tomorrow's full-page photograph, what could the future hold? 'I wouldn't give sixpence for any theatrical successes anywhere,' Ellen confided to Bealby Wright, 'and I wish she would give up ideas of that kind.'[27]

George and Mabel were married at the Roman Catholic Cathedral in Ashley Place, shortly after her return, on 30 September 1903—in the presence, astonishingly, of her erring father, who thus makes a belated and final appearance in the history of the family. Something of Bealby Wright's chivalrous nature may be gleaned from his vellum-covered, gold-tooled *Fifty Sonnets*, privately printed (the flyleaf of a unique copy carries some complementary—and complimentary—verses in her own hand by Marie, Queen of Roumania, so deeply impressed was she by the poet's selfless regard for his beloved). The sonnets 'Malediction' and 'Servitus' well illustrate this; and

> *Most grieved am I that Censure's bony hand*
> *Should tarnish thee with misdirected blame*

and

> *If thou should'st say the word I would commit*
> *All sins to please thee, and be proud of it*

are lines which hint at Hoffmanesque situations with (drifting down the Grand Canal) the voice of some enchantress for whom one sells one's soul as well as one's shadow.[28] And, like that celebrated song of Giulietta's, the marriage fades and dies away, and soon—but for Bealby Wright's enduring friendship with Ellen—might never have happened at all.

Five

Glimpses of Mabel from now on are blurred and tantalizingly brief. A letter of hers to Lane, telling him to hunt up Aubrey's 'Table Talk', which was in a black shiny manuscript-book in her revolving bookcase, belongs to 1903:[29] Lane brought out his edition of *Under the Hill*, to which, with some other pieces of miscellaneous writing, a mere ten of these aphorisms were appended, in 1904. Father Gray published his collection of Aubrey's *Last Letters* in the same year. Of about that date, therefore, must be Mabel's thanks to him for suggesting that the royalties on the book should go to Ellen.[30] One wonders how far there could ever have been room for a newcomer in Mabel's Aubrey-orientated world. Here they were, she and George, setting up home at 48 Charlwood Street,[31] almost opposite the house in which brother and sister had shared that bleak period of the Fire Office and the Polytechnic, when their dependence on each other must have been greatest. Nor would one suppose the husband as anxious as the wife to accept Raffalovich's fluttering hospitality or the ministrations of her enigmatic 'godmother', Miss Gribbell. But Raffalovich was particularly busy on Mabel's behalf in 1904. An exhibition of Aubrey's work would be held in Vienna, that December, and she looked to him to act as her agent in all matters arising. One of these was the plan Mme Strindberg* had in mind to produce a German edition of the artist's letters, a hundred and fifty of which had been purchased from Smithers. The lady Ada Leverson called 'Madam Swindleberg' was now hoping to negotiate reproduction rights of drawings for some separate venture. It was useful to be able to call upon Raffalovich, wealthy and wise in matters of business, to deal with such a formidable person.[32]

In her son-in-law, Ellen had evidently been counting on an ally who would open Mabel's eyes to the folly of pursuing a theatrical career. Ill-health, however, rather than George's tactful counsels, seems to have brought about the desired result. There is mention in a letter of Mabel's possible appearance in a 1904 production with Mrs Brown Potter.†[33] Nothing seems to have come of it. Renouncing the hardships of provincial and foreign tours and gradually ceasing to play even the smallest parts in London from now on, Mabel would lend her fine presence and waning, but still impressive beauty only to an occasional summer pageant or charity matinée. *The Idler*, for a while, and *The Saturday Review*, for longer, continued to print her articles, in the belles-lettres manner, on topics ranging from Molière to Musset and George Sand. But it was in another role, neither strictly theatrical nor

*Frida (or Freda) Strindberg (1872–1943), wife of the Swedish dramatist.
†1859–1936. American actress who became in that year manager of the Savoy Theatre.

89 'Beginners for the First Act—a Hundred Years Ago': a tableau at Drury Lane Theatre, 12 June 1906, arranged by James Pryde, the painter, and organized as part of a series in aid of the Ellen Terry Benefit. The names of the actresses taking part, from left to right, are: Mabel (foreground) Mrs Sam Sothern, Pauline Chase, Mrs H. Beerbohm Tree, Winifred Emery, Lena Ashwell, Geraldine Wilson (at window), Beatrice Ferrar, Hilda Trevelyan and Margaret Bussé.

literary (yet a bit of both), that she began to shine at her brightest.

Advancing far beyond the 'Thursday teas', Mabel now attracted to her weekly luncheon-table some of the most distinguished men of the day. Not long after the Drury Lane tableau (Fig. 89), the sculptress Kathleen Bruce* was invited to one of these occasions (still in Charlwood Street?), finding among fellow-guests, not only Max and J. M. Barrie, but her future husband, Robert Falcon Scott, newly promoted captain. Ten months later, in 1908, she received a second invitation, meeting for the first time Henry James and Ernest Thesiger,† and renewing acquaintance with the fascinating Captain Scott.[34] Mr Good has been kind enough to let me consult Walker's notes on the Beardsley family correspondence. Miss Dash possessed seven letters addressed to Mabel from the explorer, who was no mere bird of passage in her life. No doubt she charmed him as literary or artistic women so often (and inexplicably) charm men of action. He wrote to her not only from Oakley Street, but from HMS *Essex* ('No theatres or tea-parties for quite a long time!'); and, in March 1908, when conducting trials for his second expedition in the *Terra Nova*.[35] Max, Blanche, MacColl, all of the

*Later, Lady Scott; and, on her second marriage, Lady Kennet.
†Actor (1879–1961).

Cénacle, remained faithful; Somerset Maugham she added to her long list of homosexual admirers; among players and playwrights, her closest friend was H. B. Irving,* but Mrs Pat Campbell, Henry Arthur Jones and Sir Alfred Sutro were also be met at her house. Of later English artists who painted her portrait, the best-known were Sir John Lavery (Fig. 90) and Sir Oswald Birley, whose picture of her I shall return to in a moment.

Six

In May 1910, there was held at the Grafton Galleries what was called a 'high revel in Bohemia', an Artists' Ball. Those taking part included Mabel, in the character of a fifteenth-century page (Fig. 91). An injudicious choice, perhaps, and (as a photograph shows) one little calculated to conceal the alarming change in her appearance which had occurred since she played in *The Degenerates*: in less, that is, than a decade. Now, nearing her thirty-eighth birthday, she has become haggard, and the mass of Monna-Vanna hair serves only to accentuate the angular, exposed bones of jaw and cheek.

The Tatler's photographer was merciless. Fortunately, Mabel had a sympathetic portrait-painter among her friends. In 1911, Oswald Birley showed her in that same fur-edged tabard, with a goshawk on her wrist. To this picture he gave the title 'An Elizabethan Age', and the result is altogether charming (Fig. 92). It may be compared with another portrait in which flattery is used with the same tact and skill, Blanche's of Aubrey, painted in 1895 (Fig. 24). The faces show a remarkable similarity: one might say that Aubrey, in the short lifetime vouchsafed him, and Mabel, in the longer enjoyed by her, had reached, when these likenesses were taken, an identical parting of the ways, each facing the certainty of death for the first time. For Mabel was now desperately ill.

The earliest reference I have found to cancer as the disease from which she suffered occurs in the unpublished diary of 'Michael Field' (the comprehensive pseudonym adopted by Katherine

*H.B. was Sir Henry Irving's elder son (1870–1919); Mrs Pat Campbell (1865–1940), celebrated actress, made her name in *The Second Mrs Tanqueray*; Henry Arthur Jones (1851–1929) was the rival of Shaw and Pinero as a playwright; Sutro (1863–1933) also won success in the theatre, and translated Maeterlinck.

90   A portrait inscribed 'To Mabel Beardsley' and signed 'J. Lavery'.
One is reminded of Margot Asquith's quip, after meeting the painter's
wife: 'Now I know why Lavery's pictures are so poor in drawing, there
is no drawing in Mrs Lavery's face.'

91   Mabel wearing a fifteenth-century page's costume at the Artists' Ball at the Grafton Galleries
in 1910.

92 Sir Oswald Birley's portrait of Mabel as 'An Elizabethan Age', exhibited at the International Society's show in the spring of 1915, but painted in 1911. The costume is the one she wore at the Artists' Ball of 1910. Birley has idealized her growing emaciation: nevertheless, the picture made a painful impression on those who knew her.

Bradley and Edith Cooper,* even in committing their most private thoughts to paper). This establishes that Mabel had already entered a Hampstead nursing-home by October 1912. Edith Cooper (orthographically, it is possible to distinguish the younger from the older Field), in reporting a conversation with Ricketts about this nursing-home, speaks of an old Adam house under Catholic management.[36] As the description seems to have been Ricketts's—he was one of Mabel's most constant visitors—I could not believe the term 'Adam' to have been used carelessly; but neither the most extensive inquiries nor two years' intermittent field-work in the immediate neighbourhood of Hampstead Heath revealed the existence at any time of an Adam-style home run by nuns of a Catholic Order.

Then, at last, a letter from Mabel of about the right period came into my hands. It was headed: 'The Nook, Holford Road, Hampstead Heath'. This was clearly the nursing-home referred to by Edith Cooper—but the house had been built in the 1880s and it was the private venture of the Mayfair and Hampstead Nursing Corps. However, as further information showed, The Nook was associated with an eighteenth-century house next door, originally Ladywell Court, and once occupied by Colonel Horatio Sharpe, former Governor of Maryland, whose portrait was painted by Reynolds. The Nook, built on a corner site of the Ladywell grounds, had given its name to the whole property, and Mabel's room was in the 'Adam-style' building. Neither now remains, though an old, ivied brick wall from former days still marks their combined boundary at the junction of Holford and East Heath Roads. I shall be forgiven, I hope, this short excursion into artistic geography for the clearer picture it helps to establish of that remarkable court held by Mabel, during her last years, when her wit and evanescent beauty offered full compensation for the inconvenience of a journey to the northern heights.

Seven

The cause of cancer, and thus of cancer of the uterus (the form of it afflicting Mabel), was, and is, unknown. Had the cancer been

*Katherine Bradley (1846–1914) was the aunt of Edith Cooper (1862–1913). They wrote lyrics and poetic drama together and called each other 'husband' and 'wife'.

more specifically cervical, it might have lent support to the tale of a full-term child having been born to her, as Lord Tredegar believed. For cancer of the cervix is often the result of parturient scars. Yet, even so, this would not have brought us any nearer solving the problem of the embryo-motifs, finding a meaning for 'The Mysterious Rose Garden', and serving a paternity-order on the father of the elusive'Mr Watkins'.

There is impressive evidence of Mabel's courage, though she was visibly wasting and often in great pain. The first serious onset of the disease seems to have been experienced in June 1912, to judge by a remark of Yeats's; but it is most interesting that the scene for his poem-sequence, 'Upon a Dying Lady', was being set as early as April. From a reference elsewhere to the loss of the *Titanic*, which sank on the fifteenth of that month, we can assume a rough date of a few days afterwards for the following passage in a letter addressed by Ricketts to Ross:

> I have promised Mabel Beardsley a Beardsley doll. I find that neither Miss Birkenruth nor I have a reproduction of the Mademoiselle de Maupin frontispiece which is wanted for that purpose.
>
> Would you be a good chap and either lend it to me, *or* better still make a rough sketch or tracing of the drawing. This would save me the trouble of packing the book back, which is one of those tasks before which the spirit is willing but the flesh weak.[37]

Was the busy but generous Ricketts moved to make this use of his precious time to soften a doctor's gloomy verdict? One can imagine as much. And another question arises: if a doll based on one of Aubrey's drawings was to be constructed, why did the choice fall upon the Frontispiece to *Mademoiselle de Maupin*? The drawing is far from being the best of its kind, nor is it particularly characteristic. I find a curious coincidence here. At the Artists' Ball of 1910, attended by Mabel in the page's costume, a friend of hers, a Miss Glady Balby, went as Mlle de Maupin, in a costume directly modelled on this same Frontispiece (Fig. 93). The natural deduction we make is that Mabel must have had a special liking for the work and the theme of transvestism, or transsexuality, which it was designed to illustrate; and having

93   Mabel's friend, Miss Gladys Balby, as Aubrey's 'Mademoiselle de Maupin', at the Artists' Ball, the Grafton Galleries, 1910

induced Miss Balby to slip on the ambiguous frills of Gautier's 'Théodore', this carefully selected memento of her, and her brother's, interest in cross-dressing was to be perpetuated now in miniature by the nimble Ricketts.

I knew that Ricketts took a particular delight in small sculpture (there is a single figure, 'Silence', of his, cast in bronze), and that among his most treasured possessions were two little Greek clowns; so, with the gift to Mabel in mind, I asked Miss Bridget D'Oyly Carte if he had ever made any dolls when working on costume designs for her father's Savoy productions. She did not recall such a practice. So this must have been very much a labour of love on the artist's part: and, in spite of the mention of a Miss Birkenruth, Yeats thought Ricketts carried out all the sewing himself. I should add that Ricketts's affection for Mabel is all the more touching in that, rightly or wrongly, he always supposed the vogue for Aubrey's work had ruined any hope of his own success in the field of book-illustration.[38]

Eight

When news of Mabel's illness reached him, Symons wrote, reminding her that it was just seventeen years since they had first met: 'I have been fond of you,' he said, 'as I never was of Aubrey.'[39] Indeed, the opportunity had come for other old friends, besides Ricketts, to express their appreciation. They came to Hampstead in troops. There was H. B. Irving, Somerset Maugham, William Toynbee,* and always some young man or other from one of the Scottish universities, introduced by Raffalovich, himself (though domiciled in Edinburgh) in frequent attendance. The Michael Fields appeared as often as Edith's swift decline allowed. Rothenstein (the Fields' 'Heavenly Dog') had not yet left for Far Oakridge; and MacColl, in Hampstead Way, was also within easy reach of Holford Road. Other visitors were Ross, Blanche and George Moore.

The single toy-figure planned by Ricketts had become one of several, by Christmas 1912. The ceremonial presentation has been

---

*William Toynbee published a good deal of occasional verse and translation between the late 1880s and 1912. He presented a copy of his *Rhymes of City and Countryside* to Mabel.

exquisitely particularized for all time in those seven short poems
by Yeats, entitled 'Upon a dying Lady'. Yeats (Fig. 94) would have

94   The author of 'Upon a Dying Lady': W. B. Yeats, as Mabel knew
him during her last years. Photograph by Arnold Genthe, 1914.

met Mabel during the last decade of the nineteenth century: according to Max, the first meeting of the poet with Aubrey himself took
place at a supper at the New Lyric Club, to celebrate the initial

number of *The Savoy*; that is, in January 1896. Aubrey, Yeats said long afterwards, 'has never the form of decadence which tempted me';[40] and on the magazine's short life could comment, with regret: 'We might have survived but for our association with Beardsley.'[41] All the same, poet and artist were close enough for a self-confession or two on Aubrey's part, and some discussion of the 'spiritual life', including that same glimpse of the bleeding Christ vision that had been communicated to Symons at Arques-la-Bataille in 1895. And, as Yeats tells Lady Gregory,* Aubrey was one of those he had in mind when writing 'The Grey Rock', a poem that begins:

> *Poets with whom I learned my trade,*
> *Companions of the Cheshire Cheese . . .*[42]

'Strange,' he informs his Irish patron, on 8 January 1913, 'that just after writing those lines on the Rhymers who "unrepenting faced their ends" I should be at the bedside of the dying sister of Beardsley, who was practically one of us.'

The letter continues:

She had had a week of great pain but on Sunday was I think free from it. She was propped up on pillows with her cheeks I think a little rouged and looking very beautiful. Beside her a Xmas tree with little toys containing sweets, which she gave us. Mr Davis [Ricketts's patron] had brought it—I daresay it was Ricketts's idea. I will keep the little toy she gave me and I daresay she knew this. On a table near were four dolls dressed like people out of her brother's drawings. Women with loose trousers and boys that looked like women. Ricketts had made them, modelling the faces and sewing the clothes. They must have taken him days. She had all her great lady airs and asked after my work and my health as if they were the most important things in the world to her. 'A palmist told me,' she said, 'that when I was forty-two my life would take a turn for the better and now I shall spend my forty-second year in heaven' and then emphatically 'O yes I shall go to heaven. Papists do.' When I

---

*Augusta Lady Gregory (1852–1932), Yeats's patron and colleague in promoting the Irish literary and dramatic revival.

told her where Mrs Emery was she said 'How fine of her, but a girls' school! why she used to make even me blush!' Then she began telling improper stories and inciting us (there were two men besides myself) to do the like. At moments she shook with laughter. Just as I was going her mother came and saw me to the door. As we were standing at it she said 'I do not think she wishes to live—how could she after such agony? She is all I have left now.' I lay awake most of the night with a poem in my head. I cannot over-state her strange charm—the pathetic gaiety. It was her brother, but her brother was not I think loveable, only astounding and intrepid. She has been ill since June last. . . .[43]

As a character-sketch on the level of gossip this could hardly be bettered. The poems themselves were in process of composition, when Yeats wrote again to Lady Gregory on the same subject:

Mabel Beardsley said to me on Sunday 'I wonder who will introduce me in heaven. It should be my brother but then they might not appreciate the introduction. They might not have good taste.' She said of her brother 'He hated the people who denied the existence of evil, and being so young he filled his pictures with evil. He had a passion for reality.' She has the same passion and puts aside any attempt to suggest recovery and yet I have never seen her in low spirits. She talked of a play she wanted to see. 'If I could only send my head and legs,' she said, 'for they are quite well.' Till one questions her she tries to make one forget that she is ill. I always see her alone now. She keeps Sunday afternoon for me. I will send you the little series of poems when they are finished. One or two are I think very good.[44]

The postmark shows this letter to have been sent off on 11 February 1913. The poems, were, indeed, completed not long afterwards; but while 'The Grey Rock' could be included in the 1914 collection, *Responsibilities*, 'Upon a Dying Lady'—even had the title been changed—by reason of its very nature was barred from publication until after the Dying Lady's death. As an artist anxious for his best work to see the light, Yeats may even have been a little disconcerted to find Mabel so far out in her forecast

of the cancer's final, massive invasion. Medically, indeed (given
that the diagnosis was correct), her longevity is astonishing.[45]

One may pass now to the poems themselves (they first appeared
in *The Little Review* and *The New Statesman* in 1917, a little over
a year after Mabel's death), where rhetoric alters hardly at all the
broad impression conveyed by the earlier letter to Lady Gregory.
In them, the invalid's weaknesses are refined and her virtues
exalted, just as Maeterlinck, and then Debussy, refine and exalt
the character of Mélisande, frail and foolish child-wife. And if the
poems suffer a little, in the reader's mind, from what he knows
now to have been a misreading of the imminence of death, this,
too, is a needful reminder that life can never hope to emulate the
tidiness of art.

The first poem of the septet,[46] 'Her Courtesy', runs as follows:

With the old kindness, the old distinguished grace,
She lies, her lovely piteous head amid dull red hair
Propped upon pillows, rouge on the pallor of her face.
She would not have us sad because she is lying there,
And when she meets our gaze her eyes are laughter-lit,
Her speech a wicked tale that we may vie with her,
Matching our broken-hearted wit against her wit,
Thinking of saints and of Petronius Arbiter.

The reader should turn now to this book's frontispiece showing
Mabel stretched out on her day-bed in the garden of The Nook, the
wall being that which still separates the re-built site from East Heath
Road. The photograph has the appearance of having been taken
no more than three or four months after Yeats's second letter,
written in February 1913, and forms, therefore, a perfect, hitherto
unpublished, illustration to the opening lines of 'Her Courtesy'.
Any further commentary from me on the lines so far quoted
would be impertinent—and superfluous, since I have already
drawn attention to the strange contradictions in Mabel's character
—among the strangest, that so cleverly epitomized in the last line.

The second poem concerns the gifts ('Certain Artists bring
her Dolls and Drawings'):

Bring where our Beauty lies
A new modelled doll, or drawing,
With a friend's or an enemy's
Features, or maybe showing
Her features when a tress
Of dull red hair was flowing
Over some silken dress
Cut in the Turkish fashion,
Or, it may be, like a boy's.
We have given the world our passion,
We have naught for death but toys.

Ricketts, says Yeats (in his letter to Lady Gregory), made the dolls. Who, then, supplemented these with drawings? Sickert, possibly, as a very old friend; but he was constantly on the move between London and Dieppe just at this time. I would regard Shannon, with whom Ricketts was associated in all his ventures, as a likelier choice. And Edmund Dulac,* close friend of both Yeats and Ricketts, could make a third. Sturge Moore,† another friend in common, is a fourth name that readily suggests itself. If it were a question of pleasing their 'Beauty' with a drawing in the Turkish, or any other Eastern, fashion, Dulac was the very man: he must have been working at that moment on his embellishments for *Princess Badoura*, and he had already published the gorgeously decorated *Stories from the Arabian Nights* and *Ali Baba*. It is a curious fact that, according to one interview Mabel gave, her very first part on the stage had been in an oriental, trousered costume. As to the 'boy's' dress, we have seen her in the 1910 page's tabard (most likely to have been the one copied by Ricketts) and of course there was the Graham Robertson (1911) portrait of her in Aubrey's clothes.

Her admirers take second place in 'She turns the Dolls' Faces to the Wall':

Because to-day is some religious festival
They had a priest say Mass, and even the Japanese,

---

*1882–1953, French born watercolourist and illustrator.
†Thomas Sturge Moore (1870–1944), poet and wood-engraver.

Heel up and weight on toe, must face the wall
—Pedant in passion, learned in old courtesies,
Vehement and witty she had seemed—; the Venetian lady
Who had seemed to glide to some intrigue in her red shoes,
Her domino, her panniered skirt copied from Longhi;
The meditative critic; all are on their toes,
Even our Beauty with her Turkish trousers on.
Because the priest must have like every dog his day
Or keep us all awake with baying at the moon,
We and our dolls being but the world were best away.

Perhaps it was the account of these priestly visits that had led to the Michael Fields' assumption that The Nook was a Catholic nursing-home. The good-humoured anti-clericalism here takes its cue from Mabel's own teasing way with unbelievers; and, in the poem that follows, 'The End of Day', Yeats uncovers a wilful, childlike streak in her, irritating enough to fellow guests at Mrs Erskine's but now, in the changed circumstances, both charming and pathetic:

She is playing like a child
And penance is the play,
Fantastical and wild
Because the end of day
Shows her that some one soon
Will come from the house and say—
Though play is but half done—
'Come in and leave the play.'

'Her Race' and 'Her Courage' speak for themselves, Mabel fulfilling Yeats's need to find the woman he admires a natural aristocrat, one who throws caution to the wind and scorns death. Thus, in 'Her Race':

She has not grown uncivil
As narrow natures would
And called the pleasures evil
Happier days thought good;
She knows herself a woman,
No red and white of a face,

Or rank, raised from a common
Unreckonable race ;
And how should her heart fail her
Or sickness break her will
With her dead brother's valour
For an example still?

And in 'Her Courage':

When her soul flies to the predestined dancing-place
(I have no speech but symbol, the pagan speech I made
Amid the dreams of youth) let her come face to face,
Amid that first astonishment, with Grania's shade,
All but the terrors of the woodland flight forgot
That made her Diarmuid dear, and some old cardinal
Pacing with half-closed eyelids in a sunny spot
Who had murmured of Giorgione at his latest breath—
Aye, and Achilles, Timor, Barbar, Barhaim, all
Who have lived in joy and laughed into the face of Death.

In conclusion, and greatly adding to the power and immediacy of the septet, Yeats forsakes mythology to return to lamp-starred Hampstead, as one may see it still on a late December afternoon when the children are dragging home their sledges and a thrush, high up in the copse, sings its last song of the day. As the mists gathered over the bracken-broken crust of snow, and 1912 approached its end, Mabel prepared herself to receive a special delegation, as described in 'Her Friends bring her a Christmas Tree':

Pardon, great enemy,
Without an angry thought
We've carried in our tree,
And here and there have bought
Till all the boughs are gay,
And she may look from the bed
On pretty things that may
Please a fantastic head.
Give her a little grace,
What if a laughing eye
Have looked into your face?
It is about to die.

Nine

It would have been strange had Yeats, his little sheaf of verses complete, then bowed himself out. The published biographies and studies of the poet, since Mabel's name is never mentioned again, appear to accuse him of such callousness. I am glad to be the first to show that the implication is quite unjust. Through the courtesy of the University of Texas, and the kindness of Senator Michael Yeats, I have been privileged to read twenty-one letters and four photostats of letters from Yeats to Mabel. As they are earmarked for inclusion as unpublished items in the forthcoming edition of the poet's Collected Letters, to be issued by the Oxford University Press, I cannot quote from them or reproduce them here. There need be no weeping and gnashing of teeth on that account, however. The letters have the effect only of blurring the edges of the poems, and we would rather preserve these in all their pristine sharpness.

No new notes of admiration are here sounded. It is specifically Mabel's ability to be gay, in spite of pain and (as Yeats at first supposed) the imminent approach of death, that impresses him. This jesting stoicism of hers he found particularly attractive. But he was not in love with Mabel, and the letters are not love-letters. When they began, he was not even on Christian-name terms with her. Extending from very early in 1913 till sometime in 1915, the letters bear witness to this, for it was only in August 1913, close on a year after the poems had been conceived that he regularly addressed her as 'Mabel', rather than 'Mabel Beardsley'. And it was not till November 1913 that, for her, he ceased to be 'Mr Yeats' and became 'Willy': one would guess that he had seen little of her since the 1890s and not much then. Nor is he mentioned as one of those who frequented the Charlwood Street *salon*. It must have been a very tenuous acquaintance that he renewed (perhaps through Ricketts) in 1912, but one that immediately, and right up till her death, acquired the force of an irresistible poetic vision and spiritual inspiration. I think an important truth becomes apparent here: that Mabel, trivial, affected, shallow before her illness, was transformed by suffering not only into a woman of unearthly beauty, but a woman of strong and noble character.

There are letters, too, from Max to Mabel.[47] Most are brief and
of little interest (whether or not he can accept an invitation), and
none is dated with the year. A letter containing a sentence like,
'If, when I arrive, you are asleep or sleepy, your Nurse must say
"Not at home", and I will come another time,' can be placed
approximately within the earlier period of her illness; and another,
which says, 'How sweet of you to like my "Garland",' must have
been written between late December 1912, when *A Christmas
Garland* was published, and early 1913. Very busy on his flying
visits from Rapallo, Max did not find it easy to fit the journey
from Upper Berkeley Street to Hampstead and back into the time
at his disposal, but he and Florence Beerbohm* came as often as
they could.

'I have been hearing so much about you from one person and
another,' wrote Max, about the time when Yeats was finishing his
poems. 'Your wit and charm are the talk of the town.'[48] One of
his informants could have been Ross, to whom, from The Nook,
Mabel sent a pencilled letter over a year later, on 27 July 1914:

I've been wanting to write to you for some time, but have been
very ill indeed with pleurisy—I know you are overwhelmed
with letters, so you must not dream of bothering to answer this.
It's only a line to send you my love and to say how much I
have been thinking of you lately—and sympathizing with all
the anxiety and worry and suffering which this abominable
conspiracy must have caused you. Everyone, not only those
who know you, is indignant and amazed at the gross injustice
and crass stupidity of the [?] press. Juries of course always are
stupid, tho' I should have thought they wd have condemned
Crosland on his face. One comfort is he's such a scoundrel he's
sure to bring himself within reach of the law one of these days.
(He owes me 3 guineas by the way.) The other I imagine will
drink himself into a lunatic asylum. Dear Robbie, the affection
and devotion of your friends will never fail you. I've heard how
loyal people like the Asquiths are. D. S. MacColl was here on
Saturday talking with real loyalty and affection of you. He tells
me you are going away for a rest and change. I do hope you
will come back strong and well.

*Max's American wife (1878–1950), whom he married in 1910.

And she adds the postscript: 'I still go on, merely I believe to spite the doctors who gave me up long ago.'[49]

Ten

Time· had not closed the rift between Ross and Lord Alfred Douglas. The story is a long and complicated one which hardly concerns us here; but after Wilde's death in 1900, Ross took it upon himself to restore his friend's literary and dramatic credit, a mission, to some people's way of thinking, he carried out all too successfully. In the process (and not without good reason) he incurred the bitter enmity of Douglas.[50] The part played by T. W. H. Crosland,* a rather splendid Fleet Street mercenary and self-appointed guardian of public morals, seems in this instance to have been wholly venal. Paid by Douglas, in January 1914 he sent Ross a letter in which he described him, in his capacity as apologist of Wilde, as 'one dirty Sodomite bestowing lavish whitewash upon another'. The object of the letter, copies of which were sent at the same time to the Prime Minister, a couple of judges, the Public Prosecutor, and, among others, the High Master of St Paul's School, was to force Ross to action.[51]

Certainly Ross had had his measure of worry and anxiety, as Mabel says. For, having discovered damning evidence against him in the testimony of a boy called Garratt, Douglas and Crosland rubbed their hands in anticipatory glee. As intended, Ross was left with no alternative but to bring a charge, and Crosland's trial began at the Old Bailey on 27 June 1914. It was chiefly remarkable for some fine exchanges between F. E. Smith and the ferocious Crosland. Judge and jury were delighted, and Crosland went free. After a breathing-space—and a few months after Mabel's letter was written—Ross rather foolishly had Douglas arrested on further charges of libel. At this trial the jury disagreed; but in the end Ross had to put in a plea of *nolle prosequi* and pay Douglas's costs and expenses. As this was tantamount to a confession of guilt, Robbie was obliged to relinquish his post as Assessor of Picture Valuations to the Board of Trade. But there were compensations. In 1915, he was presented with a cheque for £700 from admirers and friends; and, in 1917, he was appointed to the

*1865–1924, poet and journalist and author of *The Unspeakable Scot*.

Imperial War Museum as Director and Manager, as well as to a
Trusteeship of the National Gallery. The damning notebook of
Inspector West seems to have been shut up for good. The indiscreet, yet magically invulnerable, friend of Wilde and of all
three Beardsleys died in 1918, widely mourned and respected.

It is to be our last glimpse of the *Cénacle*, and of the 'love that
dare not speak its name'. Crosland lived out his life in the way
that best suited him, Fleet Street, Monte Carlo and the Charing
Cross Hospital providing the three points of his triangle. Douglas
did not, as Mabel prophesied, drink himself into a lunatic asylum.
He survived Wilde by forty-five years, but ever—with all the day's
newspapers spread round him—on that eternal quest of his,
another suit for slander.

Of special interest is Mabel's mention of a severe pleurisy, at
the beginning of her letter. This, according to my medical advisers,
must add to our nagging suspicion that the officially recorded
cause of death, cancer of the uterus, was incorrect; though for
want of evidence to the contrary one is obliged, at least provision-
ally, to accept it. According to the Michael Fields' Diary, cancer
was first diagnosed as early as 1912, yet the disease ran for another
four years. While pre-malignant conditions like carcinoma in situ
may last an average of ten years, once the host resistance begins to
yield and symptoms appear which persuade the patient to consult
her doctor, the end comes rapidly. Mabel's survival astonished
not only the poet who addressed valedictory verses to her in
1912–13, but—as she herself points out here in her postscript—
her medical advisers as well. If no biopsy were taken, if no operation were performed during her lifetime, and no autopsy after
death (the certificate records none), then the statement on the
certificate is, as is quite proper, an expression of opinion rather
than of fact. What this leads up to must be the possibility that
Mabel suffered, not from cancer uteri, but from tuberculosis of
the womb. If the disease were pelvic tuberculosis, a *slow* downhill
path would be traced, and this might include a pleural effusion.
Of course, it is true that, in cancer, individual cases can depart
widely from the average, and it so happens that in Herman and
Maxwell's *Diseases of Women* (a new and enlarged edition of which
was published in 1913) a contemporary view is given that uterine

cancer 'may kill in four months or *extend over as many years*' (my italics). One is not, however, left relieved of all doubts, especially as tuberculosis would be the predictable condition.

Eleven

When Ricketts returned from a visit to Mabel on 2 August 1914, the streets rang with news-vendors' voices proclaiming the invasion of Luxembourg.[52] But as 1914 passed into 1915, the war ceased to have meaning for the invalid. Raffalovich speaks of her delusions, when she wrote cheques, 'giving them away, or thinking she did so, to dear compassionate friends';[53] and Ricketts, of a 'very black' last five months: 'Curiously, with the increase of pain and the loss of hope came a new clinging to life—the wish to live.'[54]

Yeats had put it another way:

> *And how should her heart fail her*
> *Or sickness break her will*
> *With her dead brother's valour*
> *For an example still?*

Was it not Aubrey *ex tenebris* who, in a sense, took possession of his sister and willed in her the wish to live?

In these last pages I propose to take my study of the relationship between Mabel and the artist a stage further: to move, that is, from the symptom of transvestism to the syndrome of transsexuality. For persistent eccentricities in Aubrey's work reflect, in my view, something more than a preoccupation with the clothing of the opposite sex and the commonly accepted rituals connected with it. And if transsexualists, united to the transvestist only through their common cross-dressing, form a minority group, this is no cause for surprise: in studying Aubrey and Mabel we were from the start presented with a pair of rare birds.

Let us consider the artist first. We have already noted the high incidence of hermaphroditic figures at an early stage, particularly in *Le Morte Darthur* where the text is ludicrously at odds with such gender confusion. Accompanying the hermaphrodite or effeminate man, in drawings up to early 1897, is the brutal or neuter woman. Either of the celebrated Messalina subjects will

MESSALINA.

95 Messalina returning from the Bath, for The
Sixth Satire of Juvenal, ?1897: first published in
A Second Book of Fifty Drawings, 1899.

serve as examples in the former category (Fig. 95); of the latter,
the flat-chested Atalanta with the dog (Fig. 96) is equally characteristic. But when we come to the illustrations for *Mademoiselle
de Maupin* (begun about February 1897) (Figs. 57, 62, 65) a
remarkable change has taken place, by no means to be entirely
explained away by the plot of Gautier's story, though this may
have helped to reveal something of the artist's own nature to
himself. Whilst formerly the emphasis laid by Aubrey upon
breast, nipple and areola was conveyed almost as a malediction, in
keeping with his general presentation of woman as animal, dominating man and anticipating his lust, in the *Maupin* set the artist's
attitude has become gentle, affectionate, honey-sweet. The
frontispiece-drawing of Mlle de Maupin shows a transvestist
'Théodore' as pretty as a Renoir (Fig. 55). The 'D'Albert', however
feminized, is equally free of satire. 'D'Albert in search of his

96   Mabel's own copy of *The Idler* for March 1897, open at the interview with her brother, showing her photograph and the Atalanta with the dog.

Ideals' (Fig. 97), though given female habitus and hour-glass body build, returns to an almost Burne-Jonesian blandness of expression, and the two incidental figures might be walking down Quality Street. At first sight, 'The Lady at the Dressing-Table' (Fig. 65) seems to bring us back to the old satiric pairing of vicious *madame* and false *vierge*. However, on closer scrutiny, it will be found that they play their parts with no sensual inter-communication or leers at the spectator. Madame has become a 'good sort', and her pupil's expression is as velvety as her flesh. So, too, the sting has been extracted from 'The Lady with the Rose' (Fig. 62). Full-lipped, languorous, she is still essentially 'nice', suffering no depreciation of moral character under the dwarf's impertinent stare. There was one further pen-and-wash drawing, 'The Lady with the Monkey', in this set, but the pretty book-plate for Olive Custance* and the 'Arbuscula' belong to the

*1874–1944, poet. She married Lord Alfred Douglas in 1902.

97   D'Albert in search of his Ideals, from *Six Drawings illustrating . . . Mademoiselle de Maupin*, published 1898.

same period and are carried out in the same manner (Fig. 63). In 'Arbuscula', imaginary portrait of a Roman actress, Aubrey had every excuse to employ his old attitude of disenchantment: far from coarsening his subject, he has not even sharpened his wits on it—this might be the ingenuous Miss Marie Tempest herself, or some other mummer whose new-found respectability had so annoyed George Moore.[55] Of greater interest, because it belongs to the Gautier illustrations and because of its altogether finer quality, remains 'The Lady with the Monkey' (Fig. 57). There is a world of difference between the brutal Messalinas and this turbaned charmer, her breasts gentled so discreetly by the draftsman.

The 'Initial M', for *Volpone*, among the very last tasks undertaken by the dying man, brings this change in Aubrey's treatment of woman to a more than decorative climax (Fig. 98). Nothing now—the drawing was despatched from Menton as late as New

98 Initial M, from *Ben Jonson his Volpone: or The Foxe*, published 1898.

Year's Day, 1898—'restrained the dark disclosure', which reads like a full confession of the artist's transsexual desires. Fetish garments are no longer of interest. The woman spurns her minimal scrap of drapery, demanding exclusive attention for her sexual characteristics: breasts prominent, belly and mons veneris swollen and emphatic. Behind, the term-like figures sprout six breasts each and perch on the same generous haunches. There is nothing, be it noted, flippant or salacious about the design. One cannot mistake the solemnity of this cry from the artist's heart.

Looking at 'Initial M', we know on the instant now why the Abbé Tannhäuser=the Abbé Fanfreluche=the Abbé Aubrey could not be 'saved' by a last-minute miracle: Heaven, for him—and in no heterosexual sense—*was* 'under the hill'. Moreover, the broad, lyre-shaped pelvis and knock-knees, which Aubrey sees fit to give his background 'fertility' figures as marks, apparently, of a super-femininity, are to be found also in two of his self-portraits: that called 'A Footnote' (Fig. 99); the other, the idealized representation of himself as 'The Abbé' (Fig. 67). We can hardly start measuring Aubrey's pelvic girdle at this distance in time, but neither Sickert's oil-sketch nor any photograph suggests the child-bearing hips of 'The Abbé' and 'A Footnote'. Those who have made a special study of transsexualism all remark upon the bizarre conviction of the male patient that he is feminine in physique when the opposite is ludicrously evident and the most he can hope for, without the knife (though surgery remains only surgery, not a change of sex), is some reduction of facial hair and partial atrophy of the testes.

If subject to something like the same self-hypnosis, Aubrey was in happier case than the uncreative queuer at the clinic: he could express his convictions as art, achieving much more satisfactory results than all the mammaplastic, vaginoplastic surgeons put together. It might be thought strange that the sublimation of this feminine personality in his work manifested itself so suddenly and

99 A Footnote (self-portrait), from *The Savoy*, No. 2, April 1896.

so late. In fact, one can exaggerate the suddenness. Apart from the 'Messalina Returning from the Bath' (Fig. 95), which most critics believe to be of a date earlier than that ascribed to it by Smithers,[56] the tempering of satire—implying anything but a decline in talent—had been proceeding steadily throughout *The Savoy* phase. From that point, the artist's jealousy of the sex difference, formerly expressing itself in spiteful indecency, is replaced by a new self-knowledge and self-confidence. The proud claim to female normality for himself (as asserted by every trans-sexualist when the 'light dawns upon him', whatever—as I have pointed out—its demonstrable unreason) would have restored Aubrey to just this kind of tranquillity, rendering superfluous all those prodromal sneers, snarls and blasphemies once necessary to defend his position. For the total 'revelation' of transsexualism to delay onset till the early twenties is, in fact, as normal as anything else in the twilit world we are exploring.[57]

Twelve

The ties between Aubrey and his sister, as we have seen, were exceptionally close. Ellen's absences, the bickering between their parents on those rare occasions when both were present, the boy's physical dependence upon his sister, had sealed the union in early days. They shared in the social ups-and-downs of the shabby-genteel, and moments of glory as child prodigies.

The banalities of Lombard Street and the Polytechnic followed these facile triumphs. The young Beardsleys gave the appearance of having settled down in a workaday world of premiums and text-book instruction; but office and classroom were no more than endured. Ellen was the humorously tolerated *petite maman*, her husband, till progressive muscular atrophy killed him in 1909, had always existed like a man in another world. Brother and sister were at one on every subject: on *The Burning Babe*; on Whistler, on Burne-Jones, on the Japanese; on *Tannhäuser*, on *Tristan*; on incense and all church ceremony; on the absurdities of sexual convention. For Aubrey, no homosexual on his own admission, the circle of Passionate Friends at least offered freedom from this last. Mabel, ranging further afield, returned always to maidenly-male households like those of Raffalovich and Ricketts.

After her brother's death she continued to cultivate his friends, to talk his kind of talk.

Always touched by something in Mabel that reminded him of Aubrey, Raffalovich must have found himself bewitched during the last months of her life. The photograph reproduced as our frontispiece here not only illustrates Yeats's poems to perfection, it enables us to appreciate how, with the malignant march of her disease, she acquired more and more noticcably an extraordinary resemblance to her dead brother. Nothing remained of the little girl with the fringe, or the round-faced actress who played Mrs Maydew in *The Queen's* Proctor. And the difference between Mabel even in *The Degenerates*, at the beginning of the new century, and the last Mabel, stretched on her day-bed, is hardly less astonishing. Illness—or some *trauma* (the word is of 1916 vintage) duplicating the ecstasies of the saints—had completely transformed her. The 'daisy', as Wilde once called Mabel, becomes the 'orchid' he had designated Aubrey. On his side, the artist of the 'Initial M' symbolically achieved his sex-change after all. The breath-starved nostalgic found his way back to the womb. Disregarding Wagner's plans for him, one might say, Tannhäuser regained his shadowy coulisse Under the Hill.

Thirteen

I promised earlier to return to Mr W. G. Good's small painting of Mabel by W. Graham Robertson (Fig. 100). It bears, besides the artist's signature and the date (1911), the curious inscription: 'To Philip Beardsley'. As no one could explain who Philip Beardsley might be, and no one understood why the name should have been associated with Mabel, the portrait was not included in the Victoria and Albert Museum's exhibition of 1966, though subsequently shown in New York.

It has never seriously been questioned that the portrait is of Mabel. Walker reproduced it in his *Miscellany*, and I was not in doubt that I should include it among the illustrations to this book. I have already discussed the likelihood that the man's clothing worn by Mabel in this picture, jacket, waistcoat and trousers, once belonged to Aubrey. But why the name Philip? To our knowledge,

100 W. Graham Robertson's oil-sketch of Mabel,
inscribed by the artist to 'Philip Beardsley', 1911.

no Philip Beardsley ever existed. The suggestion has been made
(though not published) that Mabel adopted the title of Philip
Beardsley in her transvestist role. I feel sure she did, and for a
reason which the whole argument of this book is designed to drive
home: because 'Philip' was her brother. A drawing of Aubrey's
in Volume III (1894) of *The Yellow Book* bears, indeed, the
cryptic signature: 'Philip Broughton' (Fig. 101).

*   *   *

At some point in the last stage of her illness Mabel was taken to live at 75 Lansdowne Road, the home of her mother-in-law, Mrs Wright. There, very conveniently for Ricketts and Shannon and their patron, Edmund Davis, who lived in Lansdowne House and at No. 13, respectively, she was watched over by kind friends till the end. She wore her sufferings, says Raffalovich, like a crown of gilt thorns and, round her shoulders, a vast Roumanian dalmatic presented to her by George's friend, Prince Antoine Bibesco.*[58]

101   Portrait of Mantegna by 'Philip Broughton', from *The Yellow Book*, Volume III, October 1894.

Her grave may be found in the Roman Catholic reservation of the St Pancras and Islington Cemetery. It is a neglected spot. Yet one is glad there are no fiercely viridian rock-chips to keep down the nettles; that, back in the straitened days of the First

*Prince Antoine Bibesco married Elizabeth Asquith, the novelist. The Asquiths, it will be remembered, were among Ross's warmest supporters.

World War, funds did not run to a half-veiled urn, an angelic figure pointing upward or stooping to lay its stone wreath on the sarcophagus; that one does not have to read, incised upon yet another simulated book, the words: 'Where is death's sting? Where, Grave, thy victory?' No. 38, R.C.2, is a barely traceable tumulus, woven over with wild grasses. The cross itself, reflecting nothing of the fashion for Celtic ornament and the textural imitation of bark which seems to have held contemporary monumental-masons in thrall, leans desolately off-true. Simple as the cross's design is the legend it bears: 'In loving memory of Mabel, wife of George Bealby Wright and sister of Aubrey Beardsley, who died May 8th 1916 aged 44 years. "Eternal rest give unto her, O Lord." R.I.P.'

102   The last photograph, showing the artist in his room at the Hôtel
Cosmopolitain, Menton, in late November or early December 1897.
'I had myself and my room photographed a few days ago,' he wrote to
Mabel. 'They tell me it has come out splendidly.' He was working
on the *Volpone* drawings at this time. The massed prints on the wall
are by his beloved Mantegna. The crucifix may be that given him by
Ross. The candlesticks are the celebrated pair which always travelled
with him. On the bookcase are three identifiable photographs: from
the left, André Raffalovich, the composer Wagner and Mabel.

Notes

A Young Marcellus

1 From a letter (of 7 November 1913) to André Raffalovich, in response to the latter's gift of a copy of the *Last Letters*. It was Harland, we are told, who introduced Aubrey to Henry James one Sunday afternoon early in the spring of 1894.

2 Alexander Michaelson (pseud. for André Raffalovich, hereafter named as author), 'Aubrey Beardsley', *Blackfriars*, October 1928, p. 610.

3 Charles B. Cochran, *The Secrets of a Showman*, 1925, p. 4.

4 W. G. Good, Walker papers: 'Account of Aubrey Beardsley at Brighton Grammar School given by Mr W. W. Hind Smyth.'

5 Letter to Raffalovich, February 1897: Henry Maas, J. L. Duncan and W. G. Good, editors, *The Letters of Aubrey Beardsley*, 1971 (hereafter referred to as 'MDG'), p. 249. He also told Raffalovich: 'I know how much more bitter are these [school] troubles to bear than any others that come later in life': MDG, p. 248.

6 W. G. Good, Walker papers.

7 'Extract from *Excursus on Downside*—part of the unpublished Reminiscences of Sir Ninian Comper (1864–1960)', made available to me by Mr Anthony Symondson. Walker, as Mr Good informs me, also drew attention to the interest taken in Aubrey's work at this stage by a fellow clerk, A. H. Pargeter.

8 W. G. Good, Walker papers.

9 Reading University, Beardsley archive.

10 MDG, p. 29.

11 Letter to G. F. Scotson-Clark, *c.* September 1891: MDG, p. 29.

12 MDG, 19 August 1896, p. 153.

13 Robert Ross, *Aubrey Beardsley: with . . . a revised Iconography by Aymer Vallance*, (1909) 1921, pp. 16, 17. Aubrey is reported by the writer to have explored the National Gallery in the same way; other contemporaries speak of his sketching from religious works of the Italian School.

14 September 1893: MDG, p. 54.

15 Charles B. Cochran, *op. cit.*, p. 5.

16 Arthur Symons, *Aubrey Beardsley*, (1898) 1948, p. 16 *et seq.* The essay was first published in *The Fortnightly Review* for May 1898.

17 MDG, p. 34.

18 Introduction, *Aubrey Beardsley's Erotic Universe*, 1967.

19 Letter discovered among the effects of Mr Read, successor to

Aubrey's headmaster at Brighton Grammar School. Though without date, it must have been written in the autumn of 1892.

20 Robert Ross, *op. cit.*, pp. 15, 16.

21 R. A. Walker, *A Beardsley Miscellany*, 1949, p. 22.

Passionate Friends

1 Aubrey had met Wilde during his visit to Burne-Jones of 12 July 1891; but a re-introduction was necessary to bring the two together again.

2 Sir Rupert Hart-Davis, Editor, *The Letters of Oscar Wilde*, 1962, p. 493 (note 2).

3 Margery Ross, *Robert Ross: Friend of Friends*, 1952, p. 54.

4 Lord Alfred Douglas, *Autobiography*, 1929, p. 29.

5 MDG, p. 47.

6 Letter to Ross, late November 1893: MDG, p. 58. 'I can tell you,' says Aubrey, 'I had a warm time of it between Lane and Oscar and Co.'

7 In the Sterling Library, University of London.

8 Hart-Davis, *op. cit.*, p. 348.

9 MDG, p. 58.

10 '. . . and it was further stipulated that the Art contributions to the Yellow Book should in no way illustrate the text, and further that Oscar Wilde should never be allowed to write for it whether anonymously, pseudonymously, or under his own name. Both editors made this stipulation although Oscar Wilde's plays had been published at The Bodley Head. I have recently seen a signed letter from Beardsley with the above statement regarding Wilde': W. G. Good, Walker papers.

11 Netta Syrett, in both *The Sheltering Tree* (her autobiography), 1933, p. 78, and a novel based on her recollections of the *Yellow Book* set, *Strange Marriage*, 1930, p. 94. Miss Syrett remembered Mabel, at the same time, in a dress that 'vaguely recalled a lady of the Italian Renaissance'.

12 Sir William Rothenstein, *Men and Memories*, Vol. I, 1931, p. 187.

13 'I have worked to amuse myself, and if it has amused the public as well, so much the better for me!': *The Idler*, March 1897, p. 199.

14 Sir Rupert Hart-Davis, *Max Beerbohm: Letters to Reggie Turner*, 1964, p. 84.

15 Rothenstein, *op. cit.*, Vol. I, p. 182.

16 Aubrey, in a letter to Rothenstein: MDG, p. 54.

17 Hart-Davis, *Max Beerbohm: Letters to Reggie Turner*, p. 92.

18 W. G. Good, Walker papers: 'Beardsley was the Yellow Book' (Lane); the same sentiment is expressed in E. F. Benson, *As We Were*, repr. 1939, p. 276.

19 *The Times*, 20 April 1894: '. . . possibly, however, it [*The Yellow Book*] may be intended to attract by its very repulsiveness and insolence, in that case it is not unlikely to be successful, its note appears to be a combination of English rowdiness and French lubricity . . .'

20 H. Montgomery Hyde, *The Trials of Oscar Wilde*, 1948, p. 236.

21 Frank Harris, *Oscar Wilde*, 1938 (2nd ed.), p. 94.

22 Walker, *op. cit.*, p. 80: 'No one ever took liberties with Aubrey.'

23 Letter from Aymer Vallance to Ross, 23 May 1895, in Margery Ross, *Robert Ross: Friend of Friends*, p. 38. Lane's interview on the subject was cabled by Miller of *The New York Times* to *The Daily Chronicle* (W. G. Good, Walker papers).

24 H. Montgomery Hyde, *op. cit.*, pp. 193–4.

25 Hart-Davis, *Letters of Oscar Wilde*, p. 193.

26 Wilde had personally sponsored Gray's *Silverpoints* in 1893.

27 Raffalovich, *op. cit.*, p. 609.

28 *Ibid.*, p. 610.

29 *Ibid.*, *loc. cit.*

30 Miss Brophy brought out this point in a review of Maas, Duncan and Good's *The Letters of Aubrey Beardsley* in *The Listener*.

31 Margery Ross, *op. cit.*, p. 38.

32 Letter to Raffalovich, February 1897: MDG, p. 250.

33 Alexander Michaelson (pseud. for André Raffalovich, hereafter named as author), 'Aubrey Beardsley's Sister', *Blackfriars*, November 1928, p. 670.

34 Letter to Raffalovich: MDG, p. 416.

35 *Cf*, also to Raffalovich: 'My great difficulty for some time yet, I fear, will be dryness and difficulty in prayer.': MDG, p. 290.

36 Letter of 22 March 1897: MDG, p. 282. For an investigation into the friendship with Julian Sampson, see Easton, *Apollo*, January 1967, pp. 66–8.

37 Raffalovich, 'Aubrey Beardsley's Sister', p. 674.

38 W. G. Good, Walker papers: 'It was only when the world discovered the artist's greatness that Moore became an enthusiastic admirer' (Lane).

39 George Moore, *In Single Strictness*, 1922, p. 200.

40 Miss Gribbell was the daughter of a Scots bank-agent. She began as André's governess, then became his housekeeper. Marie Raffalovich,

who found her son's ugliness too painful to bear, remained resident in Paris, while Miss Gribbell and André settled permanently, first in London, then in Edinburgh. See Fr. Brocard Sewell, *Footnote to the Nineties*, 1968, p. 25.

41 W. B. Yeats, *Autobiographies*, 1961, pp. 329–30. This passage was first published in *The Trembling of the Veil*, 1924.

42 MDG, p. 97.

43 Arthur Symons, *op. cit.*, p. 7.

44 *Ibid.*, p. 8.

45 I record here my impressions of Mr Good's Collection, which I was privileged to examine. Pink was Aubrey's favourite addition to the pen-drawings in those examples which he coloured by hand, such as 'La Dame aux Camélias' and 'Messalina Returning Home', both in the Tate.

46 Stuart Mason [Christopher Millard], *Bibliography of Oscar Wilde*, 1914, pp. 413–4.

47 *Men and Memories*, Vol. I, p. 245.

48 Sir Francis Beilby Alston himself received some coaching from Ellen, odd as this sounds. In a letter to Lane, Ellen begs him not to mention this, as it would upset her friendship with Lady Alston.

49 *Cf.* letter to Smithers, 2 November 1897: MDG, p. 384.

50 Hart-Davis, *The Letters of Oscar Wilde*, p. 627 and note 1.

51 Letter to Raffalovich, 26 July 1897: MDG, pp. 351–2.

52 Hart-Davis, *op. cit.*, p. 635, Note 2 (letter of 2 September from Smithers to Wilde).

53 The story is naïvely, but movingly, related in *The Early Life and Vicissitudes of Jack Smithers*, 1939 (Jack was the publisher's son).

54 Extracts are published in Brian Reade, *Sexual Heretics* (1970), 1st American edition, 1971, pp. 228 *et seq.*

55 Discussed by Mr Reade in a letter to me.

56 Arthur Symons, *op. cit.*, p. 13.

Ellen and the Invalid

1 In his *Miscellany*, Walker published a very useful paper, entitled 'Notes on the Family of Aubrey Beardsley', pp. 95–106. He lays emphasis on the interesting fact that the artist's paternal grandfather was a working jeweller and goldsmith; but Vincent Paul Beardsley never entered the trade, so that there was no Dürer-like background, even at one remove. Mr Good's Walker papers include the death certificate of a John Beardsley who breathed his last in the Worksop workhouse in 1838.

2 W. G. Good, Walker papers. The Crowley testimonial is dated 23 January 1883, the year in which the Beardsleys are thought to have first moved to London.

3 I have spent whole days trying to locate the '2 Ashley Villas' address, even to the point of examining old Water Board Minutes in the Westminster area. My suggestion arises from the existence of an Ashley House today in Vauxhall Bridge Road.

4 September 1893: J.-P. B. Ross, MSS.

5 I think it could be argued that the nature-denying outlines of so many women's costumes drawn by the artist may derive from earliest memories of his mother during the 1870s. The female figure was then especially heavily swathed, draped, puffed and pleated, a roomy mantle or ankle-length skin-coat ultimately filling up the last convexities. As a sick child, he would have been familiar with one shapeless female garment above all others—his mother's nightgown. We see this nightgown, perhaps, in the beautiful design for the front wrapper of the fourth issue of *The Savoy*.

6 Walker, *op. cit.*, pp. 75, 79.

7 Information from Mr Good.

8 University College, London, Lane archive. The letter, undated, was presumably written in the 1920s.

9 Letter to A. W. King, 9 December 1892: MDG, p. 38.

10 Edmund Symes-Thompson, with his father, was part author of *Clinical Lectures on Pulmonary Consumption*, 1863.

11 MDG, p. 18.

12 *Ibid.*, p. 55.

13 Copy of document (in Miss Dash's hand) given me by Mr Reade.

14 J.-P. B. Ross, MSS: published in Margery Ross, *op. cit.*, pp. 27–8.

15 MDG, pp. 53–4.

16 *Ibid.*, p. 34: letter to E. J. Marshall, autumn 1892.

17 J.-P. B. Ross, MSS. There are several letters to Ross from Mabel referring to her mother's illness.

18 MDG, p. 34. The 'chronic sciatica' was probably an acute disc lesion for which perfect rest, as prescribed for Ellen, would still be the best treatment.

19 Netta Syrett, *Strange Marriage*, 1930, pp. 92–3.

20 J.-P. B. Ross, MSS: published in Margery Ross, *op. cit.*, p. 32.

21 J.-P. B. Ross, MSS: published (as, in error, 5 September 1893) in Margery Ross, *op. cit.*, pp. 26–7.

22 Reade, *Aubrey Beardsley*, 1967, Notes, p. 351; see also MDG, p. 104.

23 W. G. Good, Walker papers.

24 J.-P. B. Ross, MSS: hitherto unpublished.

25 W. H. McMenemey, 'The Water Doctors of Malvern, etc.', in *Proceedings of the Royal Society of Medicine*, Vol. 46, 5, 1 October 1952.

26 Edmund Symes-Thompson and Charles Frederick Grindrod, 'Hydropathy: its place in Medical Science' in *The Practitioner*, 1888, Vol. 41, p. 23.

27 *The Story of Venus and Tannhäuser* is better known as *Under the Hill*, as it was called in the expurgated version which first appeared in *The Savoy* in 1896. Leonard Smithers brought out the original unexpurgated text under the *Venus and Tannhäuser* title in 1907 (the edition already described). The 'moping and worrying' passage occurs in a letter to F. H. Evans: MDG, p. 79.

28 *Men and Memories*, Vol. I, p. 134.

29 W. G. Good, Walker papers.

30 Desmond Flower and Henry Maas, *The Letters of Ernest Dowson*, 1967, p. 355. (Letter of 24 April to Henry Davray.)

31 J.-P. B. Ross, MSS: hitherto unpublished.

32 MDG, p. 126.

33 Edmund Symes-Thompson, *Clinical Lectures on Pulmonary Consumption*, p. 231.

34 MDG, p. 127.

35 J.-P. B. Ross, MSS: letter of 2 May: hitherto unpublished.

36 Or could it have been tuberculous epididymitis?

37 MDG, p. 153.

38 J.-P. B. Ross, MSS, letter of 25 October(?): hitherto unpublished.

39 *Ibid.*, letter of 19 November: hitherto unpublished.

40 *Ibid.* Four lines of this letter are quoted in Margery Ross, *op. cit.*, p. 45.

41 He was able to attend one concert only in the Winter Gardens. This took place on 18 March, when the Bournemouth Municipal Symphony Orchestra gave a performance of Beethoven's 4th Symphony.

42 MDG, p. 265.

43 *Ibid.*, p. 278.

44 J.-P. B. Ross, MSS: published in Margery Ross, *op. cit.*, p. 47.

45 One of the stay's few enlivening features had been a visit from Mrs Drummond (wife of Canon A. H. Drummond) and her son Malcolm, then a youth of seventeen. Malcolm Drummond's genius as a painter has been appreciated only in very recent years. In 1922, he executed the 'Sacred Heart' altarpiece for Gray at St Peter's, Edinburgh.

46 It seems clear that 'stupes' were not meant. A 'stupe', taking the form of a piece of flannel first wrung out in hot water, was accepted treatment for pleurisy in those days.

47 Letter to Robert U. Johnson, 15 May 1898: MDG, p. 440.

48 In the recollections of Miss Stella Alleyne and Mrs Viva King, and passed on to me in conversation and letters.

49 MDG, p. 441.

50 Walker, *Miscellany*, p. 80.

51 J.-P. B. Ross, MSS. Letter of 29 September 1893: published in Margery Ross, *op. cit.*, pp. 27–8.

52 *Ibid.*: letters of 20 April and 10 June, hitherto unpublished.

53 *Ibid.*: hitherto unpublished.

54 MDG, pp. 203, 207 (on the subject of canaries!).

55 J.-P. B. Ross, MSS, letter of 22 April: published in Margery Ross, *op. cit.*, p. 47.

56 MDG, p. 297.

57 Mr Reade thinks the pen consisted of a 'gold nib, or gold nib-and-fitting, attached to a black (?) wooden handle.' 'Unfortunately,' he adds, 'it was lost long ago.'

58 Ellen herself stated afterwards (whether correctly or not): 'The day before he died he [Aubrey] *telegraphed* to Smithers to burn the Lysistrata "Dans mon agonie".' MDG confirms that Ellen addressed the envelope of the letter, p. 439.

A Flutter of Frilled Things

1 Such a committee was formed to encourage Spitalfields brocades and other native-produced silks; its watchword was 'simplicity with artistic authority'. Messrs Liberty spread the gospel in their many catalogues.

2 In the Library of the Victoria and Albert Museum. Mrs Madeleine Ginsburg gives information on Worth in an article in *High Victorian: The Costume Society Spring Conference, 1968*, Victoria and Albert Museum, 1969.

3 Alexandre Dumas *fils, La Dame aux camélias*: Préface de Jules Janin, 'Mademoiselle Marie Duplessis' (Calmann-Lévy: *Oeuvres complètes d'Alexandre Dumas fils*, n.d.).

4 *Ibid.*, p. xviii.

5 'In the first place there were three sexes, not, as now, two', etc.: *Symposium*, 189 a–190 a (Stephanus edn.).

6 MDG, p. 286.

7 Letter H. C. J. Pollitt: MDG, p. 355.

8 Letter to Pollitt, 26 September 1897: MDG, p. 372.

9 29 September 1897: MDG, p. 374.

10 This letter survives only in a few lines' digest from a catalogue (Myers): MDG, p. 382.

11 Hart-Davis, *The Letters of Oscar Wilde*, p. 509. The long letter to Douglas was written in January–March 1897, extracts from which were published by Ross under the title of *De Profundis*.

12 *Cf.*: De l'épiderme sur la soie
   Glissent des frissons argentés,
   Et l'étoffe à la chair renvoie
   Ses éclairs roses reflétés.

   D'où te vient cette robe étrange
   Qui semble faite de ta chair,
   Trame vivante qui mélange
   Avec ta peau son rose clair?

13 Théophile Gautier, *Mademoiselle de Maupin*, (1835) 1927, pp. 92 *et seq.*

14 *Ibid.*, p. 100.

15 *The Desire and Pursuit of the Whole* was written by Rolfe in Venice, in 1909–10.

16 'I am horrified at what you tell me about "The Ballad". I had no idea it was "poor" ': MDG, p. 122.

17 MDG, p. 72.

18 MDG, p. 76.

19 *The Story of Venus and Tannhäuser*, 1907, p. 21. 'Ruff' appears for 'muff' in *The Savoy* rendering; but the illustration shows that 'muff' was intended. These quotations have been very kindly checked for wording and punctuation for me by Mr Good.

20 *Ibid.*, p. 25. Smithers's edition has, incorrectly, 'Nôtre Dame'.

21 *Ibid.*, p. 35.

22 'Therapeutic Uses of Mescal Buttons (Anhelonium Lewini)' in *The Therapeutic Gazette*, 15 September 1895, referred to in the 1896 publication of the paper.

23 S. Weir Mitchell, 'Remarks on the Effects of Anhelonium Lewini (the Mescal Button)' in *The British Medical Journal*, 5 December, 1896, p. 1625.

24 P. 1626; p. 1627.

25 Havelock Ellis, 'Mescal: a New Artificial Paradise' in the *Annual Report of the Board of Regents of the Smithsonian Institute* (*Natural History Museum*), *to July 1897:* reprinted from *The Contemporary*

Review, January 1898.

26 *Ibid.*, p. 539.

27 *The Story of Venus and Tannhäuser*, p. 20.

28 S. Weir Mitchell, *op. cit.*, p. 1626.

29 Havelock Ellis, p. 543.

30 *The Story of Venus and Tannhäuser*, p. 20.

31 S. Weir Mitchell, *op. cit.*, cited p. 1627.

32 Havelock Ellis, p. 545.

33 *Ibid., loc. cit.*

34 Maas, *The Letters of Ernest Dowson*, p. 345.

35 Aldous Huxley, *The Doors of Perception*, (1954) 1957, p. 40

36 Redwood Anderson's record of his experience is quoted at length and verbatim in Walter de la Mare, *Desert Islands and Robinson Crusoe*, 2nd ed., 1932, pp. 91–6.

37 Aldous Huxley, *op. cit.*, pp. 9, 10.

38 Walter de la Mare, *op. cit.*, p. 93.

39 Letter postmarked 7 March 1897: MDG, p. 269.

40 *The Story of Venus and Tannhäuser*, ed. cit., pp. 58–59.

41 Richard Le Gallienne, *The Romantic '90s*, (1926) 1951, p. 135

42 *The Story of Venus and Tannhäuser*, p. 66.

43 MDG, p. 53.

44 H. Montgomery Hyde, *op. cit.*, p. 192.

45 *Ibid.*, p. 281.

46 *Ibid.*, p. 193.

47 Reported in *The Times*, 21 August 1894.

48 Reported in the same newspaper, at unusual length, from 16 May 1870.

49 *Cf.* also J. Hoenig, J. Kenna and Ann Youd, 'Social and Economic Aspects of Transsexualism', in *The British Journal of Psychiatry*, August 1970, p. 164.

50 Dr John Randell, 'Transvestism and Transsexualism' in *The British Journal of Hospital Medicine*, February 1970, p. 212.

51 *Men and Memories*, Vol. I, p. 135.

52 The programmes are extensively reproduced in *The Uncollected Work*.

53 Copy given me by Mr Reade. The MS is thought to be in Miss Dash's hand, but at Ellen Beardsley's dictation. It is headed 'Mrs Beardsley—Jan. 12 1921'.

Aubrey and Mabel

1 'Aubrey Beardsley by Ellen Agnus Beardsley', in Walker's *Miscellany*, pp. 79–80.

2 *Ibid.*, pp. 82–3.

3 *Ibid.*, p. 83.

4 *Ibid.*, p. 79.

5 *Ibid.*, p. 83.

6 Copy of letter from James to Gray (from Edinburgh, undated) in the Library of University College, London, Lane archive.

7 E. F. Benson, *op. cit.*, pp. 282–3.

8 Walker, *Miscellany*, p. 75.

9 Information from the Local History Librarian, Brighton Public Libraries.

10 *The Church of the Annunciation, 1864–1964*, n.d. (1964), p. 16.

11 W. G. Good, Walker papers. As assistant curate to Father Chapman, during the years 1882–6, a Charles Greenwood Thornton is recorded. This must be the Thornton referred to by Haldane Macfall (on p. 16 of his *Aubrey Beardsley*, 1928), though the latter does not connect him with the Church of the Annunciation.

12 MDG, p. 119.

13 Mr Symondson's typescript, entitled: 'Extract from *Excursus on Downside*—part of the unpublished Reminiscences of Sir Ninian Comper (1864–1960),' p. 2.

14 *Ibid.*, p. 3.

15 Information from *The History of St Barnabas, Pimlico*, n.d. (*c.* 1931–2).

16 Information from Miss Stella Alleyne and from Comper (in Mr Symondson's typescript).

17 As may be checked in the 'List of Drawings' supplied by Aymer Vallance for Ross's *Aubrey Beardsley* in 1909, itself going back to a task connected with the album of *Fifty Drawings* published during the artist's lifetime.

18 University College, London: Lane archive.

19 MDG, pp. 21–2.

20 Walker, *Miscellany*, p. 76.

21 See also A. W. King, *An Aubrey Beardsley Lecture*, 1904, p. 32, note 1.

22 MDG, p. 15.

23 This information appears in a number of interviews, since Mabel was understandably proud of her scholastic achievements: e.g. in *The Sketch*, 10 June 1896.

24 Netta Syrett, *The Sheltering Tree*, p. 68.

25 *Ibid.*, p. 69.

26 *Ibid.*, p. 74.

27 *Ibid.*, pp. 73–4.

28 Frank Harris, *My Life and Loves*, (1923–1927) 1961, Vol. I, p. 15.

29 Hart-Davis, *Max Beerbohm: Letters to Reggie Turner*, p. 88.

30 Legrand du Saulle, 'De l'inceste considéré au point de vue de son influence sur la progéniture', *Journal de médecine de Paris*, 1885, 8, p. 784.

31 From the review of a novel, *The Other I*, by Joel Lotan, in *The Psychiatric Quarterly*, April 1963, cited by Eugen Kahn, 'On Incest and Freud's Oedipus Complex' in *Confin. psychiat.*, 8, 1965, p. 95.

32 In the recollection of Miss Stella Alleyne, and passed on to me verbally.

33 Ross, *op. cit.*, p. 23.

34 The portrait in question turned out to be of Allan Odle by Adrian Allinson.

35 Brian Reade, *Aubrey Beardsley*: Exhibition at the Victoria and Albert Museum, 1966: entry under Item No. 587.

36 Mr Reade has permitted me to quote from his letter of 5 February 1969.

37 Letter of 26 March to Smithers: MDG, p. 120.

38 It was once suggested that Sir Landon Ronald might have been the man involved. 'It is beautiful to love and be loved . . .,' he wrote in his rather sentimental autobiography, *Myself and Others: Written Lest I forget*—but Mabel is not mentioned. Ellen Beardsley had lodged, it is said, with Landon Ronald's parents, when she first came to London.

39 Saul, L. J., and Lyons, J. W., 'Motivation and Respiratory Disorders', in Wittkower, E. D., and Cleghorn, R.A., *Recent Developments in Psychomatic Medicine*, 1954, pp. 267–80.

40 MDG, p. 37.

41 Reade, *Aubrey Beardsley*, 1967, p. 22: 'Had he [Aubrey] witnessed a miscarriage of his sister's and one for which he himself had been responsible?'

42 Letter to Marshall, autumn of 1892: MDG, pp. 34–5.

43 In the Directory, the ownership of No. 114 was recorded in her name alone.

44 Interview with Mabel, in *Bon Accord*, 2 February 1900.

45 Walker, *Miscellany*, p. 83.

46 J.-P. B. Ross, MSS, letter of 5 September 1894, published (by error, as of 1893) in Margery Ross, *op. cit.*, pp. 26–7.

47 In the *Liverpool Daily Post*, 6 October 1892.

48 Discussed by Reade, *Aubrey Beardsley*, 1967, p. 347.

49 MDG, p. 65.

50 Hart-Davis, *Max Beerbohm: Letters to Reggie Turner*, p. 53.

51 *Under the Hill* (1904), 1921, p. x. The 'Publisher's Note' was written by Lane in 1903.

52 Information from Mr Good.

53 Netta Syrett, *The Sheltering Tree*, p. 73.

54 *The Lady*, 10 January 1895.

55 Mabel, in an interview: *Bon Accord*, 23 February 1900.

56 Charles B. Cochran, *The Secrets of a Showman*, p. 50.

57 From Mabel's scrapbook, cutting dated 6 April 1897.

58 MDG, pp. 204–5.

59 Printed opposite 'Atalanta', on p. 200 of the March issue of *The Idler*.

60 MDG, p. 245.

61 *Ibid.*, p. 332.

62 *Ibid.*, p. 333.

63 *Ibid.*, p. 354.

64 *Ibid.*, *loc. cit.*

65 Letter of 18 August 1897: MDG, p. 358.

66 MDG, p. 359–60.

67 *Ibid.*, p. 396.

68 *Ibid.*, pp. 400, 402.

69 *Ibid.*, pp. 429–30.

70 *The Rocket*, 26 February 1898.

71 J.-P. B. Ross, MSS.

72 MDG, p. 437.

73 *Ibid.*, p. 438.

74 J.-P. B. Ross, MSS.

The Dying Lady

1 The first Solemn Requiem was held in the Cathedral at Menton. As regards the second, I am grateful to the Revd F. Edwards, S.J., for the information that among the Notices read out at Farm Street on 4 May 1898 was the following: 'On Thursday at 10.30 there will be a Solemn Requiem Mass for the repose of the soul of Aubrey Beardsley.' There are no other references to the event in the Church's surviving correspondence, nor mention in the Minister's Log-Book. The magazine, *The Farm Street Calendar*, did not begin to appear till October 1905. A letter from Mabel to John Gray (Reading University, Beardsley archive) tells us that 'Father Chew celebrated':

she did not know the names of the other two officiating priests.

2 J.-P. B. Ross, MSS: Ellen to Ross, 13 May 1898, unpublished.

3 *Ibid.*, headed 'Wednesday' but undated, unpublished.

4 From a cutting in Mabel's scrapbook: 'My Social Diary' in the *Daily Mail*, 24 October 1898.

5 At 6c Bickenhall Mansions.

6 Burne-Jones died in 1898. The drawing figures in Ellen's will.

7 Letter to Robert U. Johnson, 15 May 1898: MDG, p. 440-1.

8 In 1921, this pension still stood at £55 a year.

9 Faith Compton Mackenzie, *As Much as I Dare*, 1938.

10 *Ibid.*, pp. 123-4. It ought to be said that there are no fauns or satyrs in the *Lysistrata*: but where else in Beardsley can one find *every* 'stage of erotic exaltation'?

11 From a cutting in Mabel's scrapbook: *The Saturday Review*, 8 December 1900.

12 Raffalovich, 'Aubrey Beardsley's Sister', p. 672.

13 I owe to Mrs I. J. Bealby-Wright's kindness my opportunity of examining this album of press-notices.

14 Undated and otherwise unidentified cutting in the above scrapbook.

15 'The Candid Friend' provided a regular feature in *The Theatre World*.

16 Cuttings in Mabel's scrapbook from *The Hastings and St Leonard's and Bexhill Amusements and Visitors' Guide* and *The Southern Yachting Gazette and Southampton Excursionist* (both of 1909) show that she toured as far afield in the South.

17 Sir Rupert Hart-Davis, *Max Beerbohm: Letters to Reggie Turner*, p. 146.

18 *Ibid.*, photograph opposite p. 152.

19 *Ibid.*, p. 146.

20 *Ibid., loc. cit.*

21 From the MS 'Ballad of Aymer Lovelace': communicated to me by Sir Rupert Hart-Davis.

22 Netta Syrett, *The Sheltering Tree*, p. 121.

23 From a review of Alfred Sutro's *The Cave of Illusion* in *The Saturday Review*, 25 August 1900.

24 *Ibid., loc. cit.*

25 From a newspaper cutting (with sketch of the dress) in Mabel's scrapbook.

26 Letter in the possession of Mrs I. J. Bealby-Wright.

27 *Ibid.*

28 I am grateful to Mrs I. J. Bealby-Wright for an opportunity to examine the copy of *Fifty Sonnets* annotated by the Queen of

Roumania. To Mr Good I owe the further opportunity of examining the same author's *A Ballad of the Night and Other Poems*, n.d., another work printed for private circulation.

29 Written from Cape Town on 1 April: University College, London, Lane archive.

30 Reading University, Beardsley archive.

31 A letter from Bealby Wright to Father Gray exists, so addressed, and dated (in a different hand) 12.12.1906, in the Reading University Beardsley archive.

32 Reading University, *loc. cit.*

33 *Ibid., loc. cit.*

34 Lady Kennet (Kathleen, Lady Scott), *Self-Portrait of an Artist*, 1949, pp. 75–6; 82–3.

35 W. G. Good, summary of the Dash collection of letters in his Walker papers.

36 Miss Riette Sturge-Moore has kindly permitted me to refer to these reserved papers. Mrs I. J. Bealby-Wright possesses a copy of *Mystic Trees*, inscribed 'Mabel with the homage of Michael Field' and dated autumn 1913.

37 Margery Ross, *op. cit.*, p. 228.

38 Cecil Lewis, *op. cit.*, p. 227.

39 Written on a sheet of paper with *The Savoy* heading. The letter is dated 2ʳ July 1912: Roger Lhombreaud, *Arthur Symons*, 1963, p. 130.

40 Letter to George Russell (AE): cit., Joseph Hone, *W. B. Yeats, 1865–1939*, 1962, 2nd ed., p. 185.

41 Some daily newspapers had even made it a rule not to mention Aubrey's name.

42 In *Responsibilities*, 1914; *The Collected Poems of W. B. Yeats*, 1967, p. 115.

43 Allen Wade, Ed., *The Letters of W. B. Yeats*, 1954, pp. 574–5.

44 *Ibid.*, p. 575.

45 Later, reference is made to a possible error in the death-certificate.

46 'Upon a Dying Lady' in *The Collected Poems of W. B. Yeats*, 1967, pp. 177 *et seq.*

47 I am grateful to Sir Rupert Hart-Davis for letting me see a number of these letters in photocopy; and to Merton College, Oxford, for permission to quote from them or to refer to their contents.

48 Letter headed 'Saturday' but undated, from 48 Upper Berkeley Street.

49 J.-P. B. Ross, MSS: hitherto unpublished.

50 The principal bone of contention was Ross's action in presenting to the British Museum Wilde's long letter to Douglas written in prison and afterwards entrusted to Ross. It contained a highly unflattering portrait of Douglas, which is excluded from the extracts entitled *De Profundis*. Under reserve till 1960, the full text can now be studied in Hart-Davis, *The Letters of Oscar Wilde*.

51 For the pro-Douglas, pro-Crosland, version of these events, see W. Sorley Brown, *The Life and Genius of T. W. H. Crosland*, 1928.

52 Cecil Lewis, *op. cit.*, p. 210.

53 Raffalovich, 'Aubrey Beardsley's Sister', p. 673.

54 *Ibid.*, *loc. cit.*

55 George Moore, 'Mummer Worship'.

56 See Note 483, p. 363, in Brian Reade, *Aubrey Beardsley*.

57 M. Roth and J. R. B. Ball, 'Psychiatric Aspects of Intersexuality' in *Intersexuality in Vertebrates, including Man*, ed. Armstrong and Marshall, 1964.

58 Raffalovich, 'Aubrey Beardsley's Sister', p. 670.

Index

1872
1871